Ou

D0302529

PRACTICAL SOCIAL WORK

Series Editor: Jo Campling

BASW

Editorial Advisory Board:
Robert Adams, Terry Bamford, Charles Barker,
Lena Dominelli, Malcolm Payne, Michael Preston-Shoot,
Daphne Statham and Jane Tunstill

Social work is at an important stage in its development. All professions must be responsive to changing social and economic conditions if they are to meet the needs of those they serve. This series focuses on sound practice and the specific contribution which social workers can make to the well-being of our society.

The British Association of Social Workers has always been conscious of its role in setting guidelines for practice and in seeking to raise professional standards. The conception of the Practical Social Work series arose from a survey of BASW members to discover where they, the practitioners in social work, felt there was the most need for new literature. The response was overwhelming and enthusiastic, and the result is a carefully planned, coherent series of books. The emphasis is firmly on practice set in a theoretical framework. The books will inform, stimulate and promote discussion, thus adding to the further development of skills and high professional standards. All the authors are practitioners and teachers of social work representing a wide variety of experience.

JO CAMPLING

A list of published titles in this series follows overleaf

Practical Social Work
Series Standing Order ISBN 0–333–69347–7

You can receive future titles in this series as they are published by placing a standing order. Please contact your bookseller or, in the case of difficulty, write to us at the address below with your name and address, the title of the series and the ISBN quoted above.

Customer Services Department, Macmillan Distribution Ltd
Houndmills, Basingstoke, Hampshire RG21 6XS, England

PRACTICAL SOCIAL WORK

Robert Adams *Social Work and Empowerment*

David Anderson *Social Work and Mental Handicap*

Sarah Banks *Ethics and Values in Social Work*

James G. Barber *Beyond Casework*

James G. Barber *Social Work with Addictions*

Peter Beresford and Suzy Croft *Citizen Involvement*

Suzy Braye and Michael Preston-Shoot *Practising Social Work Law (2nd edn)*

Robert Brown, Stanley Bute and Peter Ford *Social Workers at Risk*

Helen Cosis Brown *Social Work and Sexuality*

Alan Butler and Colin Pritchard *Social Work and Mental Illness*

Crescy Cannan, Lynne Berry and Karen Lyons *Social Work and Europe*

Roger Clough *Residential Work*

David M. Cooper and David Ball *Social Work and Child Abuse*

Veronica Coulshed *Management in Social Work*

Veronica Coulshed and Joan Orme *Social Work Practice: An Introduction (3rd edn)*

Paul Daniel and John Wheeler *Social Work and Local Politics*

Peter R. Day *Sociology in Social Work Practice*

Lena Dominelli *Anti-Racist Social Work (2nd edn)*

Celia Doyle *Working with Abused Children*

Angela Everitt and Pauline Hardiker *Evaluating for Good Practice*

Angela Everitt, Pauline Hardiker, Jane Littlewood and Audrey Mullender *Applied Research for Better Practice*

Kathy Ford and Alan Jones *Student Supervision*

David Francis and Paul Henderson *Working with Rural Communities*

Michael D. A. Freeman *Children, their Families and the Law*

Alison Froggatt *Family Work with Elderly People*

Danya Glaser and Stephen Frosh *Child Sexual Abuse (2nd edn)*

Gill Gorell Barnes *Working with Families*

Cordelia Grimwood and Ruth Popplestone *Women, Management and Care*

Jalna Hanmer and Daphne Statham *Women and Social Work*

Tony Jeffs and Mark Smith (eds) *Youth Work*

Michael Kerfoot and Alan Butler *Problems of Childhood and Adolescence*

Joyce Lishman *Communication in Social Work*

Carol Lupton and Terry Gillespie (eds) *Working with Violence*

Mary Marshall and Mary Dixon *Social Work with Older People (3rd edn)*

Paula Nicolson and Rowan Bayne *Applied Psychology for Social Workers (2nd edn)*

Kieran O'Hagan *Crisis Intervention in Social Services*

Michael Oliver *Social Work with Disabled People*

Joan Orme and Bryan Glastonbury *Care Management*

Malcolm Payne *Working in Teams*

John Pitts *Working with Young Offenders*

Michael Preston-Shoot *Effective Groupwork*

Peter Raynor, David Smith and Maurice Vanstone *Effective Probation Practice*

Steven Shardlow and Mark Doel *Practice Learning and Teaching*

Carole R. Smith *Social Work with the Dying and Bereaved*

David Smith *Criminology for Social Work*

Gill Stewart and John Stewart *Social Work and Housing*

Christine Stones *Focus on Families*

Neil Thompson *Anti-Discriminatory Practice (2nd edn)*

Neil Thompson, Michael Murphy and Steve Stradling *Dealing with Stress*

Derek Tilbury *Working with Mental Illness*

Alan Twelvetrees *Community Work (2nd edn)*

Hilary Walker and Bill Beaumont (eds) *Working with Offenders*

Social Work Practice

An Introduction

Third Edition

Veronica Coulshed
and
Joan Orme

First edition 1988
Reprinted 1990 (twice)
Second edition 1991
Reprinted 1991, 1992, 1993 (twice), 1994, 1996
Third edition 1998

Published by
MACMILLAN PRESS LTD
Houndmills, Basingstoke, Hampshire RG21 6XS
and London
Companies and representatives
throughout the world

ISBN 0–333–72730–4

A catalogue record for this book is available from the British Library.

10   9   8   7   6   5   4
07   06   05   04   03   02   01   00

Copy-edited and typeset by Povey–Edmondson
Tavistock and Rochdale, England

Printed and bound in Great Britain by
Antony Rowe Ltd, Chippenham, Wiltshire

To the memory of Veronica Coulshed

Contents

List of Figures and Tables

Figures

Tables

Acknowledgements

In producing the third edition of this text I owe much to many people, but most obviously to Veronica Coulshed for producing the original format which has proven to be universally popular and timeless in its appeal to social work students and practitioners. I was both honoured and humbled to be approached by Jo Campling to produce the third edition, knowing the significance of such a text for Jo because of her friendship with, and respect for, Veronica. Her support, and that of John Coulshed, have been invaluable and have been constant reminders of the significance of the project. I hope that I have not disappointed their hopes and expectations. Additionally, for her support throughout the production process, I am indebted to Catherine Gray at Macmillan.

However, my contribution to this text would not have been possible without the experiences of teaching social work at the University of Southampton. Over the years countless students and practitioners have shared their practice, and their reflections on that practice, with me in my many roles within the Department, and this has informed the development of my thinking about social work practice. Although all Departmental colleagues have influenced my reflections, one in particular deserves thanks. Peter Ford has contributed to this text in many different ways. From sharing joint teaching sessions, to commenting on the final draft of this edition, Peter has always provided rigorous and valuable feedback imbued with his enthusiasm for social work practice and education.

As ever, thanks and gratitude go to Geoff, Emily and Tim who are indefatigable in their ability to look after themselves – and me!

JOAN ORME

xi

Introduction

When the first edition of *Social Work Practice* was published I expressed the opinion that this was the book I had always wanted to write. At that point I was not aware that it was going to become a best seller. I had been teaching on qualifying social work courses for over ten years and the focus of my teaching had been variously constructed around what was then called social work methods. These experiences made me aware that, for good or ill, what students wanted was a text which brought together the core approaches to social work practice; an introduction to the literature and a summary of the ideas in a meaningful form. The combination of Veronica Coulshed's experience and forthright style with the format of the BASW Practical Social Work series was powerful, and the need for a third edition is testimony to the relevance of the text.

In the light of my initial reaction, the invitation to produce the third edition is both an honour, and a daunting challenge. The tragic death of Veronica Coulshed has meant that she has not been able to continue to demonstrate through her writing her lifelong commitment to social work students and the profession for which she was preparing them. The task is therefore to ensure that her original mission is continued. The purpose of this text remains the same as the earlier editions – to help students and practitioners to apply theory to their practice. In selecting a range of methods of intervention, the focus is on developing core skills which are useful across the range of settings and client groups and to show, through the use of practice examples, how theory informs and improves practice.

However, as Veronica Coulshed said in her introduction to the second edition, knowledge in social work changes so rapidly that one almost wants to rewrite as soon as the first account appears. The significant experience for me in working from the second edition is that much of what was written then is relevant to social work students today. The language might have changed (we now talk about care management as if it were synonymous with social work), but the principles and the tasks remain constant. Veronica herself acknowledged that there were things which had been omitted and things which might have been said differently. It is therefore not a criticism, nor would it be experienced as such I am sure, that feedback from readers and reviewers, students and colleagues has also suggested differences in approach and emphasis. Some changes in emphasis arise from having different professional histories. My own background as a probation officer, for example, made me acutely aware of the few references to probation practice in the first two editions. It might seem strange to advocate writing probation into a text about social work practice at a time when probation training is being removed from qualifying social work education, but for me the skills, tasks and principles discussed in this text remain pertinent to those working with offenders.

Therefore, while this revised edition will retain many of the messages and principles of the first two editions, there will be significant differences. The new edition is bound to reflect, and comment on, the changes which have been occurring in social work education and practice since the second edition was published in 1991. At the very time the second edition was being written, the policies and practices related to community care legislation were being introduced. While these were referenced in part, it was difficult for anyone to predict the scale of the changes which were heralded by these policy initiatives. Other changes were hardly on the agenda, but have been introduced so rapidly that they have impacted on social work, and might seem to challenge the project of this book. The introduction of the Diploma in Social Work in 1990 as the qualification for practice opened up a debate about the relationship between social work agencies and social work courses in educational establishments. The competence-based approach to social work practice and education precipitated significant debate in social work circles about the relationship between theory and practice, and the future of social work as a profession and as an academic discipline. The threat to a university-based education, the discipline of social work, was heralded by the Home Office's withdrawal of sponsorship for social work education and training for probation officers. The disassociation of probation practice from social work and the recommendation that the newly introduced care management does not require professionally qualified social workers posed equally grave threats. Ironically, this withdrawal from a professionally qualified workforce occurs at a time when social work educators and practitioners have become more articulate and more assertive of the theoretical and research base for social work. Despite the success and popularity of the early editions of *Social Work Practice* it could be argued that such a text, incorporating what seems like a shopping list approach to the social work task, has compounded the competence-based approach to social work practice. This was never the intention and the misuse of the text was anticipated by Veronica Coulshed. Her message was that there are no easy remedies in social work, especially when we are confronted daily with oppression and deprivation. She acknowledged that putting together an eclectic range of approaches might make it appear that they were menus for success; readers may assume that if they follow the strategies and techniques then planned outcomes will be achieved. No technique or theory can do this. As England (1986) described, the intuitive use of one's self, including the quality of the relationships which we work to build remain at the heart of what social workers do well. While it is true that people do not come to social work looking for a relationship, and while it is no substitute for practical support, nevertheless social workers are one of the few groups who recognise the value of relating to others in a way which recognises their experience as fundamental to understanding and action. This is not to advocate an anti-theoretical or atheoretical stance: those who discount intellectual scrutiny and rigour undermine the credibility of the profession (rushing about merely 'doing' might say more about needing to be helpful as opposed to trying to understand the meaning of someone else's experience).

The recognition that social work is constantly, and some argue successfully (Vernon *et al.*, 1990), trying to bridge the theory–practice divide was implicit in the second edition. This revised edition goes further than this. It revisits the introduction to the first edition by exploring the relationship of theory to practice, acknowledging the need for reflection by the effective practitioner. Social work needs to articulate, celebrate and broadcast the theoretical frameworks which inform, structure and facilitate its operation. To do this begs many questions about the theoretical frameworks; the phrase suggests a claims-making that is not uncontentious. Chapter 1 therefore deals specifically with the process of relating theory to practice, and in particular looks at some of the theoretical concepts which have fundamental significance for social work practice. In earlier writing these have been framed as values, but the issues are wider than those traditionally identified as the value base of social work, acknowledging that the process of social work is just as important as the practice.

The first edition was written because of a concern that our traditional approaches were being misshapen or lost. Social work was beginning to feel embarrassed with words such as 'casework', apologetic about looking for deeper meanings which people attach to events in their lives, and inhibited about wanting to be creative and instinctive when occasion fitted this. Veronica argued that while critics would have us start afresh, innovators who have shaped alternative practices, for instance community social work (Hadley *et al.*, 1987), are beginning to recognise the need for interpersonal as well as entrepreneurial skills (although they still criticise what they amusingly term 'client-centred, esoteric methods'). It is at this point that my convergence with Veronica is apparent. In anticipating the changes that were heralded by care management (Orme and Glastonbury, 1993) I was adamant that what was needed was not an abandoning of the skills-base of social work, but to build on best practice.

This work has contributed to the revisions to Chapters 2 and 3, which discuss the core skills of care management, putting greater emphasis on assessment, monitoring and review. The scope of assessments is widened to take into account the growing need to assess not only people but also organisational systems. New activities such as advocacy and consultation with users introduce new approaches, but also require an understanding of some of the theoretical arguments which are framing policy and practice. These are explored in Chapter 3 which identifies good interpersonal and organisational skills related to the provision of community care services. Chapter 4 focuses on core issues of communication, spending some time discussing interviewing skills before looking specifically at ways of problem-solving by using counselling methods. Social workers deal not only with people in crisis, but whole communities and systems in crisis, Chapter 5 offers some techniques and a theoretical framework for crisis intervention and disaster management in order to help individuals and whole communities to cope with catastrophes in their lives. A method of problem-solving which can similarly lend itself to many levels and size of system is task-centred work, reviewed in Chapter 6.

The later chapters focus on what might be viewed as specialist methods, though the intention is that they become part of everyone's armoury of knowledge and skill. Two major schools of thought, the psychosocial and the cognitive approach, are explained in Chapters 7 and 6 respectively. Both have been subject to challenge and criticism. Psychosocial methods are the oldest in social casework, at one time seen by radicals as a form of policing the poor, forcing them to accept and adjust to the status quo. On occasion, clients' socioeconomic positions were neglected, as was concerted action aimed at bringing about social change. However, as analysts point out (Rojek *et al.*, 1988) opponents of individual methods themselves were prone to uncritical acceptance of 'received ideas'. Marxist slogans of exploitation and oppression were bandied about; such language, as they suggest, constructs reality (just as casework language does), rather than reflects it. Similarly, behaviour modification, and its use in institutions to make people conform was rightly condemned; in Chapter 8 some current therapies are explored, whose ethics are less dubious.

The final section of the text focuses on contexts of interventions, in which many theories and interventions may apply, but which have also produced their own literature and contribution to practice. Working with families and couples is explored in Chapter 9. Family systems therapy is outlined, together with everyday skills which can be used to help families with problems of getting along together. Chapter 10 introduces working with groups, analysing different models of groupwork and ways of handling difficult dynamics. A new chapter (Chapter 11) which discusses the history, principles and practices of community work and community social work bring us almost full circle.

The notion of circularity is relevant to the concluding chapter. Social work intervention constantly deals with endings. Each interview or meeting has its own ending, and each episode or period of intervention (for example assessment) comes to an end, even if contact with the worker or the agency continues in a different form. Endings are therefore an on-going part of the dynamic between worker and client or user. Ironically, literature in social work emphasises the need for good beginnings and 'engagement' but at times forgets to address the issue of terminating help. For organisational neatness the need for good endings is explored in a concluding discussion, but is relevant to all that has gone before.

The original format, which included in many chapters frameworks which summarise the main ideas, is retained. These provide a useful exercise in comparing one approach with another and in getting hold of the focal components of knowledge and skill. Examples of practice are used to help bring the theory 'alive'. Much of that text is retained, with changes reflecting changing contexts, rather than any deficiencies in the original. That this has been possible is a testimony to the quality of the original work, and to what Margaret Yelloly (1988) rightly identified in her introduction to the first edition as the 'wisdom, clarity and freshness of the original text'. I hope I have not detracted too much from those qualities, but that I have contributed in ways that will ensure that the text continues to be the introductory text for every student of social work.

JOAN ORME

1

Theory for Practice

In social work there has always been a tension between practice and theory. At times students and practitioners have protested that it was necessary to forget theory once in practice placements, that it reduced spontaneity in caring for people. Theory implied distance and objectivity which contrasted with feelings and the living reality of social work encounters. As such it was seen to be a stumbling-block to developing individual style, and the most that could be hoped for was that students would admit that they might subconsciously be using theory which they had absorbed during training. In recent years students have become less antagonistic to theoretical ideas, naming and trying to integrate what can at first glance appear to be a smorgasbord of apparently contradictory explanations of behaviour. There is an irony that this acceptance occurs at a time when changes introduced are based on assumptions that social work is a set of functions, and that practitioners need to be trained merely to perform these functions. Education in theories which might underpin decision-making, or which might inform what action to take, is seen as unnecessary. This approach, known as the competence-based approach, was heralded by the introduction of requirements for social work education and training in the *Diploma in Social Work Studies*, but is reflected in policy implementation which is now controlling much social work activity.

In this introductory chapter it is therefore important to clarify both what is meant by theory, and why and how social workers apply theory in their practice. To do this is not merely a justification for the text. It is the beginnings of, or contribution to, the defence of social work as an activity. In Chapters 2 and 3 in describing how legislation and policy initiatives have been accompanied by sets of 'guidelines', there are examples of attempts to set limits on social work activity. The consequence of this prescriptive account of social

7

work intervention is that the emphasis is on tasks, and task performance, not on workers' abilities to analyse and process information drawn from their interactions with individuals, families or groups. The argument of this introduction, and indeed the purpose of the whole text, is to suggest that such an approach is unethical, failing to provide users of social work with appropriate interventions, and as such it is incompetent.

If such a mechanistic approach is adopted, there is no understanding that the information gleaned during social work interventions might be interpreted in many different ways, depending on which theoretical approach is used. Nor is there any expectation that students and practitioners will review their intervention in the light of the growing amount of practice-based research which is available in social work. The competence-based approach requires certainties; that if one is dealing with *A*, you can intervene with *B* and that will secure an acceptable outcome. In the history of social work such assumptions were associated with a scientific approach when social work emulated medicine in the quest for a professional identity. Now, in a climate of increased managerialism, workers are scrutinised on performance indicators which include the time taken to respond to a referral (or to prepare a report). The outcome is often that the required form has been completed. The quality of the intervention, what has occurred or might occur between the worker and the service-user while the form is being completed, is not covered in national standards for probation practice or competences for care management. For discussion of the impact of the competence-based approach on social work education, *Educating for Social Work: Arguments for Optimism* (Ford and Hayes, 1996) is a useful text.

Other implications of a competence-based approach are reflected in the development of computer-based and distance-learning materials for teaching social work practice. The first computer-based package for teaching interpersonal skills (ProCare, 1996) identifies clearly with competencies. However, the accompanying Tutor Guide argues that while computer-based learning (CBL) provides a flexible approach to learning skills, this also leaves more time for students to identify and understand theoretical and conceptual aspects of interpersonal skills. Here is the dilemma for social work. There are tasks to be performed and skills to be utilised, but prescriptions of the what and the how cannot be constructed in a vacuum. Social workers, to be truly effective, need to be constantly asking why. It is in this quest for understandings about, for example, why situations arise, why people react in certain ways and why particular interventions might be utilised, that theory informs practice.

Hence in this third edition the need to reassert the theoretical basis for practice is paramount. To do this it is necessary to explore understandings of what constitutes theory, and how social workers use theory. To illustrate the point, in debates with local agencies who receive students on practice-learning opportunities I am frequently asked why I do not teach care management. My reply is that I do. I raise all the issues that are dealt with in Chapters 2 and 3 in this text, and many more in the seminar discussions which ensue. However, I do not teach students how to complete the relevant forms, I see that as the role of Practice Teachers. Students need to question the purpose of the forms, their construction, the implications of completing them (for worker and user) and what contributes to and influences the process of gathering the necessary information. The notion of 'necessary information' is contestable. Their experience of completing forms, of undertaking assessment interviews for care management, informs their contribution to classroom debates and causes me to reflect on what I teach. This highlights the benefits of partnership between agencies and educational institutions, and the necessity for the integration of theory and practice.

However, even this description might suggest that there is a certainty about what should be taught, that theory for social work practice is uncontentious. Some educationalists have debated at length competing positions regarding social reality and the production of knowledge, in other words, theory (for discussion see Rojek, 1986; Howe, 1987). Gradually it is being acknowledged that a 'gladiatorial paradigm', that is the notion that social work theories compete and cannot be integrated since they offer opposing interpretations of social reality, ignores the commonalities and interdependence of explanations of how human beings shape and are shaped by their internal and external worlds.

Either/or arguments, such as insisting that counsellors must be either Rogerian or behaviourist, or that social workers are either radical or traditional in their approach, fail to see the underlying continuities which hold together such apparently diverse positions. Most theories have elements in common as well as elements in opposition. Howe (1992) demonstrates that the so-called eclectic helper, who claims to take the 'best' from different theories, actually holds a consistent view of people and their situations. Purists might attack this seemingly undisciplined and incoherent way of working; yet this is the way in which practice is generally conducted at present. However, exploration into how the growing proliferation of methods and therapies might be integrated, at least into 'families' which share a common vocabulary plus a pool of concrete, specific operating procedures, is going ahead (see, for example, Mahrer, 1989).

Before going any further, perhaps it would be useful to examine what the term 'theory' might mean for social work. In doing this, it is possible to discover that there is little agreement about the nature of theory that is required to intervene in social work situations. Siporin (1975), for example, believed that social workers needed foundation knowledge (personality theory, social theory and social policy theory) which would contribute to an understanding of the person in society. More recently such a view has been contested by Jones (1996) who has criticised social work academics' selectivity in identifying and privileging certain theories or, in his words, 'seeing [theory] as a resource to be plundered and pillaged' (Jones, 1996, p. 203). Another way to classify theory is to distinguish between levels of theory. So called 'grand theories' might include Freudian or Marxist explanations of what motivates human nature, giving seemingly all-inclusive accounts. On the other hand, 'mid-range theories' are not so comprehensive, they address particular phenomena such as loss, attachment, delinquency and so on, and try to explain their causes and consequences. Such explanations can be offered within Marxian or Freudian understandings of the world.

Another way of framing theory is offered by Pilalis's (1986) six meanings of 'theory' which reflect visions which are carried amongst student groups. It is suggested that some regard theory as general rules or laws testable against observable evidence. Others, similarly influenced by the physical sciences, take it to mean a probability, a hypothesis or a speculative explanation subject to research. The third and fourth meanings, specific to the human sciences, involve a system of principles which help us to understand events more clearly or to capture, for practical purposes, underlying ideological and value bases of say psychological, sociological or political ideas. Finally, popular uses of the word 'theory' are encapsulated in the fifth and sixth examples, that is the way in which it is distinguished from practice ('this is theory rather than practice'), and the dismissive 'that is all very well in theory' which sees knowledge as idealistic and unattainable goals.

A further problem when we talk about 'social work theory' is that we could, moreover, be referring to at least three different possibilities. Those identified by Siporin (1975), that is the relevant social sciences can be described as theories *for* social work. An alternative set of explanations might be theories *of* social work, what it is, who is it for and so on. Finally, the phrase might be used to mean how to do social work. Evans called the second two categories explicit and implicit theory, with explicit theory being 'the theory of practice' derived from the social science knowledge base of social work. Implicit theory is alternatively called 'practice theory', which is implicit in what social workers do and in how they make sense of their experiences (Evans, 1976, p. 179). This 'commonsense' approach is echoed by England (1986) who argues that a social worker's 'practice knowledge' involves a unique understanding of the people who constitute the clients, 'the general processes of perception and the creation of meanings which determine the individual's capacity to cope' (England, 1986, p. 34). However, in espousing a commonsense approach, England is being neither atheoretical nor anti-theoretical, but argues that 'defined' knowledge is not enough on its own. Professional learning has to be accompanied by, or mediated through, 'personal' knowledge which will inform intuitive knowledge and intuitive behaviour (England, 1986, p. 35). Again the conclusion must be that theory is inexorably tied to practice in social work, and neither can, nor should, be separated from the other.

However, as we move towards an understanding of a theoretical foundation for social work practice, the very notion of foundational theory has been called into question. As social work searches for a common base, the notion of theoretical coherence is being challenged by post-modernity (Howe, 1994). Post-modern critiques of social work theory describe attempts such as the one in this text to articulate practice theory for social work as being without any authoritative foundation and failing to provide any opportunities for reflexive self-awareness. Post-modern practice theories for social work would be 'a kaleidoscope of ideas, research findings, argument, practice wisdom, values and critical speculation, whose coherence would lie in relationships between the different parts, and between them and the reader's experience' (Tuson, 1986, p. 70).

Such an exploration is at odds with the 'modern' stance taken by Payne (1991) who argues that there are paradigms for social work, which are socially constructed and into which all current theory and practice should be fitted. He uses paradigm in the sense of it being a set of assumptions, beliefs, values and methods that make up a particular and preferred view of the world. In social work such a paradigm is informed and constructed by experimentation, research and debate which build on general views and lead to revolution and a new world view.

Accepting this notion of paradigm helps us to appreciate the many influences on the construction of social work theory, and ultimately practice. An example of this is the paper by Bottoms and McWilliams (1979) which argued for a 'Non-Treatment Paradigm for Probation Practice'. This seminal paper questioned probation practice based on psychodynamic approaches to working with offenders. The ideas contained within it changed the way that probation officers viewed their clients, and led to questioning of an interventionist approach to probation practice. This non-treatment approach found resonance in feminist critiques of the criminal justice system. Research had shown that women who offended were more likely to receive interventionist sentences such as probation orders for minor offences because they were thought to be in need of treatment or help, because they had acted in an unfeminine way (Carlen and Worrall, 1987). In Chapter 8 we see how non-treatment approaches have led to behavioural methods being used to good effect in work with offenders, and in Chapter 10 we note some of the education and skills groups which have been set up as alternatives to treatment. These are the positive outcomes. However, in recent years the demise of the treatment paradigm has been associated in policies with a more confrontational and punitive approach to offending behaviour. These policies have questioned the need for a social work approach in criminal justice, and have culminated in the withdrawal of government support for training in social work practice for the probation service.

A different example is the way over-arching assumptions that theories of the market should frame welfare services has led to both the mixed economy of service delivery and the commodification of resources and support into 'packages of care'. We will see in Chapters 2 and 3 how this has influenced social work practice.

It might be argued that these examples indicate that there is no one timeless, all embracing theory for social work, and that social work 'evolves and reforms according to local and cultural conditions of all social life' (Howe, 1994). In doing so, they also call into question who defines relevant theory, or which theories are privileged at any one time. While that is a subject of a different text, putting the question takes as given that social work practice utilises, and is framed by, theory. To paraphrase Howe (1994), this theory and knowledge is not consistent, coherent but it is cumulative and progressive. This does not mean that it is integrated and unidimensional. What is certain is that the job of social work is an intellectual one; it demands the rigour of the practitioner-researcher who can think and do, who can use heart and head, who can incorporate reading and research so as to liberate practice.

Social work theory therefore, should never become an end in itself. It serves the following functions: it should provide some explanation for the complexities observed in practice so that out of apparent chaos patterns and regularities in behaviour and situations can be exposed; it should thereby help predict future behaviour, how the problem or condition could develop and what might be the effect of planned change. Or, as Howe puts it, theory helps us to describe, to explain, to predict and to control and bring about (Howe, 1987, p. 12). But, social work theory is defined by what social workers actually do and it therefore has to be both interactive and reflexive and will change in response to practice constructions (Payne, 1991).

Having established the nature of the relationship between theory and practice it is also possible to identify what purposes are served by theory for the profession of social work. Theory ultimately provides guidance towards more effective practice, giving a measure of confidence so that workers do not feel totally at the mercy of their working environment. More importantly, knowledge gained from theory exists to inform social workers' understanding, not to dominate it. As England argues, theory is not an end in itself, 'abstract knowledge in social work, whilst it remains abstract knowledge, is utterly useless' (England, 1986, p. 35). If effective strategies and techniques are recorded and developed, then knowledge is created and can be used to direct others to what is common and regularly occurring in human experience. Theory fulfils a boundary-setting function too, assisting the identification of those domains where the theory for practice is relevant or not; and having a body of accepted theories of practice helps novices to internalise basic professional knowledge and values by which they may explain to themselves and others what they are doing and why. Some codification of behaviour also enables social workers to evaluate their practice. When social workers evaluate their efforts, be they services to individuals or whole programmes of care, they begin to engage in theory building. Much social work theory derives from someone's experience which they have written down and shared with others.

The educationalist/community worker Freire (1972) calls this ability to think and do 'praxis', again a concept which has been explored further by feminist scholarship (Stanley, 1990). The notion of praxis encourages people to perceive, interpret, criticise and transform the world around them. In social work a lot of time is spent in giving tangible, immediate, practical help but this does not invalidate attempts to look beyond the obvious to ensure that people get the thoroughness of the service they need. More importantly praxis, especially in the feminist tradition, recognises that the worker is not the expert and does not have a monopoly on understanding situations. Hence, while some have argued that because the processes of social work have become more complex in recent times and what is needed is an increase in the variety of tools in the workbag (Davies, 1985), others have identified this as technical rationality (Schon, 1987). Such approaches deny important components of social work interactions, the workers and the service-users.

Throughout this book attention is drawn to the way that the actions workers might take, the questions they ask and even the tone of voice used, will influence the process of the intervention. There are discussions about the way class, gender and race can operate to oppress or empower users of services. There is a sense in which the topics covered in this book might be seen to be equipping social workers with beginning knowledge about the how and the what to do in social work interventions. There are other kinds of knowledge, for example an understanding of legislation and policy which might inform when a social worker intervenes, and to some extent why. Possessing this knowledge might mean that technically students and practitioners are equipped to intervene in people's lives and can demonstrate or construct accounts of what we have done, in what order and the outcomes; the values, strategies and assumptions that make up 'theories' in action (Schon, 1987). Much of this is expected of students and practitioners when undergoing supervised practice, and it is to be hoped that this text will contribute in some way to that construction. However, good professional social work practice also requires that the workers are able in a 'moment-by-moment appreciation of process' to deploy a wide-ranging repertoire of images of context and action, to be able to reflect-in-action and respond to the diversity of experiences and reactions which are encountered when working with fellow human beings.

The aim of the text is therefore not to provide a recipe book, a manual of how to do it, but an array of approaches which themselves arise out of, and are constructed by, others' attempts to describe practice. It is important for practitioners to be able to utilise these constructions and to understand that each intervention in which they are involved will add to their knowledge and under-standing, and help to contribute to their own theoretical approach. In this way, and in many others, this text should be considered as a beginning, and not an end in itself.

2

Care Management: Assessment and Commissioning Services

The role of care manager was introduced with the National Health Service and Community Care Act 1990, and the title is now being used interchangeably with social worker in a way that is confusing. Its usage begs many questions; is the work of care manager and social worker synonymous, what does care management involve? If, as the guidelines suggested, it is not necessary to be a qualified social worker to be a care manager, how can they be the same task? It has been argued elsewhere (Orme and Glastonbury, 1993) that care management requires the knowledge, values and skills provided by professional education and training for social work. In this chapter and the next, the processes and practices of care management will be discussed, while in Chapter 4 skills required will be explored.

Care management

The legislation which introduced care management was the finalisation of policies of community care which had been developed over many decades, but which gathered momentum in the 1980s. The key components of community care as interpreted by the policy initiatives are:

- Services that respond flexibly and sensitively to the needs of individuals and their carers.
- Services that allow a range of options for consumers.
- Services that intervene no more than is necessary to foster independence.
- Services that concentrate on those with the greatest need.

(DoH, 1989, para. 1.10, p. 5)

16

Delivery of social services has always been complex and practitioners have been required to organise and coordinate services across a range of field, day and residential settings, drawing on natural, voluntary, private and statutory sources of help. In order to meet the requirements of community care an individual worker will be assigned to provide an overview of the arrangements made: a 'case manager' to take responsibility for ensuring that individuals' needs are regularly reviewed, resources are managed effectively and that each service user has a single point of contact (DoH, 1989, para. 3.3.2, p. 21). The care management process aims to achieve planned goals using what are familiar and central tasks in social work, namely data collection, analysis and planned intervention (what again long ago, modelled on medicine, were called study, diagnosis and treatment). In addition, care management, which is defined as 'The process of tailoring services to individual needs' (para. 7, Summary of Practice Guidance, 1991) depends on practice skills such as interviewing, communicating, assessing, recording, counselling and mobilising resources.

Before we proceed we need to address the distinction between case management and care management. Case management was the term first used in Britain in the period when the practices of North America were being introduced into the organisation and delivery of British social services. Research and writing around that time used the imported terminology. In the policy documentation which produced the blueprint for British social work practice (DoH, 1989) the term care management began to be used. (For a discussion of these developments see Payne, 1995.) The change indicated a move away from the individualised approach to service delivery which had been the focus of casework, and emphasised that it was the *care* that was to be managed and not the *case* or person.

It has been argued (Renshaw, 1988) that care management has always been with us inasmuch as it relates to social work as a problem-solving process which relies on a mixture of administrative efficiency alongside what the North Americans call 'clinical' skills, that is social work practice and human relationship skills. Discussions have ensued around the distinction between care management as a *system* and as a *practice* (O'Connor, 1988) or between care management as a method of organising service delivery or a method of intervention (Orme and Glastonbury, 1993). Community care packages are examples of systems, or methods of organising service delivery, where agencies have devised policies and programmes, designed jobs, organised staff training and made arrangements with other organisations in order to bring about the delivery of services to the individual. Care management is a practice or set of practices which involve individual workers mediating those arrangements and systems for individuals in need. As such, care management draws directly on the theory and practice which has been variously described as the unitary approach (Pincus and Minahan, 1973), systems theory, or the integrated approach (Goldstein, 1973; Pincus and Minahan, 1973; Specht and Vickery, 1977), all of which relate to a method of social work practice which identifies the worker as a change agent, and the focus for the worker's intervention as being manifold. This association of care management with systems theory is a recurring theme, and the discussion of the theoretical base of systems theory is dealt with in the next chapter.

If care management builds upon existing social work practices, it also heralds change. One of the most significant is the responsibility that care managers have for allocating and managing resources, including finance. Social workers have always had a gatekeeping function, but budgetary devolution, introduced with the community care legislation, involves skills in accountancy to assess the cost of the services required. The policies also require the separation of assessment of need from determination of the service response based on the resources that are available. This is now translated into the shorthand version of 'purchaser/provider split'. This requirement was introduced to ensure the development of a mixed economy of welfare with a greater involvement of voluntary and independent sector agencies in the provision of facilities in the community. The aim is to provide more choice for users and carers, and to find more flexible ways of maintaining people in the community.

The purchaser/provider split has had a major impact on the way that workers in the statutory sector carry out their roles and tasks. One consequence is that it is often assumed that care management equates solely with the process of assessment for the purposes of community care. However, care management is more than this. At its simplest level it can be described as a circular process of case finding and screening – assessment – planning monitoring and review – (and eventual closure). A more detailed description of these stages can be found in guidelines produced by the Social Services Inspectorate (SSI), *Care Management and Assessment:*

Practitioners' Guide (DoH, 1991) which provides a useful 'action checklist' for practitioners and identifies seven core tasks in arranging care for someone in need. They are listed below.

Case finding and screening therefore includes publishing information and determining the level of assessment, while assessment of need involves both assessment and the beginning of the planning process. Care planning includes the implementation of the care plan or 'package of care', but this can only be achieved if services have been commissioned and the voluntary and independent sector stimulated to ensure that the range of needs identified have appropriate services in place to meet them. Finally, monitoring and review includes ongoing assessment, as well as methods of quality assurance designed to ensure that the services are being provided in an appropriate manner, and to the required standard (DoH, 1994).

Stages of care management

Stage 1	*Publishing information*	} Case finding and screening
Stage 2	*Determining the level of assessment*	
Stage 3	*Assessing need*	} Care planning
Stage 4	*Care planning*	
Stage 5	*Implementing the care plan*	
Stage 6	*Monitoring*	} Monitoring and review
Stage 7	*Reviewing*	

Stages 3 onwards reflect the circular process of much social work intervention that preceded care management, and which is recognised as good practice in other areas such as child care and working with offenders. As such, care management could be said to be a codification of the social work process and that performance of all these tasks remains dependent upon core social work skills which include interviewing, assessment, negotiation, consultation and counselling. Seemingly new processes such as advocacy and working in partnership draw on many of the basic skills, but are often employed in different circumstances, or with people other than those traditionally defined as clients of the social work agencies. For example, negotiating skills may be used with line managers in order to secure resources for particular users' needs, or with representatives of a voluntary agency in order to ensure that a particular need is provided for. The various tasks and skills also differ according to the role held in the organisation. For example, programme development and service commissioning might be the main feature of a middle manger's role and involve liaison with managers in, for example, health authorities. Front-line workers (care managers) might rely more on direct skills such as those written about here. Another way of analysing or dividing functions of care management is to draw a distinction between skills which are used in planning, commissioning or purchasing, and those required for providing services in community care. Such distinctions are always arbitrary, because in both sets of activities the elements of communication which have been encompassed in interviewing skills are necessary and fundamental. However, to help clarify the practice issues of care management, this chapter will deal with skills linked to the commissioning process, that is assessing the individual, formulating the care plan and securing services (purchasing). The next chapter will look at skills and processes which are used predominantly, but not exclusively, to ensure that the user and/or carer receives an appropriate and acceptable service (providing).

Before continuing with this division, it is important to remember that while the introduction of care management has focused social work thinking both on what we do, and the way that we do it in order to achieve a particular set of outcomes, in this case enabling people to remain in the community, other aspects of social work intervention have continued. While the focus is primarily on care management, many of the skills and tasks are not peculiar to care management. The expectation that probation officers work in partnership with the voluntary sector and provide 'packages of supervision' in the community means that they too need to develop liaison skills, and have to monitor the provision. Also, the notion of partnership which is explicit in the policy documentation associated with child care legislation draws on similar skills.

In the rest of this chapter assessment is explored, and, again, although the focus is on care management it is important to remember that assessment and planning have always been part of social work intervention, and remain so in those areas of social work practice which, to date, are outside the usual definitions of care management. In child care work and working with offenders, assessment is crucial in deciding the outcome of intervention which may in both cases involve major life changes such as the loss of liberty or removal to an alternative care environment.

Assessment

Assessment is an ongoing process, in which the client participates, the purpose of which is to understand people in relation to their environment; it is a basis for planning what needs to be done to maintain, improve or bring about change in the person, the environment or both. The skill of undertaking and producing an assessment depends on administrative talent coupled with human relations skills. It takes someone who can organise, systematise and rationalise the knowledge gathered together with a gift for sensitivity in taking in the uniqueness of each person's situation. 'Hard' knowledge such as facts are pertinent, but so too are thoughts and feelings and the worker's own clarified intuition. Thus, while appreciating that documentation issued by bodies like the Department of Health and the Social Services Inspectorate (referred to above) and their very useful guidelines on assessment are essential everyday handbooks, inexperienced workers need to learn the art as well as the science of carrying out this task: for example, noting how a family interacts with you as well as what they say.

Sometimes beginners confuse the term assessment with evaluation, and while there may be an evaluative component, for example measuring if a client or a whole care programme is accomplishing goals, assessments are more akin to an exploratory study which forms the basis for decision-making and action. Similarly, assessment is not just an event, for example the production of a profile on someone or a report for the court; it is, as indicated, a way of continuously collecting and synthesising available data, which includes thoughts and feelings, in order to formulate 'treatment' plans. Assessment is therefore a process and a product of our understanding. It is on this basis of understanding people and circumstances that we reach initial appraisals or what used to be called 'diagnostic formulations' which:

- describe,
- explain,
- predict,
- evaluate, and
- prescribe.

Assessment in community care involves a shift in emphasis from assessment of an individual to assessment of the individual's circumstances.

Initial assessment

In community care initial assessment is known as *determining the level of assessment* or *screening*. This involves decisions about whether the problems that are presented, the care needs identified, are appropriate to the agency. The aims of any initial or pre-assessment process are to:

- Provide information and advice;
- Provide simple direct services;
- Collect basic information.

While these aims may be clear, the circumstances which precipitate initial assessments are complex. The requirement of community care is that publicity be made widely available describing services and inviting people to make contact with the area centre if they have certain categories of problems. It is envisaged that this will ensure that users who are in need of services feel able to approach the agencies and ask for help. However, a consequence of publicity is that people's expectations are heightened, and they come to the social work office expecting a service when this is not necessarily going to be available, or, if it is, they may have to pay for it.

Even in the climate of community care many people use social services as the last resort having considered other options such as seeking advice from friends and relatives. Also, people are referred from other agencies, especially health services, for their community care needs to be assessed. Referral of older people may come from a relative who has been providing some form of care for some time, or from friends and neighbours who have concerns.

In the areas of child care and working with offenders a further dimension is provided by referrals which are made on those who are unwilling users of the services. Situations which have raised alarms about standards of child care or the possibility of some form of abuse mean that identifying need often involves investigatory techniques to establish whether there are causes for concern. For the probation service, referrals from the court have established the guilt of the offender, but the assessment that is to be made is about suitability for certain forms of intervention.

The way in which a referral is made and received has implications for the relationship between the person needing the service and the agency providing it. Before contact is made the individual may have picked up the phone numerous times and entry into the system is, to them, a giant step. The public perception of social workers is mixed. Some view them as powerful, authoritarian figures and are fearful of the possible interventions which could lead, for example, to children being removed. In the context of community care and the need to assess resources, the threat to older people that they may have to sell their homes in order to receive a service can be a barrier to open communication.

Whatever the problem or concern that is brought to the social work office, if the person is black or from an ethnic minority background their approach will be influenced by a number of factors linked to structural oppression. They may perceive the agency as racist because of previous experiences, or because they have experienced racism in other public services. Also, if the environment alienates them by not acknowledging the multicultural nature of our society they will immediately experience the organisation, and perhaps the worker with whom they are meeting, as responsible and racist.

In the pre-contact phase, therefore, it is necessary to develop ways of reaching out especially with oppressed groups and those who are unwillingly referred. In many social work interventions the imperative is for partnership, and from the outset of contact social workers are expected to set the tone of partnership, but also to acquire appropriate information on which to make the decision. Early interviews are often concerned with screening to see if the person is eligible for service, and then if this is the case the potential client becomes an actual client or service-user. Therefore it is important to conduct the initial stages in a way which does not alienate the user, or duplicate the assessment process. The ways in which this might influence the actual interviews are discussed in Chapter 4.

Sometimes when a referral is made by another agency information comes in either written form, or by a phone call. Information is obviously available to the worker referring, and the skill here is to ensure that enough appropriate information is received in order to make an accurate assessment without being influenced by the views and perspectives of a worker who is already involved, and has their own views, albeit from a different agency perspective. It is at this point that the need for liaison and negotiation skills is paramount, recognising the expertise and status of a colleague in another service, while retaining professional and individual autonomy.

Even when screening has taken place and the decision made that the person or situation warrants a complex assessment, it may be that the experience of the user or referrer has been such that they are deterred from seeking further help, either because the time delay seems so great, the system too complex, or by the thought of having to repeat the information, or give even more details about personal circumstances. Also, as Baldock and Ungerson (1994) discovered in their research on stroke patients, even when hospital residents had had quite complex assessments carried out, such patients had little understanding that an assessment had taken place and at times confused it with all the other medical checks that were taking place. The consequence of this is that they might not return.

The mixed economy of welfare provision and the development of private sector services have made this even more possible because individuals can purchase anything from a place in a residential home to a gardener, without having to give personal details to a social worker. This is increasingly becoming an option when services provided by social services are charged for and part of the assessment has to be a financial assessment. However, there are some who do not have the means to pay, and even those who do might not want to. This has implications for the way that assessments are conducted, and practices adopted by social workers must ensure that service-users are empowered, a theme which is discussed in the next chapter.

It is important that decisions at the initial screening are not just made on basic eligibility criteria related to simple assessment. The SSI (Social Services Inspectorate) guidelines identify four categories of risk for people with disability, but acknowledge that it is inappropriate to prioritise just on the basis of, for example, disability. Assessment of the resources of the person and their situation is just as important, including the stress on both human and other resources.

Factors which might determine priority include:

- attitude and aspirations of the person,
- capacity of the individual,
- capacity of the individual carer,
- capacity of other services, and
- suitability of the living environment

Assessment process

Traditionally, social work assessments, after certifying eligibility for services (case finding and screening), tended to follow what might be termed 'resource-led' pathways rather than a broader 'needs-led' approach. Good practice stems from open-minded and comprehensive assessments, avoiding the narrow focus of service-oriented assessments (Challis *et al.*, 1990). In other words, if we develop frameworks which separate out ends and means (what needs and goals could be met and whether or not there are resources to achieve these), this larger picture will reveal service gaps, adding possibilities for filling these imaginatively. Certainly in relation to elderly, frail people, these kinds of needs assessments have enabled creative services to happen: clients can be kept in the community longer with a better quality of life for themselves and their carers. An illustration of this occurred when a group of older people who tended to neglect their food, either because they had no appetite to eat alone, forgot to eat or were too physically frail to cook, were brought together in a local domiciliary helper's home for their meals, a service that was specifically designed to match their patterns of living.

In the same way, the components of a comprehensive assessment for children require vision. A plan for long-term care would go beyond simply checking out the child's developmental history, significant people's perceptions about levels of care provided and the child's reactions. The child's own views, whether expressed verbally or non-verbally, and those of relevant participants to the assessment would be sought to get ideas about the best way of helping the child, regardless of whether such a service existed or could be afforded.

In reality, of course, needs-led principles cannot work unless there are plenty of resources; in social work we will always be in a position where demand exceeds supply, which is why so many agencies have introduced priority (that is rationing) systems. Unless we approach community care with a widened vision we might continue to make our assessments fit into existing provision. A literature search of what to explore in assessments (the content) will reveal that, depending on the circumstances of the referral, one could end up collecting vast amounts of material encompassing social, psychological, physical, economic, political and spiritual elements which compose an individual, a group, a family, a neighbourhood or an organisation. The source of the referral; details of the referrer, the client and the situation; the problem and its meaning for significant people; historical facts which impinge on the present; facts about age, ethnic origin, roles and behaviour, environment and informal networks; resources and strengths; other agencies involved and so on usually feature.

The skill in undertaking and recording an assessment lies in the ability to collect enough of the right kind of information and this can only be done in the right kind of environment. Frequently learners attempt to find out everything in a 'scatter-gun' method: they hope to find out something worthwhile by asking more and more questions resulting in confusion from an information overload. It is as well to remember that we will never know all there is to know about people or systems – assessments are always continuous and dynamic and, in this sense, never complete. In some ways, too, they are never 'true' inasmuch as they tend to be filtered through the assessor's perspective, despite attempts at exactness and comprehensiveness.

Another drawback to assessments, particularly when they are carried out by statutory agencies such as the probation service and personal social services departments, is that they could be used to control not just access to services but also disadvantaged sections of the community. Stigmatising and scapegoating of clients via negative assessments (see Jones, 1983) does occur. Dossiers are kept on so-called 'problem families' or those who have assertively sought assistance. The adjective 'aggressive' is applied to black clients who assert their needs for equitable services, yet, as A. Ahmad (1990) shows, white assessment fails to take into account black realities and environments.

Thorough assessments actually take a long time, often longer than can be coped with in most busy offices; so some of the problems to do with this function may also to related to worker stress as well as ignorance. Such experiences also affect users' attitudes to assessments. People who have had to wait can become agitated which leads to understandably difficult interactions. In one incident in the probation service, the probationer became so agitated that he threatened the worker with violence, and certainly was not able to give any account of the problem for which he had originally come for help.

Accuracy of factual content is essential. Systematic methods help, as we have seen, as does what might be called 'triangulation', where information is cross-checked with other sources. It is imperative that we do not rely on hearsay or gossip when assessments serve the purpose of planning and intervening in someone's life. However, such an approach might be deemed a *questioning* model of assessment where the care manager, seen as expert, interrogates each aspect of the care system and comes to a final decision on the basis of their expertise and the knowledge gained.

More often, evaluations of assessment in care management demonstrate that a *procedural model* is invoked, and agencies have devised rigid systems for the assessment process, often typified by large numbers of forms to be completed. These procedures have been so codified in some areas that computer programmes have been written to facilitate the process of documenting all the information required. Such assessment models are often a one-way process constructed to meet the worker's and the agency's needs and can be undertaken without any positive impact on the person being assessed. For some social workers working in community care, it is the accumulation of information that is important, and that information can be gleaned from a number of sources. Even allowing for the fact that older people, for example, have more problems with recall, Baldock and Ungerson's research found that the initial contacts with care managers had little impact on a large majority of people in their sample. For example, Mrs C, a patient in hospital recovering from a stroke, was asked if she had had contact with a hospital social worker. She replied:

Er-yes. A lady came in on one occasion and she said I'm from – I think she said I am a social worker or I'm social security And she – I don't really know why she came. And it probably might have been, although she did not say so, it might have been something to do with the pension. But she didn't say so. She just sort of said, checked up on the number, and then she said, well, I'll be seeing you again. If there's anything you need. And she disappeared . . . I mean, she didn't say why she came. I think she was just checking up. (Baldock and Ungerson, 1994, p. 14)

The description of the Department of Health funded Practice and Development Exchange (Smale *et al.*, 1993) in critiquing these assessment models provides an alternative, the *exchange* model of assessment where users and carers, as experts in their own needs, are empowered by being involved in the assessment. This involves more than merely sharing assessments with users. While emphasising that the worker has expertise in *the process* of problem-solving, the model recognises that the people in need and those involved with them will always know more about their problems. The aim is to involve all the major parties in arriving at a compromise for meeting care needs. Rather than simply making an assessment, the worker manages the process; s/he 'negotiates to get agreement about who should do what for whom' (Smale *et al.*, 1993, p. 16). The focus is very much on the social situation, rather than the individual, and recognises that people come to social services for help because other support systems may have broken down or are not available. It is argued that everyone in the social network should be involved in the assessment as they will have their own perception of the problem (see Chapter 11 for further discussion of networking). The project sees assessment and care management as a continuous process, which should be undertaken in a way that empowers people. The report outlines agency responsibilities, and the need for change as well as individual worker skills. In summary, the main tasks of assessment/care management in the exchange model are to:

• facilitate full participation in the processes of decision making;
• make a 'holistic' assessment of the social situation, and not just of the referred individual;
• help create and maintain the flexible set of human relationships which make up a 'package of care';

• facilitate negotiations within personal networks about conflicts of choices and needs;
• create sufficient trust for full participation and open negotiations to actually take place; and
• change the approach to all these broad tasks as the situation itself changes over time.

(Smale *et al.*, 1993, p. 45)

Although it is acknowledged that to get feedback on assessment does improve accuracy and provides the basis for an honest exchange, shared assessments also engage the other and begin the process of change, giving priority to each participant's views. This brings us to the idea of sharing assessments with other colleagues as a way of reducing the risk of bias or error. (Multidisciplinary assessment will be dealt with later.)

There could be value in *team assessments*, as opposed to our usual practice of leaving this to one worker. The purpose of this may be to check out our personal interpretations, and the way they might influence the presentation of the information. Shared assessments have been developed in the probation service as part of the development of anti-oppressive practice. The process of gatekeeping has been developed for pre-sentence reports. There are different models, but the basic practice is that once a report has been prepared the author shares it with a colleague or a group of colleagues who check to ensure that the language, the information and the basis of the assessment do not in any way reflect oppressive or discriminatory thinking. This is an extremely helpful process, because at times it is difficult to identify how our thinking might lead to such outcomes when we are closely involved in it.

Assessment in other settings

In circumstances as important as, say, the delicate business of child placement (see Thoburn, 1988), the amount of information required about relationships, needs, sort of placement and so on demands that this be a shared study. Everyone who knows anything about the child can contribute. One social worker, faced with an eleven-year-old boy who had been in care most of his life, first of all read his file carefully. From this she constructed a flow chart diagram showing his numerous moves from one caretaker to another, noting that there were gaps in his history (which can happen if records are not meticulously kept). Within this factual flow chart she constructed an emotional one illustrating the feelings that the child experienced and those he had engendered in others, for example, 'distressed when moved into a large family'. Alongside this assessment instrument the family placement worker used others such as a family tree, an ecomap of her own team colleagues, a planning algorithm and a framework in which to analyse larger factors such as the legal context, agency considerations and public opinion. In collaboration with a student on placement and the key worker in the children's home, the worker set out to interview as many people as she could in the boy's past in order to piece together the jig-saw puzzle of his life. In this way too, the child's capacity for attachments could be assessed for the future.

Incidentally, work with this little boy, as well as the formal tools mentioned (see Bryer, 1989, for further examples), used games, exercises and playing to supplement the knowledge gained. These assessment methods also let the child gradually, over the course of eighteen months, open the door to his past, helped him cope with his losses, reliving his grief so that he could resolve it to make way for new attachments.

The Department of Health publication *Protecting Children: A Guide for Social Workers Undertaking a Comprehensive Assessment* (1988) is just one in a set of guidelines which give social workers frameworks for undertaking comprehensive assessments for particular purposes. The guidelines give background rationale, including policy and legislation, for particular actions, providing detail on who to see and the kinds of questions to ask in order to glean the information necessary to establish whether a child is at risk. The list of topics to be covered and guidance on questions provides a wealth of information for beginning social workers, but does raise the question posed in the opening chapter of this text, and underpins concerns that a 'how to do it' manual might produce technically correct social workers who do not reflect on what they are doing, and why. Such an approach does not equip workers for reacting to complex situations. There is no easy formula for predicting, synthesising or understanding the wealth of human experience. Having said that, to collect data systematically and to record it as a basis for decision-making with individuals and families is essential.

A different approach to guidelines for assessment has been taken in the field of criminal justice work. The Home Office produced *National Standards* (1992) following the passing of the Criminal Justice Act 1991, and they were revised in 1995. A national training programme based on published training materials accompanied the first publication. The *National Standards* (Chapter 2) give a synopsis of the function of the pre-sentence report (PSR) as an assessment for the purposes of sentencing, indicating length, structure, content and activities associated with preparing the report, including guidance on who should be contacted. For workers in the probation service these provide the minimum standards to be attained, but for additional views on the purpose and preparation of PSRs the National Association of Probation Officers has produced its own *Good Practice Guide* (NAPO, 1995) and Bottoms and Stelman (1988) provide a useful discussion of the policies and practice of report writing, although they are not so prescriptive in their approach.

Assessments and oppression

Most policy documents now make explicit reference to the need for assessments to be sensitive and alert to differences in people's backgrounds, according to their race, colour or religion. It might be argued that such statements are not necessary, that if an assessment is done properly it will focus on the individual in their situation, and that situation will include their race, gender colour or religion. However, if we reflect on some of the assessment schedules referred to in this chapter it is apparent that until very recently they were based on assumptions about the way that people live their lives, including diet, clothing and child care practices all of which are defined from the perspective of white, usually middle-class, values. Jalna Hanmer and Daphne Statham (*Women and Social Work*, 1988), for example, describe how the common assumptions of good parenting in child care assessments are in fact expectations of good mothering which assume that women will devote their lives to the full-time care of their children. Bandana Ahmad (*Black Perspectives in Social Work*, 1990) reminds us that social workers have tended to view black users who did not fit into assessment schedules as *problems* as opposed to *different*. Even if

assessment schedules are being devised to recognise different approaches and lifestyles, it is important that the way the information is
collated, and needs constructed, also reflects the range of different
approaches which can be provided for multicultural communities.

Assessment of need

One of the important aspects of assessment introduced by care
management is assessment of need. Discussions about whether
community care is truly a needs-led service centre on assessment
and concerns that no distinction is made between what users and
carers *want* and what they *need* (Coote, 1992; Means and Smith,
1994; Payne, 1995). However, referencing such discussions immediately raises questions about 'who decides?' If an older person wants
to be able to go to play Bingo everyday, a worker anxious about
budgetary planning might think that this is not a need. But if this is
seen as way of socialising, relieving boredom and therefore preventing the onset of depression and possible hospitalisation, then it may
well be a need. The concern is that an assessment process which
encourages users to identify a wide range of wants and needs might
well raise expectations that such needs should be met. Would it be
realistic, for example, to make an assessment that an older person
needed to have a foreign holiday every six months in order to offset
depression? Of course, some older people may well have the means
to make such arrangements for themselves. The dilemma arises
because workers undertaking assessment are aware of the limitations of public spending, and the competing demands on budgets.
However, community care legislation argues that in the first instance
the assessment should focus on the need. The assessment process
identifies problems or causes of difficulty and how these can be
eradicated, reduced or offset. If the person does not have the means
or resources to do this themselves it may be that systems for
ensuring socialising and relief of boredom can be found through
less expensive activities, then the need can be met, although not
necessarily in the way first envisaged. What is highlighted here is the
balance between needs and resources and different interpretations of
need. The important question is; which interpretation will prevail –
the worker's or the user's?

   This approach to identifying needs, and thinking creatively about
meeting them, also allows for innovative approaches which often

depend on the collation of information from individual needs, to identify ways of meeting group needs. For example, if in a particular housing area there are a number of individuals who need special transport to enable them to do their own shopping, it is possible to devise a system of volunteer drivers who will be available on some form of rota basis. However, negotiations with the local bus company might mean that a more corporate response can be created. In one city a regular 'wheels-on-wheels' service has been created where a specially adapted bus runs a regular service for wheel-chair users. This system gives more independence, is akin to those used by other shoppers, and could be seen to be more empowering (see next chapter).

Other dilemmas arise in assessing competing needs, especially those between users and carers. This has now been formalised in the Carers (Services) Recognition Act 1995, which gives carers the right to assessment. However, formalising assessment of needs does not necessarily resolve the dilemmas. If an older person wants to remain in their own home, and to do so requires informal care, they might also want to be able to say who will care for them. The request that the daughter in the family does the caring might be at odds with the daughter's own plans for employment, or even the way she chooses to spend her leisure, or organise her life.

For a more theoretical discussion of human need, Len Doyal's chapter 'Human need and the moral right to optimal care' in the excellent publication *Community Care: A Reader* (ed. Bornat, Pereira, Pilgrim and Williams, 1993) is a good starting point. Doyal argues that there are no easy resolutions to some of the conflicts around community care needs, but that a 'procedural theory of need' might facilitate communication and acceptable compromise and that 'those participating in policy formulation must include all parties in the dispute' (p. 284). This will involve users and carers as well as workers from voluntary, statutory and independent sector agencies. Such a theory links directly with the discussion of user-involvement and user-empowerment in the next chapter.

At the end of the assessment users should know:

- who has taken the decision on eligibility;
- which needs are, or are not eligible for assistance, and why;
- which needs might be eligible for assistance from other care agencies;

- when, and under what circumstances, they may request re-assessment; and
- the means of complaining if dissatisfied.

(SSI, 1991, p. 54)

However, such a linear approach suggests that assessment is a one off-event, a neat progression from beginning to end. We know that the process is more fluid than this. Circumstances might change during the period of assessment, because the person has become more incapacitated as in the case of older people, or may be making greater progress than was anticipated (for example, in the case of people who are recovering from strokes). Also, perceptions of circumstances change as both workers and users/carers acquire more information. Hence the emphasis on the circularity of all assessment. The approach is reflected in monitoring and quality assurance mechanisms of care management, and recognises that even if an assessment event can be said to have been completed there is a need to be vigilant, and to ensure that both worker and user have the opportunity to request a review or re-assessment.

Arrangements for assessment

If we are to ensure that an optimum assessment can be done, given the detail implied in this section, then, as indicated, we need time. Assessments clarify the balance between need, risk and resources for intervention. In community care they become the blueprint for the services provided, the standard against which the services are measured for quality control, and may make the difference between a person living independently or in a residential establishment. Reports for the court prepared by probation officers have to take into account due process, justice and welfare and often make recommendations which have consequences for people's liberty, while child care assessments can have consequences for the placement of children. It therefore behoves organisations not to treat such assessments on an assembly-line basis, but to recognise that an appropriate allocation of time is needed to produce a high quality professional document which is the product of a supportive assessment relationship. For further discussion of workloads and assessments see *Workloads: Measurement and Management* (Orme, 1995).

Other arrangements for assessment include formalised schedules and computer packages. For example, schedules of risk factors in child abuse have been produced for computer analysis and community profiles can be constructed noting the correspondence between rising crime rates and those for unemployment. While computer-aided assessments can save time they are not necessarily the answer to everything. In community care, the computerisation of assessment schedules was piloted in one county, and while this did allow for the collation of material to identify community profiles, the technology did not assist the users to the extent that they were able to construct their own packages of care. However, in another project the use of assessment and action records in a research project evaluating child care practices proved to be so useful that they were adopted by agencies (for an account of this see *Looking After Children*: Ward, 1995).

To recapitulate before we consider multidisciplinary assessments: an assessment is a perceptual/analytic process of selecting, categorising, organising and synthesising data. It is an exploratory study which avoids labels and is reached as a result of systematic and careful deliberation of needs, not simply what services are available. As well as facts it spans feelings, intuition, judgement, metaphors and meanings. Priority is given to the person's perceptions of their circumstances. Hasty prejudices are seen as undermining to particularly oppressed groups. Tools which are used may include questions, self-perception ratings, role-play, problem checklists, pen pictures, diaries and other instruments found valuable by the consumer or the working team.

All assessments contain the risks of error or bias which might be partly counteracted by cross-checking data; extra suggestions for reducing worker bias include:

1. Sharing the assessment with those who participate in it.
2. Improving self-awareness so as to monitor when you are trying to normalise, be over-optimistic or rationalise data.
3. Getting supervision which helps to release blocked feelings or confront denial of facts or to cope with the occasional situation where you have been manipulated.
4. Being wary of standing in awe of those who hold higher status or power and challenging their views when necessary.

5. Treating all assessments as working hypotheses which ought to be substantiated with emerging knowledge; remember that they are inherently speculations derived from material and subjective sources.

Multidisciplinary assessments

Central to the community care arrangements is the creation of individualised, flexible packages of care, requiring workers to arrange and provide services from independent, voluntary and statutory groupings: a key responsibility is collaboration with medical, nursing and other caring agencies (DoH, 1989). The care manager is the person who facilitates and coordinates a multidisciplinary assessment. In the case of health assessments of older people, these can take place at home, in a day or residential centre or in a hospital setting. Various professionals (for instance, health visitors, occupational therapists, physiotherapists, general practitioners, district nurses and social workers) work together in shared assessment of older people, but this does not mean shared perceptions.

Professionals might agree about categories for assessment, but research carried out by Runciman (1989) revealed differences in perspectives – difficulties in rising from a chair, for example, might be assessed by a GP as arthritic hips, by a health visitor as a low chair, or by a physiotherapist as poor hand function. Similarly, interesting differences in starting points or foci for assessment were noted, the social workers homing-in on attitudes and feelings, or practical problems such as housing; occupational therapists, not surprisingly, starting with mobility. The groups differed as to whether or not they carried a framework for assessment in their head; where a particular theoretical framework had been adopted, for example amongst district nurses this proved to be a barrier to more detailed considerations of need.

From this it is apparent that multidisciplinary teamwork is crucial whenever we attempt to pull together a rounded picture of someone's circumstances. Multidisciplinary teams consist of a number of different disciplines, whether or not in the same building, sharing their knowledge and expertise about a specific client with the objective of identifying and using those services which most effectively meet assessed needs (see Department of Health, 1989). If we concentrate on the role of the social worker in such a team, the kinds of skill called for include:

- *Partnership* – the ability to engage with colleagues, allocate tasks and give feedback.
- *Negotiation* – making clear what outcomes for self and others are desired; compromise and confrontation.
- *Networking* – gathering and disseminating information, linking people and establishing mutual support groups.
- *Communicating* – writing effective reports, speaking and writing in a non-jargonised way.
- *Reframing* – offering different perspectives by placing the problem in a wider frame of reference and discussing alternative ways of seeing the problem.
- *Confronting* – assertively challenging a dominant view.
- *Flexibility* – learning from the skills of others.
- *Monitoring and evaluation* – measuring outcome and modifying methods or goals accordingly

This list appears in a publication on multidisciplinary teamwork, produced by people who had worked in or received the services of multidisciplinary mental health teams (CCETSW/IAMHW, 1989). The writers argue that legal, social science theory, organisational and resource knowledge are a must for the social worker who wishes to be equipped for this kind of work: respect, openness and client-centredness too are requisite values if the worker is to make a distinctive contribution to the team. Otherwise, as they warn, the social worker could become either a hostile or marginal figure or, chameleon-like, opt to fit in with the view of the rest. They point out that consensus is not the goal of interdisciplinary working – conflict is central to success so that honest dialogue can expand everyone's skills and horizons. Just as important, perhaps, is that the worker is aware of funding complexities and respects the different management structures. Often these are forgotten in the blurring of team members' roles and tasks.

Many of the tensions that arise amongst interdisciplinary team members relate to the myths and stereotypes that we hold about other professions. Stereotyping can be overcome via joint training, working and peer supervision activities in multidisciplinary teams.

Commissioning services

Commissioning activities in community care involve ensuring that services are available so that identified needs can be met. Commissioning of services is undertaken by social workers in the statutory agencies from among voluntary and independent sector facilities. As well as liaison skills to work with the other agencies, workers need to be able to collect information from individuals and collate it into sets which will identify population or area needs. They will also need to identify and assess possible facilities to ensure that appropriate contracts can be made.

Part of the social work task involves an ability to assess and understand organisations, not only our own but those with which we interact. As stated earlier, effective care management concerns the matching of choices with resources. Let us take as a case study those older people who decide to live in residential homes as a positive solution to loneliness, increasing frailty or a desire for fulfilment through the use of recreational facilities. So, if such a plan is part of a designed 'package' then how do we go about ensuring that quality care is 'on offer'? The Social Services Inspectorate teams in their report *Homes are for Living In* (Department of Health, 1989a), and later guidance from them and the Department of Health (1990), provide useful indicators. Residential and day-care centres for other client groups equally may have the following criteria applied when assessing for quality assurance purposes. Readers may wish to peruse the organisation and management literature (Social Information Systems, 1990) for a broader analysis of quality assurance.

The main features to look for are:

- *Choice* – the opportunity to select independently from a range of options; sensitivity to ethnic and religious dimensions; the environment, such as choice of furnishings, adaptations, and so on.
- *Rights* – for instance in relation to care practices such as handling one's own affairs, confidentiality, respect, consultation.
- *Independence* – including a willingness to accept a degree of calculated risk, such as being able to make meals for oneself and others.
- *Privacy* – recognising the need to be alone, to 'own' a bedroom, to have an opportunity to discuss problems in private.

- *Dignity* – which recognises one's intrinsic value and uniqueness; for example mode of address, access to bathing, sensitivity of admission procedures (see Neill, 1989).
- *Fulfilment* – whereby all aspects of daily life help in realising personal aspirations *and* abilities.

Each of the above sets yardsticks for measuring tangible and intangible elements. In the arrangements for community care, commissioning services is often carried out by specific workers, usually in the management structure. Care managers need to be aware of the processes for commissioning, but also have the criteria in mind when working with users and carers to set up a package of care. In preparing for a stay in residential accommodation, for example, the users and carers need to have their expectations regarding personal care, mealtimes, diet, sleeping arrangements, smoking and use of alcohol norms, medical support, nightstaff support, gender of staff carrying out intimate care, frequency of bedroom cleaning, laundering facilities, and so on, clearly written down and agreed. Any quality-assured home will ensure that the individual's service expectations and plan are regularly monitored and reviewed, perhaps by a designated practitioner, who ensures that all the other care staff implement these processes with clients and relatives.

Case example

The following referral was analysed by a student in placement, relying on a model of assessment which is an adaptation of that suggested by Vickery (1976). This was an initial assessment, the start of thinking through a situation prior to deciding on appropriate action. The referral came from a volunteer, the latest in a series of visitors, who had called on ninety-year-old Mrs Moore a few times. Mrs Moore lived alone in a sheltered bungalow, visited regularly by her daughter and son-in-law and occasionally by a son who had had to move away to find work. Home care was supplied daily; meals on wheels had stopped as Mrs Moore did not like them. The volunteer was concerned that the home was looking neglected, the client was 'confused' and incontinent and said that her home carer spent a lot of time talking to her. The warden's job description limited her involvement to occasional shopping and being 'on call' for emergencies. *cont. p. 41*

Table 2.1 Initial assessment

Definition of the problem	Client	Goals	Target	Role/task of social worker
Mrs M's need for care patterned to her daily needs	Mrs M	Coordinate efforts of helpers. Review and develop services	Helpers Services	Coordinator Care manager Networker
Rapid turnover of volunteers	Mrs M Home carer Family Future clients	Persuade voluntary agency to try to match volunteers to client need for stability	Voluntary organisation	Educator Advocate Broker Public Relations
Role of wardens in housing i.e. sheltered schemes	Tenants	Liaise with housing welfare department to reconsider policy	Housing	Liaison Negotiator Policy researcher
Need for 'package of care'	Service-users	To present own agency and SSD with ideas for care management	Own agency/SSD Rest of multi-disciplinary team	Researcher Manager Planner Budgeter
Break up of natural networks and pressure on carers	Natural helpers Future consumers and carers	Explore extent of loss of natural helping networks	Politicians Local decision-makers	Campaigner Investigator Community Developer Resource mobiliser

Vickery's (1976) unified assessment asks us to take into account the assets and liabilities in the situation at the level of the individual, the group, the neighbourhood, the organisation and the wider environment. Questions to be asked include:

1. What are the problems in this situation?
2. Who are the clients (that is, who will benefit)?
3. What are the goals from each one's perspective?
4. Who or what has to be changed or influenced?
5. What resources are available to create that change?
6. What are the tasks and roles of the social worker?

In this instance, the student was working in a health centre as a member of a multidisciplinary team; he was able to draw on their expertise and gain the community's respect with relative ease. Having sought the permission of Mrs Moore (whose health assessment revealed that she was forgetful – not confused, which is a confusing label in itself; whose occupational therapist (OT) assessment revealed a broken toilet seat, which could account for some of the incontinence), the student called a meeting of the helping network to the health centre to help Mrs Moore and himself answer the above questions. The home carer, daughter, Mrs Moore and the volunteer attended and drew up the assessment shown in Table 2.1. What was interesting was that, normally, these helpers never met one another. This had led to some duplication of effort, miscommunication and distorted perceptions, especially about acceptable risk and lack of knowledge of various roles. Sharkey (1989) writes that the size of someone's network is less important than the notion of density, that is if people know each other well or not. Following the meeting, Mrs Moore's network had changed from a loose-knit to a closer-knit one without involving many new, confusing helpers.

Monitoring and review

Legal enforcement giving users access to their records dates mainly from 1984: the data protection law gave statutory right of access to files held on computer. Since then the Access to Personal Files Act has extended this to manual records in housing and social services departments. Thus, from 1 April 1989 people have had a right to see their manual records (though there is no legal obligation to show manual records before that date). Anyone wishing to look at their files must give notice to the authorities who are allowed 40 days to respond: any information about third parties, excluding professionals, should not be shown unless they give consent: pre 1 April 1989, files should block out the names of such third parties. An approach to good practice is portrayed by Neville and Beak (1990). They found that asking people to countersign their records gave a boost to the working relationship and enshrined a commitment to consulting the users of our services, that is 'doing with' rather than 'doing to'.

Although at one time seen as a troublesome chore which reduced the time available for contact with users, record-keeping is recognised as a core skill and an important part of case monitoring and review. This is particularly important in community care within a mixed economy of provision where services may be provided by a variety of sources. Then contract compliance is crucial for financial reasons, but more importantly to ensure the quality of services provided to users and carers.

The record registers significant facts, evidence, feelings, decisions, action taken and planned, monitoring, review, evaluation and costing information. It may take the form of a detailed verbatim account, a concise summary of each incident or contact, a proforma/chart on which to tick or highlight coded information, or it may include lengthy social histories, individual programme plans, community profiles, video/audio material, or any of the tools mentioned earlier in the assessment section. Sometimes the record, whether in manual or computerised forms, is split into specific sections reflecting the intake, ongoing and ending phases of the work; it may hold letters, medicals, documents from other agencies and, for instance in the event of using a goal-oriented form of practice such as task-centred work (see Chapter 6), contain a working agreement or contract with the client. Here we are talking about formal agency records which are usually confidential, permanent and occasionally transferrable to other organisations. (Social workers may make personal records or jottings which are not official registers of service given.)

Because of the especial vulnerability of black clients who are more likely to be discriminated against, A. Ahmad (1990) stresses that reports must be accurate, relevant, portray strengths, address culture in a constructive way and provide the person or the family with the opportunity to record their own perspectives. Despite good intentions, records are highly selective accounts of data remembered and thought to be significant by the worker.

The team who were responsible for developing community care case management at the Personal Social Services Research Unit (PSSRU) in Kent devised a set of documents by which social workers can plot their activities (see Challis and Chesterman, 1985). These consist of four separate items for systematic recording: an Assessment Document, a Monitoring Chart, Periodic Review forms and Costing Information. The Assessment Document was designed to strike a balance between structured precoded information and space for recording individual personal characteristics of each elderly client. Its six sections covered basic details such as age, address, source of referral; formal and informal contacts including inputs from carers and statutory services; housing and financial circumstances with details of heating, toilet and benefits; managing daily living covered key activities such as personal care, night care and household jobs; physical health and mental health in the fifth and sixth parts was concerned with immobility, instability (falling), incontinence, intellectual impairment and the client's attitude to help including informal carers.

In the development of arrangements for care management, best practice is to give users a copy of the final assessment. This enables them to monitor the services offered and that they are relevant to the needs identified. This is particularly important when, as we have seen, sometimes the services offered are different from those that were initially wanted. Also, the assessment can then become a framework for the user to identify sources of service provision other than that provided from the statutory agencies (see Chapter 4 in *Care Management*: Orme and Glastonbury, 1993).

The Monitoring Chart consisted of a single sheet showing a matrix of the seven days of the week on the vertical axis and critical periods of the day such as meal-times and bed-time on the horizontal axis: seeing who was meeting needs at various times revealed periods of solitude and risk so that plans could be modified accordingly, especially when the care manager was absent. The chart was left in the client's home so that all involved could communicate and coordinate their activities (Challis *et al.*, 1990). Periodic Review forms, while useful say every three months to check the process of care, were found to be more valuable at times of change or crisis: these covered details such as problems and changes achieved; changes intended; social worker activities; outside agencies; practical services; and finally resources required but unavailable (which also gave management information about resource deployment). The fourth document was the Costing Sheet. This recorded expenditure from the social worker's budget used to pay helpers, home help, meals on wheels, day care or residential care. The information was divided into thirteen weekly units; each sheet covering the costing per client over one quarter of the year.

These kinds of recording systems have now been adopted in one form or another by most social service departments, and descriptions of computerised recording systems are discussed regularly in the *Journal of the Centre for Human Service Technology*. This focus on recording as part of monitoring, review and quality assurance reminds us of the other aspects of care management, which are discussed in the next chapter.

3

Advocacy, Empowerment and Negotiation

Care management as a strategy for organising and coordinating services at the level of the individual user has to concentrate on the minutiae of interactions between helper and helped. In this, interviewing and counselling play a pivotal role, but before we consider these in some detail we need to look at other processes involved in care management, especially in the development and provision of the care plan or package of care. These include advocacy and user-involvement both of which require new approaches which build on established social work values. Additionally, the capacity to negotiate, with agencies, organisations and individual users and carers, is essential to ensure that appropriate services are made available. Some of the necessary skills and strategies for commissioning services are similar to those employed in community work and community social work outlined in Chapter 11. While it might seem strange to separate skills in community care from community work, to do so highlights that the policies of community care do not necessarily depend upon understandings of community work. It could be argued that notions of working with communities, of empowering individuals and groups, runs counter to the philosophy of community care which focuses on individuals with need, and recommends that these needs are met by individualised packages of care. This is certainly true of the assessment stage, but if appropriate services are to be available for these packages, if the voluntary and independent sector are to be stimulated and encouraged to provide services as alternatives to statutory services, then some of the skills and strategies of community work will be required.

The consequences of using community work skills might be to bring together groups of users, to encourage them to make demands for services, to see them as their right and to require more active consultation. In this way we see opportunities within community care policies for empowerment which were not necessarily the intention of the policy-makers. The extent to which the policy guidelines actually herald a real shift towards user-empowerment is a matter for debate. *Caring for People* (Department of Health, 1989) used the language of choice and user-involvement, much of which was seen at either the level of the individual, or as a mechanistic bureaucratic process within community care planning. The extent to which true empowerment was envisaged is questionable, and as we shall discuss in this chapter, the shifts required in the practice of social workers and others are significant.

While we have argued that packages of care are constructed on an individualised basis, in all aspects of community care the individual is considered in their context. The involvement of family and friends as potential carers, and the capacity of local volunteer groups to provide support services, are all part of the user's network or system. We discuss networks in more detail in Chapter 11, but the notion of systems is basic to a number of social work interventions, not just those used in community care. In Chapter 9, systems theory is used in work with families where what is happening to one member in, for example, employment or school can have an impact on the whole family, and members adjust to cope with it. In Chapter 5 we will see the notion of systems can apply to communities in crisis where events such as natural disasters like a flood, or more horrendous experiences such as the Dunblane massacre, cause the whole community to respond in ways which enable individuals to keep functioning in some way.

Systems theory

The core of systems theory comes from biology and engineering, and has been translated into social work practice by the identification of social systems as open systems. The significance of this is that:

- all parts of the system are connected and what happens in one part of the system will have an effect on all other parts of the system;
- the system needs to keep in a steady state and will always adjust itself or adapt to try to maintain that steady state; and
- there is a feedback loop within the system, which provides the capacity for change.

Among the first to apply systems theory to social work were Pincus and Minahan (1973), but their approach has been developed by Goldstein (1973) and, in Britain, Specht and Vickery (1974) have written about an integrated approach. All of these writers recognise that if the analysis of social systems as open systems is accurate, then it is possible to reframe the way that social workers approach their work. The focus does not have to be on bringing about change in the individual; other parts of the individual's social system can be the target for change. But the analysis is wider than this. Pincus and Minahan identified four systems within social work:

- *Change agent system* – includes social workers, their agency and the policies they work with.
- *Client system* – involves individuals and their networks including family, community and other groups with whom the change agent system might work.
- *Target system* – is the part of the system which the change agent system is working for change.
- *Action system* – people with whom the change agent system works to achieve its aims.

It is possible for the change agent system, the target system and the action system to be the same. In this way, it is not necessarily the individual who is seen as 'the problem'; it might be the way the individual interacts with different parts of his/her system, or the way that the individual is influenced by the social, or other, system. A systems approach therefore allows for an analysis which encourages workers to be more innovative in the way that they approach situations. This is particularly relevant to care management where the focus is on the person and their situation, the problems and the strengths and resources.

Case example

Mrs C is a 70-year-old woman suffering from arthritis who also suffered a stroke which affected her mobility even further. She lived in a council house where the bathroom was upstairs. Even though she had an active network of family and friends who provided meals and company and ensured that she was helped in and out of bed, her increasing inability to climb the stairs meant that she was threatened with going into residential accommodation. The problem was that the local social services department were being very careful about spending their community care budget and would not sanction the expenditure on the work necessary to fit a downstairs toilet. After some intervention by her son, the social worker lobbied her manager and the decision was reversed, and after negotiations with the housing department the necessary alterations were made.

This illustrates how the approach focuses on problem-solving and change. The work involves identifying the particular system, or part of a system, in relation to which the worker carries out his/her role. In this case the focus for the work, after the son's intervention, was not on encouraging the woman to accept residential accommodation, that is seeing her resistance as a 'problem', but on the social services department itself.

In systems theory there are phases of planned change which include problem-solving over time and require analytic and interactional skills such as interviewing, assessment and counselling. The eight practice skills differentiated for working with systems theory are:

- assessing problems;
- collecting data;
- making initial contacts;
- negotiating contracts;
- forming action systems;
- maintaining and coordinating action systems;
- exercising influence; and
- terminating the change effort.

This approach does not preclude individual work; in some situations it may be that the assessment is that the individual needs some sort of support or counselling. It does ensure that an individualised approach is not the only form of intervention considered. It is for this reason that a systems approach is relevant to care management which involves identifying the resources within the network of the person requiring the service, and being aware of the range of agencies that might be able to provide the relevant help. If, for example, it is identified that a carer needs regular respite to enable them to continue caring, then some sort of rota may be required to provide a 'sitting' service. Work may then focus on recruiting a volunteer or liaising with a specialist voluntary or independent agency to provide the service.

This brief overview of systems theory and the opportunities it gives for different approaches to assessment and intervention indicate why, in service provision in care management, the capacity to negotiate with users, carers and their advocates is necessary to ensure that there are flexible and appropriate responses to meeting need.

Negotiating

In care management, consultation processes are established in order to inform purchasing or commissioning decisions, to ensure that when a package of care has to be constructed there are appropriate services within the community. The next stage, therefore, once consultation has taken place, is for the purchasing or commissioning agency to negotiate with provider organisations to ensure that services are provided at a global level. Negotiation is also a core skill used by care managers when constructing packages of care on behalf of user and carers. Appropriate levels of service from, for example, individual volunteers or independent care agencies have to be agreed, to ensure the quality of care provided. This process raises questions about whether care management as currently envisaged by policy-makers can be truly empowering, because at this stage users and carers are not necessarily directly involved in the process, and can only comment on services provided or advocate for changes, if they are not appropriate. True empowerment might involve giving users and carers the means to negotiate their own services, and we discuss this later in this chapter.

Commissioning services for care management or negotiating packages of care are not the only situations in which social workers are working with parts of the system other than that traditionally called the 'client' system. All social workers spend about one-third of their time in face-to-face client work, the rest is spent in intra-organisational and interorganisational communications. A great deal of this effort is connected to mobilising resources. What was once identified as the 'hidden face' (Bar-On, 1990) of social work is now a core function within care management with the expectation that services will be provided from many sources: family, friends, neighbours, volunteers from the community, voluntary and private sector organisations, as well as the statutory sector. However, it is also relevant in work with children and families and is central to the work of the probation service where negotiations with different parts of the criminal justice system constitute a great deal of indirect activity (Orme, 1995).

The practice skills required for indirect activities include: negotiation, bargaining, resolving conflicts, mediation, liaison, planning, advocacy, consultation, setting up new projects and coordinating resource provision. Below we discuss how the development of self-advocacy has contributed to user-empowerment, but here we consider the worker as advocate in negotiations on behalf of users and carers.

The purpose of negotiation is to influence in order to get a just outcome; thereby, negotiation can be both competitive and colla-borative (Payne, 1986). Where the social worker is having to fight to secure justice or combat the abuse of power, perhaps by a higher authority, then competitive tactics are in order. Where parties are negotiating towards agreement rather than to gain advantage then collaborative elements are to the fore. In both instances, however, it is important not to lose one's temper but to use anger constructively, and not to stray from the point but to keep in focus each part of the bargaining process. Many of the skills of daily practice are about negotiation with different parts of a wider system, whether this concerns stimulating voluntary sector community care services, welfare rights work, persuading schools to cope with disruptive pupils, constructing appropriate community sentences for offenders, inducing policy-makers to fund new projects, or helping to resolve staff disputes in day and residential centres. Thus, many of the abilities we have already can be relied on in becoming a skilled negotiator. There are a growing number of publications, in the management field and elsewhere, which address this subject: they ordinarily suggest the following ideas.

1. *Negotiating for agreement* relies on:

- good preparation, that is knowing what you want to achieve, having the facts, and planning priorities;
- creating a cooperative climate;
- agreeing the purpose and procedures for any contact;
- exploring via brief opening statements your understanding of the situation, your aims, priorities and contribution so that there is seen to be joint advantage;
- listening, clarifying and summarising what the other party's opening statement seems to say;
- generating creative, interdependent suggestions and then deciding which of these are realistic possibilities; and
- agreeing on the action necessary to achieve mutual interest.

2. *Negotiating to get justice* may involve having to fight for resources, getting the best deal for one's clients by:

- preparation as before, but being more specific about what one is bidding for and not being prepared to be exploited by power games such as giving to get something, appeals to higher authority, being deflected by numerous questions or dominated by angry outbursts or red-herrings;
- creating a climate of goodwill;
- exploring in a probing way what is important to the other;
- reaching agreements on a broad front before tackling the detail of what your are asking for;
- being prepared to make compromises if this does not involve loss of integrity and equity; and
- remaining task-focused rather than attacking someone's personality.

Case example

This situation could be referred to agencies for many different reasons but in fact Paula was referred anonymously by her neighbours who complained that her children were at risk, being brought up in a house which was used by drug addicts, dossers and other down-and-outs. Before the social worker could visit, the police became involved and insisted that the children be taken from their mother. When seen in her home, Paula was indeed at the mercy of delinquent groups, who exploited her limited intelligence, refusing to move out until forced to do so by the police. In the meantime her home had been wrecked, savage dogs had ripped up most of her furniture and other belongings. The crisis was so severe that, coupled with her lack of social skills, Paula was quite unable to discuss her situation with the social worker, despite the latter using various communication approaches to help the woman tell her story.

The social worker used all her powers of persuasion to make the two policemen who were at the house let her help the client without resorting to the need to receive the children into care. She bravely asked for their help to deal with the dogs and later to take some of Paula's belongings in their panda car to a homeless families' unit, where Paula and her children were to stay until the social worker could negotiate alternative housing with the housing department. The police and the housing department were identified as part of the system where social work intervention was necessary, rather than focusing only on Paula as the source of the problem and the part of the system that had to change.

This goal of rehousing demanded the most careful of preparation, especially as Paula lived in the district's worst quarter, where the poorest tenants were housed until they 'proved' to the housing department that they were 'fit enough people' to be transferred into less-temporary property. Knowing it was politic, the social worker did not make the mistake of attacking council policy or of challenging the attitudes of housing personnel. She presented a clear, well-thought-through plan for preventing Paula and her children needing to be kept in the homeless unit; the offer of another house, though not much of an improvement on the former, was a start, from which longer-term work with the client, whose husband had recently left her, could begin. All this time too, the social worker had to negotiate with her own department and other agencies as part of Paula's system who were concerned at her capacity for good-enough parenting. Again, influencing and negotiating with integrity, listening to other points of view and not resorting to pushing people to see her point of view, together with a business-like and confident attitude, helped. Wisely using supervision, she checked that she was being realistic, asking her senior to give a second opinion on the social work assessment that, once out of the noxious network and helped to form new ones, Paula would have the potential to cope.

Advocacy

In the case of Paula the social worker could be said to act as an advocate, as well as a negotiator, in that she was operating on Paula's behalf. However, it is apparent that in making decisions and taking risks the social worker had views about what was in Paula's best interests, and also had to take the needs of the child into consideration. Over the last decade advocacy has been used in a much more radical way. These changes have been brought about by the activities of individuals and groups whose needs will now be addressed under the policies of community care. The policy changes did not introduce advocacy, they have made the need for advocacy that much more important.

The philosophy of care management is that the starting point should be users and their carers. They should be enabled to play as active a part in both the assessment and the implementation of the care plan or package of care as their abilities and motivation allow. However, there are circumstances when this is not possible and an advocate may be necessary. Such circumstances include working with users who are unable to express their views, for example those with severe learning difficulties or dementia. Also groups who have previously been disadvantaged in service delivery because they have not been consulted may feel reluctant to express their views, distrusting any invitation to do so. Users who are black or from ethnic minority backgrounds may feel that they have been consis-tently ignored, and see little point in participating, or feel deskilled. In these circumstances they should be supported in ensuring in-dependent representation. The notion of an independent advocate is significant. In North America, for example, advocacy is seen as part of the case management role, and is synonymous with negotiating and securing the services for the user. There they find the notion of an independent advocate strange, they do not see that even if the case manager is acting in the best interests of the user, there may be dilemmas, situations where users are dissatisfied or difficulties in communication.

In the British system of care management practitioners are responsible for mobilising, allocating and monitoring resources for users and carers. Workers might find it difficult to act as advocates because of possible conflicts of interest. In the case of Mrs C above, the social worker responded to pressure from Mrs C's son, even though it meant challenging the decisions of her own managers. If there had been no response from the worker, Mrs C's son might have felt it necessary to act as advocate with the social services department and the housing department. However, it should not automatically be assumed that relatives and/or friends could or should act as advocate. Often people come to the attention of statutory services because they are without friends or relations, or are currently not in contact with them. Where a relative or friend is available they might not always be independent; they may be involved in the caring and support in some way, and therefore might have a vested interest in the outcomes of decisions.

Consumerism

Advocacy is often described as synonymous with empowering users but also with consumerism. We discuss empowerment below, not because it is different from advocacy, but because advocacy is only one way of empowering users. Consumerism is about consultation and information gathering. The National Health Service and Community Care Act 1990 (NHS&CC) requires social services departments to consult with users in the care planning process. It has also been argued that the only effective and efficient way of commissioning services is by identifying what users and carers need (Orme and Glastonbury, 1993). However, most systems set up by agencies are at best consultation, and at worst public relations. Users and carers are told what is available, and asked to give their opinions. As such, the mechanisms are patronising, being led totally by the needs of the service providers (Croft and Beresford, 1990; Orme, 1996). Also, the rhetoric of consumerism arises directly out of a market approach to welfare provision which assumes users and carers ('consumers'), on the basis of information given, will make choices about services.

There are, however, factors which influence and restrict the choices that are available to users and carers of services, and structures and processes which deny some people choice (Braye and Preston-Shoot, 1995).The notion of consumerism is therefore an empty rhetoric which affords only limited user-involvement and does not empower.

Types of advocacy

Advocacy is associated with a rights-based approach to meeting need, and a more radical approach in community care (Braye and Preston-Shoot, 1995). Advocacy, especially self-advocacy, is user-led and arises directly out of a recognition that services have traditionally disempowered users (Mullender and Ward, 1991). More positively it depends upon understandings of citizenship which recognise the rights of all to participate in definitions of need and decisions about how those needs may be met. This does not assume that all needs will be met, but that the processes of decision-making will be transparent and informed by the views of those who have the experienced need operating as active agents within the system (Doyal and Gough, 1991).

The most well-established form of advocacy is legal representation, where expertise, knowledge and experience combine to ensure that arguments are put in such a way as to ensure that the individual is presented appropriately to the particular system, be it court, tribunal or organisation. Other forms of advocacy have included the notion of befriending, that is being with someone to offer support, rather than act on their behalf, and representation. The Disabled Persons Act 1986 provided for local authorities to recognise and formally respond to representatives of people with disabilities. Also, although advocacy is now seen as a central principle of care management it is not confined to this area of social work. In the field of child care the notion of advocacy is complicated because the representative, be they legal or otherwise may be acting for one party, either parent or child against the other, or against the social worker. Nevertheless, the emphasis on partnership in the 1989 Children Act reflects the need for all in social work practice to address the principles of advocacy, and for examples of effective advocacy on the basis of partnership with children the account of the Dolphin Project (Buchanan, 1994) is a useful starting point.

In Britain advocacy has not always been separate from care management. The Case Management Project (CMP) was set up by the King's Fund as a special independent project along North American lines, where the case manager was seen as the advocate. This meant they did not merely 'broker', that is connect people to services which addressed their needs, they negotiated and fought for services. (Dant and Gearing give a useful overview of this project and others which outline the role of advocacy in *Community Care: A Reader*: ed. Bornat, Pereira, Pilgrim and Wiliams, 1993). However, in the arrangements for community care there is now a clear distinction between advocacy and care management. The care manager will undertake the assessment, negotiate the package of care and then maintain an overview, calling regular reviews and responding to information and requests from the user or those providing services for special reviews when necessary. At any one time, the social worker/care manager may well be intervening for the needs of the user in negotiations about the services to be provided, but they have other issues to consider and may well have to make judgements about what the service user wants and what they as a professional think might be in their best interests, paying attention to issues of risk. An advocate can be involved in any part of this process. They can accompany the user at the point of assessment, make representation when the package of care is being developed, intervene with, and on behalf of, the user with service providers to insure quality care and can initiate reviews or attend those called by others in the process. At whatever point of the process an advocate is involved their sole purpose is to represent what the user (or carer) wants, and they do not deviate from that.

For certain user groups, for example those with mental health problems, their situation might require intense periods of advocacy combined with an assurance that the service is available at short notice. There will be times, of course, when they are able to act as self-advocates. Older people and people with disabilities may have a more sporadic contact with independent advocacy services and may be more ready to advocate on their own behalf. However, it is important not to make assumptions about the situations in which advocacy might be effective, or the forms of advocacy that might be utilised. For example, Monach and Spriggs (1994) report that there has been a significant increase in the number of self-advocacy groups in the field of learning disabilities, which is a major advancement since the Disabled Persons Act when it was assumed that certain groups would always need someone to advocate on their behalf. These distinctions need to be clarified further by looking as the main categories of advocacy: citizen advocacy, self-advocacy and group advocacy.

Citizen advocacy works on a one-to-one basis, where volunteers act on behalf of those who require services, representing their views where needed. It is a form of lay advocacy developed in the USA to promote the rights, interests and acceptance of people with learning disabilities, but has now been extended to other groups. It specifically recognises that long-term service users were unable, or had been denied the means, to speak for themselves and that this led to users experiencing powerlessness and devaluation. Basic to citizen advocacy is the belief that all people have value and rights, and its objective is to empower those who have been kept powerless and/or excluded (Monach and Spriggs, 1994). Its function therefore is to include the excluded, empower people, and enable them to obtain the rights of citizenship – as far as is possible.

The main component is partnership between an individual who has a disability (partner) and another who has not, but who is independent and unpaid (citizen advocate).The one-to-one relationship is important, as is the understanding, that the person with the disability has been devalued, but it means that the citizen advocate works on an individualist level both in terms of the advocacy relationship, and the relationship of the user/carer to the service delivery organisations. The citizen advocate primarily performs an *instrumental role* which can focus on, for example, solving welfare benefits problems, or negotiating the care plan. There is also an *expressive role* to be fulfilled which involves meeting emotional needs, befriending, sharing family and friends and providing support. The four key characteristics of successful citizen advocacy are:

- the individual advocate must be independent of any service provision used by the person requiring the advocacy;
- a one-to-one relationship between the advocate and partner;
- the relationship is a long-term and continuous one; and
- the prime commitment and loyalty of the advocate should be to their partner, not the advocacy organisation or the partner's family

(Butler and Forrest, 1990)

Self-advocacy involves training and group support to help people learn skills and gain emotional strength to advocate for themselves. This may be achieved by being assisted by a citizen advocate in the initial stages. Self-advocacy is also about personal and political needs, about being involved in a range of activities and utilising skills which ensure participation. The self-advocacy movement is associated with a reformist approach focusing on participation in all areas of service planning and delivery as well as responding to the needs of individuals at any one time. The aim, therefore, is not just to improve services, but to improve the status of service-users.

Self-advocacy has the important function of facilitating collective action, as well as making it easier for individuals to be assertive. There are criticisms of professionals who might display 'benign paternalism' towards users and carers, but it is apparent that if self-advocacy is to be effective professionals need to be prepared to recognise it and, more importantly, make the necessary changes in their practice to ensure not only that advocates have a voice but also that they have access to the necessary information and training to make that voice effective. The barriers to such changes in professionals have been associated with professional fears, professional mistrust, fear of change, organisational constraints, and legislative ambiguity (Braye and Preston-Shoot, 1995).

Group advocacy brings together people with similar interests, so that they operate as a group to represent their shared interests. Groups can include users, carers and professionals and advocacy is usually at the collective or organisational level, rather than at the individual level. However, the aim is to be involved in service delivery decisions, to reframe how certain problems or groups of users are perceived, and to ensure that users and carers are involved in decision-making shared with other forms of advocacy. Group advocacy may well be subsumed under the umbrella of campaigning organisations operating in the voluntary sector. There is growing concern that the policy initiatives to involve voluntary sector organisations in service provision may well have the effect of de-politicising them and reduce their advocacy role. As they become dependent upon contracts for service provision in order to survive, they have to be less adversarial or critical of commissioning agencies. Also, as service providers they themselves become the focus or target for advocacy. However, as we note below, there are some important advocacy projects emerging at the level of citizen and group advocacy which are also involved in training and supporting individuals to become advocates.

While in practice there may be limitations to all forms of advocacy, common to all are the processes and practices which have to be utilised to ensure that users at least have the opportunity to make their voices heard. Whoever acts as advocate, the necessary skills are in line with the general principles of working in partnership (Dalrymple and Burke, 1995) and include:

- retaining the flexibility to adapt the process to the wishes of the individual involved;
- ensuring the user feels in control of the process and trusts the advocate only to take action which has been agreed;
- empowering the individual;
- supporting people to speak for themselves;
- ensuring that people are able to make informed and free choices; and
- advising, assisting and supporting, not pressurising or persuading.

Organisations for advocacy have pre-dated the NHS&CC Act; disability-rights groups became visible in the late 1980s, and organisations such as Survivors Speak Out in the area of mental health were formed in 1986. Since the advent of care management in community care many independent advocacy schemes have been developed. For example, an independent advocacy service for users of mental health services in Hampshire was set up in 1992 on the impending closure of a local mental health hospital. The project, although funded by the Department of Health and the local Social Services Department, aimed to provide on a short-term basis information and advice on issues such as, housing, tribunals, benefits, treatment and medication, access to and quality of social and community services. Apart from the requirements of the community care legislation and the crisis caused by the impending closure of the hospital, the service also reflected the basic principle of the 1983 Mental Health Act that users should be treated, or cared for, in such a way that promotes as far as possible their self-determination and personal responsibility, consistent with their needs and wishes. This is summed up in their acronym:

Acting on behalf of oneself or another person
Duty of independence and loyalty to Advocacy Partner
Voicing the needs, concerns, and views of the Advocacy Partner
Open to everyone
Challenging oppressive and discriminatory behaviour
Advising on rights and how to enforce them
Commitment to equality of opportunity
You can be an advocate

(Fareham and Gosport Advocacy Project
Information Leaflet, 1994)

Discussions about who provides an advocacy service make a distinction between the focus and function of advocacy. For Rees (1991), *cause* advocacy involves arguing for reform of the system, and *case* advocacy involves advocating on behalf of an individual for resources and/or services. It has been argued that it is cause advocacy which is difficult for care managers, employed by the systems that they are expected to change. As we have seen, systems theory offers a role for social workers as change agents and illustrates the potential for identifying employing agencies as the target for change, it is still done on behalf of individual cases. Independent advocacy services, often acting on behalf of user groups, are more likely to advocate for causes such as resistance to closure, withdrawal of services or changes in the procedures for user-involvement. These services are increasingly staffed by people who are, or have been, users of community care services.

As well as being equipped with skills for acting as advocates themselves, care managers have to work in an environment which ensures that they are prepared to put users in touch with independent advocates when this is in the users' best interests, and are able to work with those who are advocating on behalf of users and carers. The skills involved in this include:

- ensuring all involved have access to necessary information;
- being available to meet with the advocate;
- giving advocates a role in relation to the decision-making;
- acknowledging that different user/advocate relationships will have different balances of involvement, liaison and consultation, but recognising confidentiality, and respect for the user.

More particularly, professionals can support advocacy projects making skills available and accessing resources and information, but some argue that it is impossible for professionals to avoid playing the dominant role and to take over the services, or at least to limit their power and direction (Chamberlin, 1988). Much of this assumes that the advocate will be someone other than the user and carer. The response of professionals to individual users who are advocating on their own behalf requires a shift of emphasis in the relationship, recognising the power imbalances which have traditionally existed within social work practice. The real test of effectiveness is the extent to which advocacy movements can challenge the power of professionals, not only in terms of service delivery, but in the conceptualisation of disability, or the particular problem or user group (Monach and Spriggs, 1994). Often, the furthest that agencies will go is some tokenistic procedure for involving a 'representative' of users and carers in generalised community care planning.

User involvement

A requirement of care management in community care is that users have to be involved at all levels. To ensure that services are relevant and appropriate local authority social service departments are required to consult users and carers in the community care planning process, and the assessment of each individual for a care plan adds to the sum total of information about community and group needs. While the principles of user-consultation and participation cannot be disputed, the practices need to be carefully considered to ensure that they are truly empowering. Models of consultation where services are provided and users merely asked what they think of them do not involve true participation. As Nina Biehal (1993) argues, the fact that an agency has a value base which espouses user-involvement will not guarantee that users will be involved in decision-making: 'Such "mission statements" will be little more than window dressing unless accompanied by specific strategies to ensure that service users participate in decision-making' (Biehal, 1993 p. 445). At an individual level we have already identified that strategies for involving users include:

- encouraging users to describe their own needs through the construction of jointly constructed problems, goals and tasks;
- sharing the assessment with the user (including the written assessment) and explaining why particular services are being offered, giving users the right to refuse what is being offered; and
- ensuring that users have sufficient information both about the decisions made, and the services available.

User-involvement requires more than this. Consultation should involve full participation in decisions about the way services are to be offered. This might include the range of services available, policies on eligibility criteria and charging for services; policies which will impact directly upon how services are delivered. If they are consulted at this level then users will feel fully involved. There are, however, many barriers to such levels of involvement. The first is that statutory agencies are not practised in open decision-making with the consumers of their services, and because of this workers are not used to asking the opinions of the users. Below we discuss the SWIP project which encouraged professionals to reflect on the ways that they defined needs, made assessments and decisions *on behalf of* rather than *in partnership with* users. However, the evaluation of the project highlighted the difficulties. Significantly, workers were concerned about involving users when they thought the case was 'difficult'; where the needs were complex, or resources limited or where there was some element of risk. But it was the workers' assessment that cases were difficult.

There are situations where the users themselves do not expect to be involved in decision-making – and indeed might not want to be. This may be linked to views of professionalism by both workers and users where there is an expectation that workers should know the answers. However, there are also users who have not normally been consulted or involved, despite the fact that they would wish to be. The Association of Directors of Social Services (ADSS) and the Commission for Racial Equality (CRE) have undertaken two surveys of local authority social service departments in 1979 and 1989, and in both they found that services were not always relevant to the needs of black people and those from ethnic minority backgrounds. In some areas the basic services required to ensure that needs could be identified and met, for example translation and interpreting services, were not in place. In any system of user-consultation that is set up, it is therefore necessary to ensure that the processes are accessible to as wide a group of users as possible.

There is also some reluctance or resistance on behalf of workers to deviate from routine approaches because they recognise that this might be time consuming, and they have no spare capacity to respond to the extra demands. Stevenson and Parsloe (1993) identify that some managers recognise that to empower users, first the staff have to be empowered. In *Care Management* (Orme and Glastonbury, 1993) the workload implications of the introduction of care management are discussed.

Perhaps because of the difficulties of working at an individual level to facilitate user-involvement many social services have resorted to what are commonly called procedural models of consultation which involve:

- open days;
- public meetings;
- documentary consultation (responding to the plan);
- surveys;
- involvement of users and carer on committees; and
- setting up forums.

(Hoyes and Lart, 1992)

There are many problems with such methods. First, they require that people are both mobile and able to communicate in readily accessible forms of communication. This can immediately exclude many users of community care services. Second, they require that people are aware of the particular events or processes; they need to be on the relevant mailing list, or part of a network or circulation list that means that they receive the information about the event, or the documentation which requires comment. Third, even if these two requirements are met, users do not necessarily feel assertive enough to attend a meeting, or give their views when they do. Consultation is therefore confined to a small group of people who feel confident enough to address public meetings, or engage in debate with managers and policy-makers. If consultation only occurs with existing users and not with potential users, this further complicates the alienation that some groups in the community might feel. For example, if black people are not accessing services because they see them as not relevant or potentially racist, how will they be able to communicate that to the organisation in order to bring about change?

There are methods which can be used to access a greater number of users and pre-users. These include postal and telephone surveys for those who are housebound, accessing people via GPs, housing departments or benefit payments, or having a link worker to work with community groups which include those other than current users of services. For example, in a research project trying to determine how users and pre-users of services for older people wanted to be consulted, one research team visited luncheon clubs and adult education classes (Avison *et al.*, 1995). Some of the views expressed about the consultation process by users and pre-users in this project process included:

- involve users in the issues for consultation;
- ensure all communication is jargon free;
- access a truly representative sample of users; and
- be clear to users how their views will be put into effect.

All of these are at one level very simple, but depending on the context and culture of organisations it may be very difficult to adhere to them. While they require changes in organisational procedures, they also require each individual worker to uphold the principles of empowerment. In many ways empowering practice reflects the value-base of social work, but also demands a more radical approach which include notions of participation, citizenship and empowerment (Braye and Preston- Shoot, 1995).

Empowerment

It is significant that the social work literature on empowerment (see Adams, 1996; Braye and Preston-Shoot, 1995) resists giving simplistic definitions of empowerment but concentrates on the processes. As a conclusion to this chapter we will reflect on how strategies such as negotiation, advocacy and involving users contribute to our understanding of empowerment in social work practice

We have considered how advocacy is one way of giving users a voice in the arrangements that are made for community care. Robin Means and Randall Smith (*Community Care: Policy and Practice*,

1994) discuss 'voice' as a model of user-empowerment, seeing it very much as case advocacy on behalf of those who want to remain, or have no choice about remaining, with existing providers of community care services, but wish to change the nature of the relationship or the services provided.

Both 'voice' and 'exit' are approaches to user-empowerment, with voice mechanisms being important for potential users who need to influence services right from the outset, before becoming part of it, for example to ensure that they get access to a full assessment. Exit mechanisms are for those who are receiving services; to express dissatisfaction by leaving, you have to be in receipt of the service. For some groups (for example those who are users of mental health services against their will) exit is not an option, but they have a right to be heard, to have a voice. A clear example of this is the patients' equal opportunities committee at one of the most secure mental hospitals, Broadmoor. Here, women in particular were able to question policies and procedures which they experienced as oppressive. Similarly, coalitions of people with disabilities have exercised their voices to great effect in ensuring that new legislation acknowledged their rights to services and to an enabling environment, rather than treating them according to medical criteria. Even though the Disability Discrimination Act 1995 was not as radical as was hoped, it did change the emphasis. Such activities can be clearly seen as cause advocacy, but are also clear examples of user-empowerment

Another means of empowering users is by conferring rights, an approach which has been at the centre of the campaign of the disability movement, and is often linked to discussions about citizenship. Discussions of the Institute of Public Policy Research about community care focus on the notion of citizenship as participation. They argue that it 'entails being able to participate in society, to enjoy its fruits and fulfil one's own potential, and it follows that each individual citizen should be equally able (or 'empowered') to do so' (Coote, 1992 p. 4). It is this definition which encourages us to look at processes which have been developed for user-empowerment. Such processes must incorporate a set of assumptions or values summarised by Mullender and Ward (1991):

- all people have skills, understanding and ability;
- people have rights to be heard, to participate, to choose, to define problems and action;

- people's problems are complex and social oppression is a contributory factor;
- people acting collectively are powerful; and
- methods of work must be non-elitist and non-oppressive.

(Mullender and Ward, 1991)

When evaluating projects which have tried to involve users it becomes apparent that while we might espouse the theory, the practice is not always easy (see Lindon and Morris, 1995, for a overview of projects).

One of the clearest statements about worker responsibility for empowerment in community care is the Joseph Rowntree Study undertaken by Olive Stevenson and Phyllida Parsloe (1993). Here the term empowerment is used for both a process and a goal: 'Step by step the worker acts to empower the user; the user becomes more powerful. Both work together in a continuous process, the goal of which is to shift the balance of power' (*Community Care and Empowerment*, 1993, p. 6). Empowerment involves the articulation of needs. Two models of empowerment, the *Strengths Model* and *Social Work in Partnership*, based on case studies, provide guidelines for staff identified as care managers.

Strengths model

Based on a project for users of mental health services:

- The focus of the helping process is upon consumers' strengths, interests and abilities; not upon their weaknesses, deficit or pathologies.
- People with mental illness can learn, grow and change.
- The consumer is viewed as the director of the helping process.
- The consumer–care manager relationship becomes the indispensable foundation for mutual collaboration.
- Assertive outreach is the preferred mode of working with consumers.
- The community is viewed as an oasis of potential resources for consumers, rather than the obstacle. Naturally occurring resources are considered a possibility before community or hospital mental health services.

Social Work in Partnership (SWIP)

This project collaborated with managers, social workers, home care organisers and occupational therapists in two social service departments to develop a model of practice which allows greater participation by users (for a fuller discussion of this project see *Good Intentions: Partnership in Social Services*, Marsh and Fisher, 1992):

- Investigation of problems must be with the explicit consent of the potential user(s) and client(s). (A client is an involuntary user.)
- User-agreement or a clear statutory mandate are the only bases for partnership-based intervention.
- Intervention must be based upon the views of all the relevant family members and carers.
- Services must be based on negotiated agreement rather than on assumptions and/or prejudices concerning the behaviour and wishes of users.
- Users must have the greatest possible degree of choice in the services that they are offered.

(Stevenson and Parsloe, 1993, pp. 38, 39)

Such frameworks provide excellent guides to the way that we must approach our practice to ensure that users and carers are viewed as partners, whether we are assessing someone for a package of care, or providing a service in a care plan that has been devised. For a more extensive account of the values, policies and processes and how these can inform and challenge our practice, *Empowering Practice in Social Care* by Suzy Braye and Michael Preston-Shoot (1995) provides an excellent overview and has many examples, case studies and exercises. Similarly Robert Adams (1996) describes how the process of empowerment can be undertaken *with* individuals, groups and communities and *through* processes of evaluation of effective relationships between users and professional workers. Later in this text methods of intervention have been identified as contributing to empowerment of users of services. For example, Audrey Mullender and Dave Ward's (1991) model of groupwork as an empowering practice is referenced in Chapter 10.

Early 'empowering' projects which developed locally-based teams (for example Bayley *et al.*, 1987) had to grapple with conflicts between statutory duties and control of services by local people;

whether participation applied to service-users only or included other people who lived locally; the worry of delegating powers and duties to those who do not have to be held accountable, as well as the complexity of managing joint health and social welfare services. In discussing systems theory we noted that interventions can be directed at resource controllers on whom we might be dependent. This challenges organisational structures where decisions about the nature and quantity of services have been non-negotiable. With the introduction of care management and devolved budget arrangements, front-line staff have had to learn organisation and management skills. This may provide more opportunities for flexible resource mobilisation. For example, the introduction of care management has allowed for the development of experimental projects such as Self-Operated Care schemes (SOCS), for people with disabilities, many of which have been broadened into Direct Payment Schemes. Here it is recognised that for certain groups true empowerment comes when they have the financial means to arrange their own services, but more importantly the power to influence the range of services available. This affords the status of active citizen having choices about involvement, not just a passive consumer who chooses from a range of services available. However, for a variety of reasons purchasing power will not be available to all users of community care services. Because of this they are frequently excluded from decision-making which directly impacts upon them. It is therefore vital that agencies' practices, processes and procedures ensure that users are afforded the rights of citizens irrespective of, or more importantly because of, their social and economic circumstances.

4

Interviewing and Counselling

The previous two chapters have concentrated on the processes of care management, and in doing so have sought to identify the practices which are incorporated into those processes. We have frequently identified that, while care management might reflect a new policy approach and involve a new social work discourse, many of the processes involve practices which have been core to social work for some decades. Those practices draw upon sets of skills which are basic to the approaches outlined in the following chapters of this book, namely communication skills. Communication occurs in many ways in social work and in this chapter we focus on interviewing and counselling as two aspects of communication which are common to many social work interactions.

Interviewing

Both in early referrals, and in ongoing contact, much depends on the quality of interviewing. Guidance on interviewing is timeless, as evidenced by the popularity of texts such as Garrett (1972). Social work interviews have been described as conversations with a purpose, but they are more than this. An interview is a process which involves a combination of social psychology and sociology, where theories and information about people in their social circumstances, their motivations and their responses in interpersonal relationships can be used to help the worker understand the individual in their situation, and to gain relevant information and offer appropriate support.

Only by carefully listening and observing the way that people seek help can objective facts and subjective feelings be part of an interpersonal exchange which correctly receives overt and covert messages, decodes them and responds to the various levels of communication therein. People can say one thing but their behaviour says the opposite. Advanced practitioners such as those who are expert in family therapy, moreover, are able to use the literal message alongside what is known as the 'metamessage' (which are messages about the message) as part of their interviewing. An illustration of this might be the crucial stage of leaving home for adolescents; here mixed messages are frequently sent by them to their parents which the bracketed phrase, 'Can I [let you let me] leave?' reveals. Even if beginners cannot use this level of communication in interviews it is worthwhile at least being able to spot these kinds of underlying motivation.

Having said that, it is important to recognise that a criticism of social workers has been that at times they have used this capacity to interpret messages to disempower those who come to them for assistance. The feminist and radical critiques of social work have parodied such an approach as 'What you are really saying is. . .', suggesting that the worker knows best and will refuse to accept the message that the person is claiming. This was a particular source of concern when social work was highly dependent upon a psychosocial approach, and messages were interpreted as having subconscious meanings. Such responses, especially at the beginning of contact, can be off-putting to those who bring problems and issues to the agency, either because the messages are not being heard, or if the issue that is being brought is the beginning of a more complex problem the person might not be ready to share all, and may be resistant to what might be seen to be an invasion into their privacy.

In discussing assessment we recognised that the first stage of care management, the screening process, was crucial in that it formed the basis for decisions about whether contact would continue and whether assessment for further services would be undertaken. Similarly in other social work activities the first contact with an individual is often of greatest significance.

Initial interviews

The first meeting between a potential service-user and a worker has four major aims. The first is to gather information which will be used jointly in decision-making about the nature of the difficulties and how to intervene. It also is an opportunity to try to secure a 'treatment alliance' whereby the worker conveys a wish to understand the other's thoughts and feelings. The third aim is to try to include a sense of hopefulness about being able to tackle the circumstances. Finally, it demonstrates to the applicant some of the ways in which the worker and the service works. Unless these factors are taken into consideration subsequent management of the situation could prove sterile; this is especially so when there is an apparently negative response to the interviewer.

At the beginning of contact, in particular, there is a fine line between the need to gain enough information to make an appropriate assessment and to identify whether, and to what extent, help can be offered, and not to be seen to be inappropriately inquisitive or not prepared to accept the explanation given. Let us just consider the daughter who approaches the social services office for help with day care for her elderly parent. In order to decide whether services can be allocated the worker has to assess both the level of need and the resources that are available. However, in doing this s/he may have to ask about the employment of adults in the family, and caring and other responsibilities of all concerned. Ultimately, there will also be questions about financial circumstances. Such information-gathering has to be conducted in ways which do not invoke feelings of guilt, or make the daughter feel that she is becoming a 'client' of the agency, in the worst sense of the word.

Situations which involve those who are reluctant participants, that is offenders, or parents who may be suspected of abusing their children, bring other sets of dilemmas. In the former the level of motivation for participating with, for example, supervision or compliance with a community sentence has to be assessed, while recognising that a driving factor will be the desire to avoid a custodial sentence. In situations where accusations and allegations have to be investigated or suspicions followed up, information has to be acquired, but it has to be remembered that the person being investigated may be innocent, and even if they are not they will need a continuing relationship with a social work agency in order to ensure the appropriate outcome for all involved.

In other circumstances, where individuals have come of their own accord to the agency, they are motivated by all sorts of factors. Practitioners can get frustrated or anxious when service-users do not return after one interview, feeling that somehow they have failed. In fact, research shows that up to 50 per cent of help-seekers do not return for a second interview, and while the quality of the initial session is related to a positive response other reasons for noncontinuation are possible (Marziali, 1988). Many people are quite satisfied with the first session and decide that they do not require further assistance. Others are not ready to commit themselves to ongoing intervention, while a high proportion of people prefer to ask for help on an as-needed basis rather than have a regular series of meetings. Finally, some people are so overwhelmed by the intensity or chronicity of their problems that they cannot use the help which is offered.

On the other hand, in the arrangements for community care where eligibility criteria have to be employed, it may be that at the end of the interview the worker has to inform the person seeking help or support that services are not available. This could be because they have come to the wrong agency, and need to be referred to a benefits agency or to a health service; it may be because they do not fit the eligibility criteria, or it is thought that the problem is not acute or sufficiently chronic to warrant further assessment at this stage. In these circumstances the person has to be given clear and full information about why the decision is made, and this has to be done in such a way that they feel validated and not rejected. In circumstances where people are involved in caring, it is likely that the situation will deteriorate and at some point in the future another referral will be made, it is therefore necessary to ensure that the person will feel able to come back to the agency.

Such approaches are all part of good social work practice, but they are also part of the quality assurance mechanisms inherent in community care plans and charters for community care, where the nature and timing of the response is monitored by managers in the service and users have the opportunity to invoke complaints procedures if they are not satisfied with the way the service is delivered (DoH, 1993). However, such initiatives often mean that there is a bureaucracy associated with screening, or determining need, which can influence the interviewing process. As we considered when discussing assessment, the use of paper or computerised systems for screening or assessment involves the worker in a whole set of other activities while conducting the interview. The purpose of such systems should be explained clearly to everyone who participates, and the use to which information is put made clear.

There are ways of conducting an initial interview (or phone call) which are more likely to establish a favourable climate for a purposeful alliance, such as ensuring that there is congruence, that is agreement between worker and client, about expectations of what can be done and being open and honest about what cannot be done. From the outset all parties should be aware of why they are meeting (or talking). Successful interviews do not merely depend on content (what was said) or whether the client got what was asked for. A significant outcome for the first interview is for the worker to be perceived as someone who is able to understand what the client's concerns are and how they feel about their difficulties, and to be open about both the agency and their own role within it. Additionally the worker will have demonstrated some of the basic values of social work, including acceptance and a non-judgmental attitude.

Skills in interviewing

The basic skills in interviewing involve the ten principles listed by Davies (1985) namely: letting the interviewee know how much time there is; starting where the client is in their understanding of the situation; trying to be sympathetic so as to help make the atmosphere a relaxed one; trying to see things through the other person's eyes; knowing the danger of passing judgement rather than acceptance; developing social skills such as smiling to help open up communication at the outset; avoiding questions that can be answered 'yes' or 'no'; not putting answers in the client's mouth; not probing too deeply too quickly and learning to cope with silences (which are usually the interviewee's best thinking times).

Each interview tends to have a focus, such as an exploration of someone's financial needs, illnesses, offences, relationships or whatever; at the same time every interview ought to have a structure (that is a beginning, middle and end). There is a circularity in the interviewing process if it is to make sense to the person being interviewed and provide the information necessary for assessment. The person bringing the problem or issue will set the initial agenda, but this can be explored by the interviewer asking more questions which might lead to further information and other avenues to be explored. However, at the close of the interview the interviewer should ensure that the original topic is returned to and reviewed in the light of the information that has emerged during the interview.

The first words at the beginning of any encounter are often quite significant, for example, 'My wife thought that you could help me'; equally, the last things said could reveal what attitude the person leaves with, for instance, 'I think I can cope now I've got the information'. The language that is used often reveals emotions, as of course do the bodily positions and non-verbal gestures displayed during the interviews. In single interviews and in a series of interviews, references to difficulties may be returned to, or repetition even of denial that something is worrying may give clues to helping. Inconsistencies and gaps may be spotted, for instance mentioning one parent but never the other, or concealed meanings such as the sexually abused client who fears interference (being interfered with?). Also sudden changes in topics of conversation may either reveal too hurtful material or the person may have associated one idea with another, so these too are worth noting.

The above list of 'triggers' or cues indicates that each interview needs to be reflected upon, reviewing aspects of the content later, if possible via a detailed record or (in certain agencies such as those using family therapies), by means of a video recording. This reflection should include an awareness of the powerful role that the interviewer plays, both in helping the person explore the issues fully in a way that they want to, or in the potential to block communication.

Sometimes students are worried when they encounter people who are uncooperative and who, despite saying that they want help, seem to do all that they can to block it. Often the reason for this is that approaching a stranger for help could be an occasion for shame, high expectations, a sense of failure and an admission of dependency. The worker does not have to reveal intimate, embarrassing or frightening facts about her or himself and so there is understandable reluctance and anger on the part of the interviewee, which may, indeed, remind them of times past when similar interpersonal contacts proved unhelpful.

A positive outcome in interviewing relies also on trying to eliminate some of the barriers to communication which can result in misunderstandings. Apart from clients who have evident comprehension, hearing or speech impairments (which may require study into alternative methods of communicating), errors which even experienced interviewers make include anticipating what the other person is going to say or assuming that you have understood the meaning of the words and non-verbal cues. It is better to let the client talk freely at first if possible; this can counteract any tendency to be sure in advance what the other is saying or is about to say. When individuals are allowed to tell their story in their own way it is surprising how often they come up with their own solutions.

Interviewing through an interpreter is another way of opening channels of communication. While this might be seen as something of a specialised and advanced skill it would be wrong not to address it in an introductory text. It is important that all students and social workers are equipped to work in multi-cultural society, and to acquire the necessary skills. Specialist texts have been written (see, for example, Bandana Ahmad (1990) *Black Perspectives in Social Work*) and below is a summary of the advice given in an article by Freed (1988). She sees the interpreter as a conduit, linking interviewer and interviewee and thus careful preparation of the interpreter for this role is necessary, emphasising confidentiality, neutrality, conveying the emotional tone of the interview and transmitting accurately what is being communicated. The social worker (whose experience may resemble watching a foreign film without subtitles), must pay attention to the seating arrangement, discuss with the client the interpreter's presence, provide assurances of confidentiality, be patient as the pace may be slow, respect the attitudes about social work in the person's country of origin, avoid working through children or relatives if this is indicated, and review the content and process later to ensure that a proper level of understanding was reached. Agencies should fulfil their obligations to offer services to non-English-speaking clients by recruiting and training interpreters to function within that role, but this is not unproblematic. The use of interpreters means that the person giving personal information is now having to give it to more than one person. The trained interpreter offers objectivity in a way that using a family member or friends does not, but they may still be experienced as in some way judging the individual. This might be particularly so where the crisis or problem has been precipitated by cultural dilemmas. For example Muslim women may feel reluctant to speak about domestic violence to a female interpreter, because of cultural expectations of the role of women within marriage. Freed's paper is concerned with the unique skills of interviewing those who do not speak English, much of what she writes could well refer to communicating through an interpreter for service-users who have hearing and sight impairment.

Other barriers to communication include the attitudes and actions of workers who are unskilled, or unprepared. For example, stereotyping can lead to sets of assumptions which block the individual and this can create defences. Assuming that because someone is black, or middle-class, or confused or inadequate they will have certain characteristics encourages premature judgements and hasty conclusions; people are too complex, subtle and dynamic to sum up rapidly. On the one hand, being antagonistic because someone is aggressive can exacerbate situations which are not helpful for the user and could ultimately lead to risks for the worker (Brown, Bute and Ford, 1986). On the other hand, warming to someone because of their charm, ability to verbalise and their seeming cooperation can lead to a false sense of positiveness, to collusion and denial of significant factors (for example child abuse or domestic violence).

Using jargon is another obvious obstacle to good interviewing; it distances worker and client. Using the client's own words and phrases is often useful; it demonstrates that you are listening attentively and at the same time conveys acceptance and respect for their way of putting things (this is discussed in more detail below).

Interviewing children and adolescents requires particular skills. Specialist literature is available (Rich, 1968; Redgrave, 1987) and should be consulted, and practice gained through experience, courses and maybe micro-skills teaching via video and live supervision. Interviewers who are skilled in adult work can find it hard to communicate with children because of a tendency to concentrate too much on the formal elements of the interviewing task. For instance, using questions is different with children with whom, in fact-finding, one may need to be quite specific and direct. Letting the child talk freely while gaining facts takes expertise. Gaining cooperation, timing, overcoming confusion, managing hostility, being spontaneous, getting the right surroundings, communicating through 'third things' (toys and analogies), awareness of cultural appropriateness and so on are perhaps more crucial than they already are when interviewing grown-ups. A text which has proved valuable for those investigating the protection of children, in order to plan for their long-term care, which contains common sense but vital areas for exploration and ways of unearthing sound assessments through appropriate questions is that by the Social Services Inspectorate (SSI) (Department of Health, 1988).

Questioning

The purpose of interviewing is more often than not to gather information. This is especially so at the beginning of any contact and in the processes of assessment, review and quality assurance. Information can be gathered by observation and listening but the most common way is to ask questions which get at both facts and feelings. Writers on interviewing have compared the different techniques associated with questions asked in classrooms, courtrooms and by researchers, clinicians and social workers (see Dillon, 1990), and these illustrate the ways in which the method can either hinder or aid the helping process.

An interviewer who poses questions accusingly or in a suspicious tone rather than in an interested and friendly way will arouse fear and antagonism. The wording of a question in this respect is less material than the manner and tone in which it is put. Try asking the question, 'Are you looking for work?' using a range of inflections to illustrate this.

Asking too many questions could sound nosey or interrogative or asking too few may leave relevant features hidden. The pace at which questions are put needs to be at the client's pace otherwise more might be revealed than the person intended resulting in annoyance or reluctance to return to the agency again. However, it is sometimes possible to assist the person to say what they want to, or give you the information you need to be able to help them by a process of funnelling. This encourages someone to speak quite generally about a subject, encouraged by the prompt to 'Tell me about . . .'. You can then ask them to give a specific example of what they are talking about, and then focus on that example, but also check out how frequently such events or experiences occur.

It is very common amongst inexperienced people to avoid asking probing questions when clients hint at what they are worried about deep-down. Failing to pursue some areas in an interview might be related to needing to protect ourselves from pain or fear of unearthing material which is threatening or distressing; over-cautiousness or reticence can be a hindrance. Accordingly, if someone hints that they are so depressed that they wonder if life is worth living and then quickly moves on to another subject, it might be worthwhile coming back to that idea again later, saying something like, 'Can you tell me more about that?' or 'I'm not sure I understood earlier when you said . . .' which allows for elaboration if the person wants this; it also lets the worker check out perceptions and it conveys to the client that the worker can cope with the 'unacceptable' thoughts and feelings.

Avoidance can also occur when suspicions are raised about behaviour and attitudes which are unacceptable, inappropriate or even illegal. This is particularly sensitive in relationships where the worker has a responsibility for monitoring behaviour. For example the requirements for the probation service to confront offending behaviour, or for child care workers to ensure the protection of children can precipitate dilemmas for workers if they receive information in interviews which clearly indicates inappropriate or unacceptable behaviour. In these circumstances there is sometimes an appeal to confidentiality, an expectation that the worker will not act on the information. It is therefore important to be clear about the parameters; if the person then chooses to reveal information they do so knowing that the worker will have to act upon it.

The response of some workers to dealing with issues of race has been to avoid challenging black and ethnic minority people in the same way as white people might be challenged (Ahmad, 1990). It is appropriate to challenge the behaviour that is deemed to be unacceptable, as long as the worker has checked out that their judgement is not framed by cultural norms which may misinterpret that behaviour and/or actions.

Obviously, questions have to be asked to get some information, especially when it has not been forthcoming in the interview. A general rule for social work is that more information is gleaned and more is learnt about people's reaction by asking open questions. These are questions which require more than the answer 'yes' or 'no'. The question 'Do you have any children?' will elicit the answer yes or no; the question 'How many children do you have?' will get the information about the number of children, and might also encourage the person to give details about them, thus avoiding the need for further questions about sex and age of the children. It is often recommended that the 5WH (Why, What, Who, Where, When and How) are useful to help us think about open questions. A blend of enquiries which address these areas will reveal a lot of fundamental information: 'What is the problem?'; 'When did it start?'; 'Who could help?'; 'Where should we aim to sort things out?; 'How do you think we can help?'. Obviously these would not be asked all at once, or in quick succession!

Careful thought needs to be given even in the use of open questions. The overuse of the question 'Why?' might seem to imply that someone should explain their behaviour and cause defences to go up. In any event, people often do not know 'Why?' and may be seeking help to understand themselves and their situation more clearly. A 'What?' alternative is preferable and may reveal information useful to all involved in the interchange as happened when a worker, instead of asking an elderly person why she was afraid to go out, asked what she thought might happen if she did.

Skilful use of questions is sometimes overlooked in social work, as if it is something anyone can do. As an alternative to questions to collect information which appears to only have value to the organisation (which increases resistance, for example in involuntary clients in probation), probing questions are a way of actually starting off processes of change. It is worth studying the range of good questioning techniques which can help others identify their experience, raise consciousness, solve problems and so on. A number of these are written about in the literature: Henderson and Thomas (1980) describe how community workers will deliberately ask naive questions to prompt local residents to begin to question what they assume they cannot influence. Reporter type questions can sometimes achieve the same goal, as can the devil's advocate approach. Here the respondent is intentionally confronted with the arguments of opponents in order to trigger a change. Other ways of employing questions which hold the germs of possible change involve taking a one-down stance by saying, 'I could be wrong but . . .'; 'I wonder . . .' or, 'I don't quite understand . . .', all of which stimulate people to step outside of their usual frame of reference to consider new possibilities, without the worker dragging out information. Another general guideline is to log awkward moments and return to them later when the client can cope with a specific question, perhaps acknowledging the awkwardness and underlining an earlier question by asking it again. Cognitive therapists, whose ideas stem from behaviour therapy, have expertise in asking questions which challenge negative thoughts or false assumptions to which those who are depressed are prone (see Scott, 1989); thus a patient who says that he has no friends will be queried about this, 'When you say that you have no friends do you mean that or do you mean that you have only one or two?' and, 'Is it true to say that you are always depressed, your diary indicates a slight lifting of mood in the mornings?'; so questions need to slow people down to check out the way that they automatically construe their world. These are somewhat specialised techniques and will be dealt with in more detail in Chapter 8.

A further style of asking good questions is that known as 'circular questioning'. Developed within the family therapy field it assesses family functioning and interaction by asking one member of the family to comment on the relationship or behaviour of two other members. Thus, 'When your mother tries to get Andrew to go to school, what does your grandmother do?' and, 'Who do you think is closer to your father, your sister or your brother?' and so on. Circular questioning highlights different viewpoints giving feedback to everyone present while introducing new information about how each third party views relations between other dyads (Penn, 1982). In essence, it sets behaviour within context.

Hypothetical questions, starting with, 'What if?' are additionally revealing for all, as are those which ask someone to describe their ideal solution (giving clues to people's goals and the way in which work might move forward). They also provide a challenge to people's assumptions. An adolescent who is being fostered, but is in conflict with his family and threatening to leave home, could be encouraged to explore 'What if you left home, what do you think would happen?', thus enabling him to explore his worries or fears that his foster parents did not (and would not) care about what happened to him.

Problem-posing questions are preferable to those ready answers which invade the competence of others. People often have their own ideas which can be 'unlocked': for example, a despairing group of unemployed people at a Probation Centre who said, 'We can't change their policies' were induced to rethink their powerlessness by a group leader who asked, 'Who are *they*, and what do we know of their policies?' In sum, asking good questions saves time, helps to engage rather than alienate clients and can be a tool for actually beginning to change a situation.

Responding

Interviewing is not just a one-way process; it is not just about asking questions and listening to the answers. Nor is it about venturing opinions or advice-giving, as we shall see below when we discuss counselling. Most people when they listen give some indication of the fact that they have heard, saying nothing can appear disinterested or even hostile. There are ways to demonstrate that you are listening: sitting attentively or nodding at appropriate points are two ways, but much more significant are the responses that are made. Five type of responses have been identified, not all of which are good practice:

1. *Evaluative* responses are those which say how you judge the person, or what is being told to you. Many remarks in ordinary conversation carry evaluative overtones. These are to be avoided. A good listener will learn to accept people, and hear information without passing judgement about what they hear.

2. *Interpretive* responses analyse what the person has said, and give it new meaning. This is often an intellectual response and is often attractive to students who are encouraged to link their practice to theory. Almost always, interpretive responses lead away from what the person is saying, but represent what is going on in the listener's mind. Interpretations should be used sparingly – even when we are asked directly what we think.

3. *Sympathetic* responses might seem appropriate if the person is sad or upset, or what they are talking about seems painful. However, there is a danger that in expressing sympathy you are reacting to how you think you might be feeling in the circumstances. Accurate empathy is listening to the emotions that the person is expressing, however unexpected they might seem. If you name an emotion for them, you might block them being able to express what they really feel because they think the emotion is 'inappropriate'.

4. *Probing* responses are those which seek more detail about what is said, but often they are based on the listener's interpretation of the situation and seeking confirmation of this. As has been said, a good use of probing is when the person is encouraged to explore their own feelings about what they are saying. This helps us to understand what they are experiencing.

5. *Understanding* responses are those which you need to be a good listener. There are three kinds of understanding responses:

- Reflection   This is usually demonstrated by repeating what the person has said. This is not done merely in parrot fashion, but more as an echo of their thoughts. It acts as a prompt enabling them to change or clarify the words that they have used and encouraging them to say more without directing or probing. It is also a clear indicator that you are actively hearing what they say.
- Paraphrase   If you repeat back what a person has said, perhaps using different words or joining together two or three things that they have said without changing the mean-'ing, this is paraphrasing. It is important if summarising a complicated set of events or feelings that you do not interpret or evaluate them. It is also necessary to check out with the talker that what you have paraphrased is accurate.
- Feedback   This is given when you want to indicate that you have heard accurately what has been said, and that you accept the person, whatever the emotions expressed or information given. So, for example, it is possible to tell a bereaved person that it is alright to feel angry with the person who has died, if that is the emotion that they have expressed. But it is always important to check out with the person that you have fed back accurately.

This analysis of possible responses involves demonstrating accurate listening and understanding and links closely with the principles and practices of counselling. These are discussed below, but for those who want to look in detail at the theory and practice of interviewing, and other forms of communication, the text by Joyce Lishman (1995) is recommended

Counselling

The British Association for Counselling defines counselling as 'when a person, occupying regularly or temporarily the role of counsellor, offers and agrees explicitly to give time, attention and respect to another person, or persons, who will temporarily be in the role of client (*Membership Notes*, 1990). The task is to give the client an opportunity to explore, discover and clarify ways of living more resourcefully and with a greater sense of well-being. This is a very broad description which allows for the fact that counselling has many schools – behavioural, psychodynamic and humanistic, as well as feminist and transcultural versions.

The aim here is to introduce the basic principles of counselling, and to illustrate these from two models, those of Carl Rogers and Gerard Egan. Both of these draw on social work values of accepting the individual, use skills in listening and attending to the information that is given and work towards a joint understanding and decision-making about ways forward. Not all intervention is so person-centred. As we shall see in Chapter 8, sometimes the focus is on behaviour. In that chapter we reference rational-emotive therapy (RET), which believes that people are essentially hedonistic and pursuing two major goals of staying alive and pursuing happiness (Ellis, 1962). The focus of intervention is on people's cognition, the way they understand and interpret events, and the therapy is fairly structured. An alternative perspective is pursued in gestalt therapy. Here it is argued that behaviour is determined by the relationship between the person and their environment (Perls, 1973). This interpretation requires the counsellor or 'therapist' to focus on the relationship between themselves and the person being helped (the I–thou relationship). This means that the approach can be confrontational, as well as accepting and supportive. These and other therapeutic approaches are described and discussed in greater detail by Windy Dryden (1984).

Whatever the school of thought or model of counselling that is followed, generically workers need to be able to listen, observe and respond. As has been outlined above skills need to be acquired in attending, specifying, confronting, questioning, reflecting feelings and content, personalising, problem-solving and action-planning. Nelson-Jones (1983) recommends that to become a skilled counsellor takes more than being caring and understanding; one has to show this through technical expertise as well. Once acquired, constant use of the skills is necessary to prevent them becoming 'rusty'. In order to be effective in active listening and appropriate responses, counsellors must own the following seven qualities:

1. *Empathy* or *understanding*, the effort to see the world through the other person's eyes.
2. *Respect*, responding in a way which conveys a belief in the other's ability to tackle the problem.

3. *Concreteness* or *being specific*, so that the counsellee can be enabled to reduce confusion about what he/she means.
4. *Self-knowledge* and *self-acceptance*, ready to help others with this.
5. *Genuineness*, being real in a relationship.
6. *Congruence*, so that the words we use match our body language.
7. *Immediacy*, dealing with what is going on in the present moment of the counselling session, as a sample of what is going on in someone's everyday life.

Books which offer exercises for practice (Corey, 1986) help develop technical expertise. Rather than attempt to do the same here, a check-list of micro-skills which seem to create special difficulty is given below, and readers are encouraged to reflect on where they may have limitations and accordingly need to keep practising. Many of these have been discussed in more general terms in the section on interviewing.

The micro-skills check-list requires counsellors to consider whether they are able to:

• Let a person finish talking without reacting?
• Accurately reflect back content and feelings?
• Paraphrase what someone has said?
• Summarise to move interviews forward'?
• Clarify your own role to the other person?
• Use open questions?
• Use prompts to encourage the person to continue? Draw out feelings?
• Offer tentative understanding?
• Tune into how the other person affects you? Tolerate silences of about five seconds?
• Control your own anxiety and relax?
• Focus on the 'here and now' as well as 'there and then'? Provide direction and keep focus in the session?
• Recognise and confront ambivalence and inconsistencies? Set mutual goals?
• Tolerate painful topics?
• Discuss and generate alternative plans of action?
• Evaluate costs and gains of what was achieved?
• Begin, sustain and end well (each session and the whole contact)?

Advice and directions are all right when this is timely and when they are sought. But, in counselling, one's own perspective can interfere with the counsellee's journey into self-assessment, self-awareness or self-determination. Whenever we are tempted to begin a sentence with 'I think . . .' or 'My feelings are . . .', it is worth pausing. By talking about 'me' and 'my' we step outside the other person's frame of reference which is at the heart of the counselling encounter. In fact, when situations are still being explored no clever responses are called for. Usually, all that is needed is to reflect back the other's statements beginning with 'You think . . .' or 'Your feelings are . . .' to *allow people to listen to themselves.*

Workshops to develop counselling skills usually reveal that inexperienced people have a tendency to cover up their uncertainty by trying too hard, interrupting too much (what Jacobs (1985) calls 'having two mouths and one ear'), and feeling responsible for someone else's difficulties. Unhelpful tendencies appear too, such as preaching, falsely reassuring, judging and offering unasked for interpretations. In sum, we are never helpful when we do not allow the other person to be different from ourselves. Self-monitoring, live supervision or peer counselling could be useful ways of changing habits.

Other factors which could affect counselling relationships and which should be considered are those of disability, class, gender and race differences. If counselling relies so much on understanding the client's experience and frame of reference then when the therapist comes from a different background it might be assumed that empathic understanding is not possible. There are problems with this assumption. For instance, white social workers could become blinkered by the issue of a so-called black culture, feeling deskilled by a lack of knowledge of religious beliefs and daily living habits. As A. Ahmad (1990) asks, how relevant is the aspect of the client's culture to recognising their needs and the nature of the counselling interaction? Do we check the cultural realities of all our clients? How do we guard against oversimplistic explanations which ignore underlying emotional (and, indeed, structural) factors which, for example, contribute to someone's depression? In interpersonal contacts where the worker is white and the client black, while both are aware of this significant factor, both participants possibly agree to a conspiracy of silence, the worker feeling guilty about being the 'oppressor'. Alternatively, assuming that being black is a disadvantage could result in ignoring clients' strengths. The major elements in counselling, particularly Rogers' 'client-centred' approach, which aimed to facilitate the self-actualising potential of people, is about equalising the distribution of power. This requires white workers accepting clients correcting their preconceptions and being open to confrontation, for example that they could never know what it is like to live continually with rejection, humiliation and discrimination, which can so undermine self-respect.

Black workers similarly may feel uncomfortable with white clients, concerned that they will never be able to understand the others' realities. If both worker and client are black this could create barriers to openness and self-disclosure, especially if the client believes that the worker has 'sold out' to the establishment,' or if the worker overidentifies because of the common bond of racial experience. On the other hand, beneficial counselling opportunities exist when white clients welcome the chance to share feelings of exploitation with black helpers or when a black counsellor's positive self-concept (Maximé, 1986) offers a sense of hope to the black client.

Having said this the very notion of counselling as a model of helping, developed according to Western values, beliefs and perspectives, could be inappropriate to different cultures or to immigrant groups such as Asian Indians, Chinese and Vietnamese people. For instance, the concepts of self-determination, individualisation, independence and self-disclosure may conflict with values such as interdependence, acceptance and self-control. Because of this some writers (Hirayama and Cetingok, 1988) favour empowerment of the family or whole community rather than focus on an individual: goals would then reflect loyalty, solidarity and cooperation, the worker taking a more active role as teacher, resource consultant and mediator.

In relation to gender differences, some feminist literature has stressed that women clients should be seen by female therapists as only women can understand women. While it is recognised that some feminist counselling has not incorporated black perspectives and is somewhat middle-class-bound (Dominelli and McLeod, 1989)), feminist literature has provided some useful guidelines for working with women, which can be applied to working with any service-user. In particular Hanmer and Statham (1988) suggest an exercise which helps the worker identify commonalities and diversities with the person with whom they are working. This is an effective way of facilitating an empathic and genuine response (see below for more discussion of these terms). Such an exercise also draws attention to the power balances within counselling relationships and helps to avoid stereotypical assumptions about, for example, sexual orientation. The evidence seems to indicate that counsellors – both male and female – are affected by prevailing sex-role stereotyping (about men and women). Thus Hall (1987) points out that, amongst other changes, practice should address the allocation of workers to clients as an important issue in establishing a relationship. So, we know that in the initial stages of counselling women who have been beaten, raped or subject to incest there is a preference for women counsellors; but later, the female client may gain more from a male counsellor who provides a different role model. Such decisions should not be forced on women, but should be arrived at as part of the counselling relationship. More recently feminist literature has explored the work that has to be done in challenging aspects of masculinity, especially violent behaviour (see Lupton and Gillespie, 1994; Cavanagh and Cree, 1996). While it is recognised that having a woman counsellor allows men to develop skills in making positive relationships with women, this has at times been oppressive for women workers. The need for male workers to offer more positive models of masculinity to male clients has been recognised. This brief discussion illustrates that research into gender matching, and matching client and worker more generally, is complex but should not be ignored. The literature quoted here is an introduction to looking at this phenomenon in more depth.

Another group for whom counselling is just as important, but who are sometimes ignored, are older people. Too frequently we assume that problems occur merely because of old age rather than the unique conflicts which face each of us at any age. Ageism makes us fail to see when older people are depressed, abusing alcohol and drugs, having sexual problems, wanting to develop self-awareness or trying to modify behaviour and attitudes. A fruitful book is that by Scrutton (1989).

To move on now to the actual theory and methods of counselling two models are looked at in more detail, those of Rogers (1980) and Egan (1981), starting with Carl Rogers' humanistic approach to client-centred (also called person-centred) counselling.

Rogers' client-centred approach

Carl Rogers, who died in 1987, developed client-centred therapy which implied that those who sought help were responsible people with power to direct their own lives: in fact, he had originally called his approach 'non-directive therapy' but later was convinced that there is a tendency towards growth and change and that, given the right climate in the therapeutic relationship, people can discover and direct their personal power. Rogers' whole attitude was grounded in the belief that the client is the only natural authority about her or himself; he trusted human beings to be able to move towards constructive growth with the help of a worker who demonstrated empathy, congruence and positive regard. Thus, the counsellor does not know best and cannot operate in a superior or expert way. As Rogers hoped, his ideas continue to develop, though there is a danger seen by some (Merry, 1990) that therapists might start to trust their techniques more than they trust their clients.

The goal of this approach is the greater integration and independence of the individual: the focus is on the person rather than on solving the presenting problem. Through the counsellor's attitudes of genuine caring, respect and understanding, people are able to loosen their defences and open themselves to new experiences and revised perceptions. As the helping relationship progresses, clients are able to express deeper feelings such as shame, anger and guilt, previously deemed too frightening to incorporate into their sense of self.

Frequently, people come to us in a state of incongruence; there is a discrepancy between how they see themselves (self-concept) and how they would like to see themselves (ideal self-concept). Or, as in the case example below, a contrast exists between self-concept and experience in reality. In the interview the worker is helping Linda to explore her sense of who she is, separate from the feedback which she apparently receives from those in her environment. This conflict, about the way we are and the way we want to be, or the way we feel we are compared to what others say we are, is sometimes at the root of all sorts of problems. While assenting that busy social service agencies may not have the time to let clients peel away the layers of their difficulties so as to work things out for themselves, it would be shortsighted to overlook the value of motivating clients towards self-management; it can help prevent problems worsening and can reduce the need to return to our departments again and again.

Case example

Linda is sixteen, living at home with her mother who is a single parent. There are two older children, grown up and living away from home. Linda attends the local Further Education college, studying a business course. She calls in the office of social services to ask for help, desperate because her mother is asking for help with the housework as she too works outside the home. Yet this leaves little time for Linda to study for her exams which are looming. In general, without an efficient duty system and easy access to the department, the client would be redirected to seek help from a student counsellor (assuming one exists). Although allocated low priority this is the kind of referral which, with minimum but sufficient attention, could prevent more serious difficulties later. Respecting the client's wishes, no contact with anyone else is planned at this stage.

The transcript is taken from the first interview of Linda (L) with her counsellor (C), in the first half hour. Linda unloads all of her mixed-up feelings towards her mother, but really towards her *self*. Her mother, burdened by her own duties, tells Linda that she is selfish and lazy: adolescents in particular seem to internalise others' opinions (Noonan, 1983) which can result in confusion about differentiating between 'me' and 'not me' phenomena.

L (despairingly) I can't do anything to please my mum.
C How does that make you feel?
L (after a pause) I don't know.
C You look sad about it.
L Well, it makes me feel miserable . . . (struggling).
C . . . Not knowing what pleases your mum.
L Nothing I do pleases her.
C Are you saying that the things you do for your mother are not appreciated? Is that what makes you feel miserable?
L I just wish she'd stop picking on me. I'd do anything for her but she only wants it done in her time.
C Can you give me an example of something that has happened this week?
L This morning she asked me to do the breakfast dishes. I was late for 'Tech' and said I'd do them when I got home. But she ranted and raved so I had to do them then.
C You sound angry about that.
L I think she is being unreasonable.
C (neutral tone) You feel *you're* not unreasonable.
L *She* says I am.

C   What do you think?
L   About not doing the dishes?
C   Yes. Do you feel that you are unreasonable as a person?
L   I don't know.

Often people who seek help feel a great deal of ambivalence towards significant others in their lives; in Linda's case, she feels only conditional acceptance that she is a 'good' person in her interactions with her mother. Because the counsellor is wise and mature, no sides are taken and no blame attached to anyone as this would detract from the aim to help the youngster work through a reflective re-cognition (recognition) of herself. The counsellor realises too that counselling is a two-way process where worker and client need to take each other into account: at times we overlook how much clients affect our feelings (Kell and Mueller, 1966).

Framework for understanding counselling

To give a framework now which summarises Rogers' client-centred approach (1980):

- *Theory base and important concepts* devolve from a philosophical background of the existential tradition which respects an individual's subjective experience and places emphasis on the vocabulary of freedom, choice, autonomy and meaning. It is a humanistic approach which is concerned with growth and 'becoming', recognising the importance of the self-concept and the potential for self-actualization, that is a 'fully functioning person'. Given appropriate nurturing conditions such as authentic, warm, empathic, unconditional relationships with significant others, people automatically grow in positive ways. It forms a 'third force' theoretical alternative to the psychoanalytic and behavioural approaches considered in Chapters 7 and 8. The theory also draws on phenomenological perspectives – the way in which a person's experience of their self is congruent or otherwise with the way they 'experience their self in the world'.
- *Problems* which arise include psychological disturbance owing to the inner conflict between self-experience and the way one is perceived by others: conditional acceptance from important

relationships puts limits on the extent to which one can really be oneself.

- *Goals* of therapy are to assist someone in their growth process; to help an individual become a fully functioning person by openness to experience and ambiguity, self-trust, developing an internal source of evaluation and learning that growth and revision are ongoing processes, not once-and-for-all end-products of therapy.
- *The client's role* is to move away from 'oughts' and 'shoulds', that is, living up to the expectations of others. A person decides their own standards and independently validates the choices and decisions which are made. In a climate of acceptance clients have the opportunity to experience the whole range of their feelings thereby becoming less defensive about their hidden, negative aspects. They develop 'a way of being'. At times, clients are instrumental in helping counsellors develop away from 'doing something' into 'being there' for others as Bhaduri's (1990) account of work with the Rahman family showed.
- *The worker's role and techniques.* Rogers' views gradually shifted away from techniques towards the personhood of the worker and the therapeutic relationship which communicated acceptance, respect, understanding and sharing. The counsellor does not use techniques in the creation of an accepting climate as this would depersonalise the encounter and the counsellor would not be genuine. In some ways this approach has built-in safety features for novices who do not have to offer interpretations and the like: staying within the other's frame of reference offers some assurance that clients will not be harmed by this caring approach which thereby encourages the client to care for her/his self.

Egan's three-stage approach

Another model of counselling, which counteracts some of the limitations of the above when counsellors listen and reflect but do not challenge, is the three-stage approach attributed to Egan (1981). He has extended the three stages of *Exploration*, *Understanding* and *Action* to add a fourth stage of *Evaluation*. Each of these stages is diagrammatically represented below. The four adjacent diamond shapes signify the widening and narrowing of focus within each

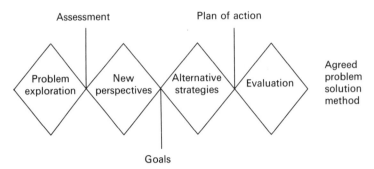

***Figure* 4.1** *Four stages of Egan's model*

interview and along the total helping process. Accordingly, following a wide exploration of the problem based on the foundation of a relationship of trust and mutual endeavour, the counsellor helps the counsellee to narrow down their discussion so that an assessment can be formulated. Following this, enquiry opens up again so that the client and helper can gain an understanding and maybe a new perspective on the difficulties. This reveals which goals to aim for but, in order to consider a range of alternative change strategies, the interview has to be wide-ranging again, prior to focusing down later on a specific plan of action. Finally, a broad-ranging discussion opens up as a way of evaluating 'how did it go?' before closer examination of the chosen problem-solving method is undertaken. Then, if necessary in a circular fashion, the first stage of wide exploration is resumed as part of the helping process.

Some skills which can be used in each stage are as follows.

- Stage 1: *exploration skills*. The worker aims to establish rapport, assisting in the exploration of thoughts, feelings and behaviour relevant to the problem in hand. Asking 'What is the difficulty?' the counsellor tries to build trust and a working alliance, using active listening, reflecting, paraphrasing and summarising skills. Open questions are used before the client is asked to say which concrete problem they and the helper need to understand.
- Stage 2: *understanding skills*. The counsellor continues to be facilitative, using Stage 1 skills and in addition helps the person to piece together the picture that has emerged. Themes and patterns may be pointed out to assist in gaining new perspectives:

this alternative point of view aids clearer understanding of what the person's goals are and identifies strengths and resources. The skills lie in offering an alternative frame of reference, using disclosure of oneself appropriately, staying in touch with what is happening here-and-now and using confrontation. This latter skill is not to be misunderstood as an attack. It is an act of caring of encouraging clients to consider what they are doing or not doing, challenging inconsistencies and conflicting ideas in order to tap the person's unused resources. Egan would view confrontation without support as disastrous and support without confrontation as anaemic. The timing of confrontation is vital when the relationship can endure such a challenge.

- Stage 3: *action skills*. The worker and the counsellee begin to identify and develop resources for resolving or coping with the causes of concern, based on a thorough understanding of self and situation. The skills lie in setting goals, providing support and resources, teaching problem solving if necessary, agreeing purposes and using decision-making abilities.
- Stage 4: *evaluation*. An action plan having been chosen and tried, all ideas are reviewed and measured for effectiveness. The counsellor's skills rely again on active listening plus all those of the previous stages.

As we can see, the worker's use of influence and expert authority is acknowledged in Egan's approach which contrasts with what was said about the Rogerian school of thought. Not all clients are willing ones; in social service and probation departments, despite critical argument (see Rojek *et al.*, 1988) and whether we admit it or not, we act as agents of control. Even when help is sought, there is natural resistance to dependency and the power of professionals. Social workers use authority which stems from their statutory powers, their position in an organisation, as well as the authority which derives from their knowledge and skill. Apart from abuse of power, supposedly anathema in our profession but not unheard of, authority can be used in counselling for setting limits, just as staff in Young Offender projects do to help teenage offenders to gain control over themselves. Equally, we gain authority on occasion from the strength of our relationships and skills in persuading and negotiating. Yet, it needs to be remembered that in using all kinds of authority, we are only as powerful as others allow us to be: influence has to be validated by others. There are ways, furthermore, of sharing power with users by explaining the skills and techniques which are used, for instance in counselling, networking and other interventions.

So far, in these first four chapters, we have dealt with some overarching themes of social work practice, identifying how that practice is now described in a number of different ways, but arguing that many of the processes are similar. We have also recognised the skills of interviewing and counselling as fundamental to any social work intervention and have considered these in some detail. In the following chapters specific social work approaches are discussed, and the skills used described in greater detail. Some of these approaches are framed by the purpose of the intervention, for example helping someone to deal with a crisis, while others are framed by the context of the person or persons being helped, for example family work, groupwork and community work.

5

Crisis Intervention

In this chapter we explore what is meant by the word 'crisis' as it relates to social work intervention. Brief case examples are used to clarify the distinction between crises and emergencies and to offer as role models practitioners who were able to 'stand still', that is remain calm, in the face of such situations. The stages of crisis resolution, the signs and symptoms to look for and the difference between stress and crisis are noted. A framework which summarises the main ideas of the approach is followed by a detailed description of the techniques which may be used in the initial, continuing and closing phases of intervention. Related literature associated with disasters, catastrophe and bereavement is introduced; increasingly such incidents have stirred agencies to set up coordinated after-care systems and preventive intervention services.

What do we mean by 'crisis'?

Social work interventions repeatedly occur with clients in crisis, and yet the word is generally misunderstood and used in something of a dragnet fashion, indefinitely describing a variety of problems, needs, stress and emergency states. Teams talk about crises when they mean that an urgent referral has come in or that they can only 'do crisis work', that is engage in minimal activity because of overwork. This signifies a lack of understanding of the concept of crisis and methods of intervention: inaccurate use of the term may have actually prevented a more thorough testing of the model such that we cannot yet dignify the crisis approach with the status of 'theory'. It is hoped that, having read this, the reader will avoid uncritical and undifferentiated use of the concept so as correctly to understand, apply and develop the processes.

Nevertheless, defining crisis is difficult (O'Hagan, 1986), hampered further by the lay-person's portrayal of crisis as a drama, panic, chaos, the 'economic crisis' and so on. The concept of crisis was formulated chiefly by Erich Lindemann and Gerald Caplan who in the 1940s and the 1950s studied the ways in which individuals react to psychologically hazardous situations: for our purposes, therefore, we can accept the definition provided by their student Lydia Rapoport who suggests that 'a crisis is an upset in a steady state' (Rapoport, 1970, p. 276).

This is a simple way of portraying how a sense of loss associated with accidental or life transitions throws an individual into a state of helplessness, where coping strategies are no longer successful in mastering problems and where the person's psychological defences are weakened. The steady state (also called 'homeostasis' or 'equilibrium') is maintained by human beings through a series of adaptations and problem-solving processes – Charles Darwin might have expressed this as a biological survival mechanism since new solutions are usually needed to manage the hazardous event which precipitated such disequilibrium. Crises are not necessarily unusual or tragic events, they can form a normal part of our development and maturation. What happens in crisis is that our habitual strengths and ways of coping do not work; we fail to adjust either because the situation is new to us, or it has not been anticipated, or a series of events become too overwhelming.

If a human being is overpowered by external, interpersonal or intrapsychic forces (in other words, conflicting needs) then harmony is lost for a time. One important thing to remember is that crises are self-limiting, they also have a beginning, middle and end; Caplan (1964) postulated that this period lasts for up to six weeks. In the initial phase there is a rise in tension as a reaction to the impact of stress; during this time habitual ways of trying to solve problems are called on. If this first effort fails, this makes tension rise even further as the person gets upset at their ineffectiveness. This state of mind results in the final phase when either the problem is solved or the individual, needing to rid themselves of the problem, redefines it for instance as something less threatening; or, alter₁atively, the problem is avoided altogether, for example by distancing oneself from it. (The same phenomenon of protest, despair and detachment is familiar to workers who understand the separation traumas of young children.) It can be seen that crises have a peak or turning-point; as this peak approaches, tension mounts and energy for coping is mobilised – we 'rise to the occasion' (Parad and Caplan, 1965, p. 57).

As indicated, during the disorganised recovery stage people are more receptive to being helped because they are less defensive and need to restore the predictability of their worlds. We all seek some kind of balance in our daily lives. Having said this, there are some families and clients who seem to thrive on living in a constant state of crisis; they lurch from one appalling state of chaos to another, on the precipice of eviction, fuel disconnection, abandonment and despair. Unfortunately, this chronic state may be part of the lifestyle and not to be confused with concepts of crisis discussed so far. Later, in Chapter 9, some methods of helping continually disorganised people, whose disasters seem to flow into one another in circular patterns which can almost be predicted, are discussed.

Crises can be perceived as either a threat, a loss or a challenge: the threat can be to one's self-esteem or to one's sense of trust, for instance; the loss might be an actual one or may be an inner feeling of emptiness and isolation; when viewed as a challenge, a crisis can encompass not only danger but also an opportunity for growth. This is especially so when new methods of solving problems are found or when the person finds that they can cope. Similarly, because crises can revive old, unresolved issues from the past, they can add to the sense of being overwhelmed and overburdened (a double dose); at the same time, however, they can offer a second chance to correct non-adjustment to a past event. A couple of case examples will illustrate this vulnerability which runs alongside increased mental energy made available for coping when no longer being used to repress ill-resolved old problems.

Case examples

1. Mrs Todd was admitted to an older persons' home following the death of her husband and at the request of her daughter, aged seventy, who could no longer manage. Six months after admission Mrs Todd refused to get out of bed for a week saying that there was no point. Physical explanations were ruled out. Sensitive questioning by the residential social worker revealed that Mrs Todd had never come to terms with the loss of her

husband. On top of this she had been unable to put into words her feelings of being abandoned by her family. Mrs Todd's denial of her grief, plus the perception that she had lost control and independence, despite high quality care in the home, had resulted in confused thinking, distortion of grief and withdrawal.

2. The ward sister of a nearby hospital contacted the field social worker who had spent some months working intensively with the Smith family in order to plan the return home of the Smith's nine-year-old daughter who had become disabled following a road accident. Adaptations and equipment were installed in the home and community care services organised. On being given a definite discharge date, perhaps the first impact of reality, Mr Smith had become uncontrollably tearful, refusing to take his young child home saying that he could not cope. In working through this period of crisis the social worker helped Mr Smith to 'think straight', to recognise his emotional outpourings as normal and to explore all the resources which would be made available. This little bit of help, given at the right time, prevented Mr Smith from drifting into worries that the family would be abandoned once the little girl was home. In fact the specificity of a discharge date had triggered off inner conflicts in Mr Smith, only partially resolved, that his wife would leave him as she had done many years before.

Rather than seek help with their unhappy marriage, the couple had resigned themselves to their disappointment in each other, never talking about the past and trying to pretend that their problems had never existed. In order to uncouple the symbolic links between past and present needs and fears, the social worker re-negotiated her agreement with the Smiths; following short-term crisis intervention a longer-term, more open-ended approach to marital counselling was offered.

Neither of the above referrals would have been high priority on many caseload weightings; they were not the stuff of drama or danger. A 'fire-fighting' response was not called for and yet these clients were in crisis. They perceived themselves as having no autonomy or command over their problems, tension had mounted and thinking had become disintegrated so that little mental energy was left over to use inner and outer resources. Without help, either of these clients could have deteriorated into a major state of personality and behavioural pathology – what is commonly termed a 'nervous breakdown' could have occurred when magical thinking such as 'If I don't think about it the problem will disappear', could have led to a loss of touch with reality or a serious medical condition (a broken heart?). Because of this, it is important for all social workers to be aware of crisis theory and to be attentive to it in all interactions. The appearance of a persistent offender before the court, the need of an older person for assistance with home care may not necessarily constitute a crisis; but it might represent a change in circumstances for some which does affect their self-perception and their coping mechanisms, or makes connections for them with other difficult circumstances.

Before we compare stress with crisis and learn to recognise the signs of someone in crisis we need to sum up. Crises occur throughout life, they are not illnesses; we constantly make adaptive manoeuvres in order to cope and maintain our steady state. If we meet a novel situation, experience too many life events, or become overloaded with old, unresolved conflicts, then a crisis occurs. This is a time-limited process during which we become disorganised in thinking and behaving. Mounting tension can result in the generation of mental energy for getting the problem solved. Crises can be perceived as a threat, a loss or a challenge; the concept encompasses danger together with opportunity. On a positive note, improved mental health can be the outcome when new methods of coping are found or when there is a second chance to tackle an earlier hazardous event. Equally, the outcome of the crisis can depend on the quality of the person's social support network (Parry, 1990).

Crisis and stress

Occasionally, the word 'stress' is used interchangeably with crisis. However, the concept of stress tends to evoke only negative connotations, for instance that stress is a burden or a load under which people can crack. In comparison, we have seen that the state of crisis need not have this harmful outcome. Crisis contains a growth-promoting possibility; it can be a catalyst, raising the level of mental health by changing old habits of problem-solving and evolving new ways of coping. In addition, the concept of stress carries within it a sense of longer-term pressures, which may largely derive from external pressure as opposed to internal conflict. Crisis, on the other hand, appears as a short-term phenomenon where the individual rapidly tries to re-establish previous harmony. Earlier levels of functioning may have been inadequate, but that is where the person's perception of equanimity lay: where crisis resolution is less than optimum then lower levels of coping may result.

Nevertheless, there is a relationship between life events and stress as research shows (Schless *et al.*, 1977). A state of crisis can occur when making social readjustments such as moving house, having a first child, becoming unemployed and so on. What is important is that what constitutes unbearable stress for one person may not be so for another. Students are always surprised when they compare their views of stressful events with their colleagues; some dread Christmas, others lose their sense of coping when faced with academic work. Thus, it is the *meaning* which people attach to these 'uneventful' events which matters – maybe someone links Christmas symbolically to an unsatisfactory time in the past; or someone whose self-esteem was bound up with academic success attaches great significance to results. The same is true when we meet clients; what the event means to them is what matters, not whether we think it is serious or not.

Anyone working in the mental health field should be interested in discriminating between stress and crisis. Specifically, when working in crisis intervention mental health teams, where there is a request for compulsory removal to a hospital or other safe place, it is vital that a correct assessment is made. Where the situation involves black clients or those from ethnic minority backgrounds, disturbing evidence has emerged of stress being misinterpreted as madness: the rate of admission to psychiatric hospitals is about five times greater for people from the West Indies – greater than would be expected given their percentage of population (Rack, 1982). One analysis (Aros-Atolagbe, 1990) is that second generation black people in the UK suffer tremendous crises of cultural identification; alienation produces more stress which may precipitate a temporary breakdown.

Although individual and ethnic-group variations exist, many immigrants similarly go through a pattern of adaptation to an unfamiliar, and probably discriminating, environment. The loss of support networks together with a sense of powerlessness means that the process of emigrating goes through critical phases such as:

excitement – disenchantment – perception of discrimination – identification crisis – and marginal acceptance

(see Hirayama and Cetingok, 1988, and Marris, 1986, who discuss the loss of one's homeland).

Alternative explanations include the misinterpretation by workers of the reactions to stress by people from different cultural backgrounds. On the one hand, some groups may be able to express their reactions by overt demonstrations of emotion. In some cultures holding a wake or similar event to allow the outward expression of grief is the norm, while in Britain such displays of emotion are frowned upon. On the other hand, cultural expectations of what has to be tolerated without comment or expression of emotion may be interpreted as depression by workers who expect clients to be prepared to 'talk through' situations. Similar misinterpretations may occur on the basis of gender where stereotypical assumptions lead workers to expect that men and women cope with difficult situations in different ways. The social worker in the case of Mr Smith, for example, was able to accept that his uncontrollable tears were a perfectly normal reaction to the events with which he had to cope. This is an important message in a culture which has deterred men from using tears as an appropriate means of stress relief.

Therefore we can see that the signs of someone in crisis actually might be difficult to spot, or the behaviour may be open to different interpretations. However, like grief, some of the responses follow a typical or classical pathway and this can give us some clues. We know that in the period of distress the person is striving to gain control and is open to suggestions which will aid recovery: phrases may include 'I can't cope', 'I feel a failure', 'I don't know where to turn' or 'It is hopeless'. With Paula (the case example in Chapter 3), she did not even know which words would express her crisis. Often thoughts and behaviour are agitated, confused, hostile, ashamed or helpless. People may become irritable or withdrawn from their friends and relatives. Attempts to solve difficulties seem chaotic and unfocused. One client, unhappy in his new department at work, walked around all day muttering to himself; this could have been mistaken for a form of mental illness rather than the man's anxiety at losing his previous well-known routines. Other signs may be physiological, so that complaints about sleeplessness, tension and headaches (see Parry, 1990) may be mentioned by someone in crisis.

Techniques of crisis intervention

The techniques for intervening in crisis situations are sketched now which help in the initial, ongoing and final stages. In the first interview it is essential that the focus is kept on the present circumstances of the crisis event. Asking 'What happened?' thereby encourages the person's *cognitive grasp* of their situation. Comments such as 'You must feel awful' or 'No wonder you are upset' help to draw out the *affective* responses (that is feelings) which block thinking. The worker and client together try to make an assessment of the actual event and the causes which seem to have triggered it. It is necessary to gauge what ego strengths someone has so that their normal coping resources can be gleaned. Often this can be done by asking how the person has reacted in other, similar situations.

Having gained some idea of available and potential resources, the worker outlines the next step, asking 'What is the most pressing problem?' or 'What is bothering you most?'. The client is then asked to settle on one target area, the worker confirming this by saying 'So the most important thing is . . . ? Obviously, these are not formulae for copying, they are suggestions as to what to cover in the initial period of disorganisation when the worker conveys hope, shows commitment to persevering while cutting the overwhelming problem down into manageable bits (known as partialising the problem). A contract for further work is spelled out in specific, concrete terms such as 'Let's concentrate on . . . You do . . . I'll do . . .'. Optimism is used to reduce the client's anxiety and perception of hopelessness: concreteness helps to keep the person in touch with reality. The aim at this early stage is to start to build a relationship based, not on time, but on the worker's expertise and authenticity, again to restore the client's sense of trust.

As the client's thinking is clarified, it is necessary to re-establish a sense of autonomy, by giving him/her something to do before the next meeting. This can be achieved, for instance with someone frozen into inaction, by getting them to say when next you need to meet again. In any event, letting individuals decide on the schedule for help such as 'I think I need to see you four more times over the next two weeks' builds self-reliance into the agreement and prevents undue dependence in the longer term.

Further contact in the middle phase sees the worker centring on obtaining missing data, for example, 'Can you tell me more about . . . ?' Although the emphasis is still on the here-and-now there may be links with past conflicts not recognised in the earlier phase of staying with the presenting issues. Pointing out possible connections helps the person to correct cognitive perception while keeping the problem, rather than fantasy or distortion, in the foreground. Also, one way of helping someone keep a perspective is to recognise that they have had past crises and that they have coped with these. Discussing those coping mechanisms sometimes gives good indications about what approaches might work in the current situation. The helper has to be the voice of reality (Golan, 1978) showing the difference between 'what is' (real) and 'if only'. Maybe the client Mr Smith would have wished he could have his 'whole' daughter back as if the accident had not happened; but that was not possible and plans had to be made to assist her and others to live with her disability.

Letting the person talk helps to relieve tension; ventilating feelings can release mental energy for tackling past worries. Help is given to sort out what worked and did not work in attempting to solve the problems; 'So you did . . . Did it work . . .? ' Alternative solutions are weighed; exploring overlooked resources assists in restoring equilibrium and also develops a pattern (that is new habits) in being able to use such help in the future. By sorting out specific tasks together, aiming for achievable goals, the social worker acts as a role model for competent problem-solving; for instance, setting home-work, 'Before we next meet I'd like you to think how you could . . .', sets the stage for encouraging a change in thinking, feeling and action.

The termination phase of crisis intervention, perhaps the last two interviews, should have been built into the original agreement. Once the state of crisis is overcome and homeostasis restored, it would be harmful to prolong this type of approach as it could ignore natural growth potential present in all human beings. Reminding the client how much time there is left, reviewing progress and planning for the future prevent dependency (that is lowered functioning). However, premature termination, 'I can cope now, so I don't want to see you anymore', could be a 'flight into health' (Rapoport, 1970) not a well-thought-through decision. We shall explore endings in more detail in the final chapter.

Bereavement and loss

Throughout this chapter we have made reference to the fact that crises are not necessarily dramatic or unusual events. Developmental crises might be avoided by anticipatory grief work. In work with pregnant women attention can be paid to the crisis of childbirth, not as a biological event, but in terms of the changes which will occur in the social situation. As we have said crises can be associated with loss. For women who are giving up work there is loss of economic independence and loss of the social environment of the workplace. For women who plan to return to work, there are other losses to face; loss of independence and freedom and, if in a relationship, the loss of intimacy. Similar senses of loss occur in other crisis situations. In the case of Mr Smith, above, he mourned the daughter he had previously known, and this precipitated confusing emotions and other senses of crisis.

It is this concept of loss present in many crisis situations which makes bereavement theory so important for helping understand crisis and to anticipate the reactions in some of the developmental crises: birth, marriage, retirement and, of course, death. Other situations, often more difficult to anticipate, similarly involve loss and therefore the sense of being bereaved: divorce, separation from children or partners (for example probation officers and other workers recognise the symptoms of bereavement when working with prisoners' wives), disability either by accident or the onset of illness such as stroke or multiple sclerosis, often mean that workers have to deal with the range and complexity of emotions associated with bereavement.

Situations which involve change, no matter how much that change is welcomed, usually involve losing something, giving up something. As Noel and Rita Timms suggested (*Perspectives in Social Work*, 1977), one of the basic functions of social work is conducting interviews with those who are facing loss and change. For this reason, the theories of bereavement are explored here.

One of the earliest texts to discuss the physical and emotional effects of grief and bereavement was Colin Murray Parkes (*Bereavement: Studies of Grief in Adult Life*, 1976). He identified five stages of typical reactions to grief. In identifying these it is not intended that they should be used in a mechanical way to chart people's progress through them, but that they are an aid to our understanding to people's reactions to loss, and provide a basis for formulating the kinds of intervention which are empathic and facilitative to people who are in crisis. The stages are:

- Alarm.
- Searching.
- Mitigation.
- Anger and guilt.
- Gaining a new identity.

In each of these stages physical and emotional changes occur which are associated with coming to terms with the loss, with the separation from the person who has died, or left. Symptoms occur which are physical such as disturbance of appetite and/or sleep, palpitations and breathlessness. Behaviour is displayed which may seem bizarre or morbid, such as searching for the person, denying their death and continuing to live life as if they were still present. Emotions expressed can be extreme and include anger with self, the deceased person and professionals who may be held responsible for the loss, guilt at not being able to prevent the loss or at feelings and behaviour just prior to the death. These can be painful and powerful.

The importance of the work of Murray Parkes (and others, including Lily Pincus, 1976) in identifying the range of experiences associated with grief and bereavement is that workers can accept the bereaved person with all their ambivalences, contradictions and complexities. In accepting and understanding the stages of grief work, they can give reassurance that while each grief experienced is personal and unique, the person experiencing it is not abnormal in the ways that they express themselves. Having said that, there are occasions when people, for a variety of reasons, become fixed in a particular grief reaction or display extremes of behaviour. In these circumstances having a framework to help assess an individual's coping strategies and to identify particular ways of working with these to develop and strengthen the person's own resources is helpful. Knowing when to stay with a person and listen, when to offer practical tasks and when to introduce them to a support group such as Cruse, or to more specialised help, is part of understanding the stages of grief and bereavement.

Having explored some of the theory of bereavement and its links with loss, change and crisis we can return to crisis intervention

Framework for understanding crisis intervention

A framework for understanding crisis intervention in summary form follows:

• *Theories* and important concepts which contribute to the identification of crisis developed from:

    (a) Psychoanalytic theories of personality (see Chapter 7) where the ego directs energy for problem-solving, appraises reality and helps us to cope, adapt and master conflicts.

    (b) Erikson (1965), building on ego psychology, suggests that we grow by managing psychosocial crisis points, which are transitional points in our life-cycle towards maturity.

    (c) Learning theory contributes in relation to ideas about cognitive perception, role modelling and repetitive rehearsal of effective problem-solving (see Chapter 6).

    (d) These contributions fuse with those from research into grief reactions (Lindemann, 1965) and those of time-limited, task-focused work dealt with in the following chapter.

• *Problems* for which this approach is applicable may not even seem like problems. They can be changes such as becoming a teenager, as well as situational or unanticipated crises such as promotion or illness. Furthermore, as we have seen, crises can occur at any time when a person perceives a threat to their life goals. It is the meaning of the event to the unique individual which matters. Problems are usually current and pressing ones; routine early history-taking would be inappropriate. So too would organizational arrangements such as waiting lists or long-drawn-out allocation procedures. Chronic crisis situations cannot be dealt with by this approach – longer-term, in-depth work is often necessary.

• *Goals* are kept to a minimum. They include relief of current life stressors, restoration to the previous level of coping, learning to understand what precipitated the condition, planning what the client can do to maintain maximum autonomy and contact with reality, and finding out what other resources could be used. When current stresses have their origins in past life experiences, the goal might be to help the person to come to terms with earlier losses to reduce the risk of future vulnerability.

- *The client's role* is to review and question the hazardous event in order to understand how the state of crisis occurred. At times, clients take unwise decisions or make inappropriate suggestions for solving the problem so the worker takes advantage of the person's lowered defences and willingness to take advice, thereby inhibiting flight, e.g. premature plans for the future. Indeed, a lot of the work for the client is to remember that there *is* a future. By 'telling the story to themselves' cognitive awareness is improved. Sharing the experience and the feelings with family or others in the support network strengthens these resources which, in their distress, some clients forget are there. Disintegration is also prevented when the client assumes responsibility for some small practical task.

- *The worker's role* is to give information and advice, to be active, directive and systematic, if need be. It is essential to be authentic as part of the promotion of reality-testing and adjustment. Setting time limits, for example four to six contacts, encourages the person to face up to the future without fear or shame that they will never be independent again. While cognitive restructuring and release of tension are the aims of this approach, self-understanding need not be part of the worker's plan for the client; rather, teaching how to split problems into manageable pieces and acting as a role model for effective problem-solving in the acute stage is what is required. To do this, the social worker must put themselves into a position of 'standing still', that is remaining calm and being able to 'bear it' when confronted with someone in crisis. The danger in crisis intervention is that the caregivers, surrounded by people who want something done, usually a 'plea to remove someone' (O'Hagan, 1986), will almost go into crisis themselves, not thinking clearly about what needs to be done

Prior to introducing the literature on coping with catastrophe, which is related to crisis concepts, there needs to be a brief consideration of *preventive work*. Over the years it seems to have been a neglected aspect of crisis intervention; if there are two types

108   *Social Work Practice*

of crisis, those which can be foreseen such as life-cycle transitions and those which are accidental or unforeseen such as sudden bereavement, then there is scope in the former to prepare for the change. Because maturational-crises can be anticipated, public health systems which operate services to maintain mental health could be developed further. Of course, politically, any preventive service is likely to be threatened when there are cutbacks. But it is somewhat short-sighted of social policy planners and social services to simply react to crises on a case-by-case basis. And yet, when economies are made they frequently hit hardest at agencies which actively deal with health education, preschool experiences, antenatal support, preparation for retirement, drugs information bureaux, marriage guidance counselling and schemes for preparation/consultation when large-scale rehousing schemes are planned.

When tragedies such as those considered below occur, many are actually 'man-made' such as wars, traffic accidents and toxic waste disasters – here too preventive action, known as *primary prevention* is possible with coordinated services made ready to prevent longterm psychological and other effects. We know that on an individual level, 'anticipatory worry work' helps later grieving, as do ceremonial rituals practised for a long time after a death by some cultures (Raphael, 1984; Parkes, 1976): so why are our services not geared to lowering the incidence of mental disorder?

Crisis intervention at a *secondary preventive level*, that is help geared to people who are in crisis, equally is at risk from unenlightened policy-makers. For instance, funding threats continually face organisations such as women's refuges, rape crisis services, suicide prevention centres, and substance-abuse rehabilitation units. The changes brought about by the community care legislation mean that voluntary sector agencies are concentrating on providing services which are commissioned as part of community care planning, to ensure they receive funding. Government grants to voluntary sector organisations are now replaced by spot or block purchasing, which means services are reactive. One consequence of this is that some preventive work, for example individual counselling, is now being offered in the private sector. Individual workers set up as therapists, charging for their services. This means that access to such services is only available to those who have the means to purchase them. It also means that there is no regulation of the provision, or accountability of those offering it.

As we have seen, help given at the right time, when a person is psychologically amenable, can prevent long-term use of any of these systems. Fortunately, some recognition of how we can set up *tertiary prevention* services (the help given to those people who have actually been made worse by earlier intervention), can be seen in the efforts to re-establish long-term patients from psychiatric hospitals back in the community. Community care could provide the opportunity to practise primary, preventive crisis intervention, not simply by putting right harmful interventions but by interfering with destructive forces affecting health. The mixed economy of welfare provision could offer the opportunity for services to be provided by/commissioned from women's groups or groups from within specific ethnic groups, but only if the statutory agencies can provide the means to purchase them.

Coping with catastrophe

In recent years literature related to managing severe trauma and coordinating all the support services for major incidents has been produced (Raphael, 1986; Hodgkinson and Stewart, 1991). While the horrors of kidnaps, famine, floods, fires, epidemics, mass murder, transport and technology accidents are not new, might not high standards of safety have been traded for cost-cutting making these events more likely? In any case, certainly in many welfare departments, emergency strategy meetings used to occur only occasionally. Now large personal social service organisations have to ensure that they constantly monitor their disaster plans, learning from tragedies such as the deaths caused by the crush at Hillsborough football ground, the Lockerbie air disaster or the sinking of the ferry, the *Herald of Free Enterprise*. These incidents have revealed the long-term psychological effects of trauma and how early counselling of survivors, bereaved relatives and friends and those in the rescue services can prevent pathological outcomes in the years which follow.

While the definitions of disaster imply extraordinary seriousness and great human suffering, there are many overlapping characteristics of relevance to both crisis and catastrophe: both are marked by rapid time sequences, disruption of usual coping responses, perceptions of threat and helplessness, major changes in behaviour and a turning to others for help (Raphael, 1986). Similarly, personal tragedies such as the loss of a loved one by violent means or someone who has been diagnosed to have AIDS will produce reactions such as shock, disbelief, denial, magical thinking, depersonalisation, sleep disorders, depression, anger, guilt and isolation. Sudden death or losses of any kind produce syndromes characteristic of disaster responses. Thus, a colleague whose father had been murdered endured a complicated and prolonged bereavement process.

The time phases of disaster, that is:

threat – impact – taking stock of the effects – rescue and recovery

resemble those of crisis reactions, though there tends to be post-disaster euphoria at having survived and immediate convergence from far and wide to help the stricken community. Nevertheless, the predominant need for people in states of crisis and those affected by disaster is for *information* by which to make meaning of such overpowering experiences, seeking to understand by describing what happened, and trying to restore some sense of command over the powerlessness which the very thought of extraordinary destruction brings.

So, even though many practitioners may never encounter catastrophes, they are of interest to any agency who is interested in providing sensitive, compassionate treatment and drawing up preventive programmes alongside those which manage psychosocial care in the aftermath. (One of the reasons that we know so much about the dimensions of grief is due partly to people like Lindemann, quoted above, who studied survivors of a night-club fire.) Raphael (1986) suggests that we should study these phenomena because:

- They give an insight into the common responses of individuals and groups, revealing universal themes of survival, loss and long-term adaptation.
- Prediction and counter-disaster activities together with guidelines for coordinating help can be drawn up.
- Knowledge can be applied to individual, everyday disasters, stress and life events.

Also, with the more interventionist approaches of the media, images of such tragedies and disasters are being made more imminent for all of us. The sense of grief and outrage that can be felt at the reporting of events may well trigger unresolved grief reactions in individuals who then present at GPs' surgeries or even social work agencies because they do not understand the strength of their own reactions. The events of the tragic massacre of school children at Dunblane led to a renewal of grief reactions in those who had suffered loss in similar circumstances at the Hungerford massacre.

When setting-up post-disaster aftercare, those involved in counselling the survivors need to assess and understand background variables related to the nature of the community which has suffered the impact. Their patterns of communication and access to it; their view towards the authorities and agencies which give direction; cultural and ethnic issues; how dependent/independent and urban/rural the community is; how integrated/loose-knit are networks; the interpretations made of the disaster; any special individuals whose qualities could influence responses are some of the factors to be taken into account. An overview of welfare systems is required as is epidemiological data such as mortality and morbidity rates so that public health planning and coordination of the relief services such as police and ambulance is effective.

There are many different ways in which people attempt to gain command in the immediate post-disaster phase. These can include:

- *Talking through*, putting into words (and therefore outside oneself), the meaning of the experience. On the other hand, someone who tells their story again and again with no emotional abreaction can become locked into the experience.
- *Giving testimony*, wanting to write about or talk on the media about the process is a further attempt to gain control over the events and to guide others in the future. Such testimony has also led to people becoming actively involved in campaigning to help prevent the situations which led to the disaster recurring. The involvement of the parents of children massacred by Thomas Hamilton at the Dunblane primary school in the anti-gun lobby is just one example of this.
- *Feelings* are often the most difficult to release, perhaps only coming later when the catastrophe is safely behind. Long after

impact sensory perceptions may remain as frightening memories. For instance, the awful noise accompanying any event or the terrible silence and stillness; vivid visual experiences and the smell of the disaster haunted those who survived the Bradford fire.

• *Tears* are important in the release of feelings, maybe triggered by others' grief and distress, though, as we have said, sometimes difficult for some men or cultures where they are viewed as weakness. Caregivers, such as ambulance personnel, doctors or social workers are sometimes hidden victims of disasters when they are assumed to be invulnerable. Communal rituals and public acknowledgement of suffering may also help tears and anger but generally feelings have to come out bit by bit when the person can gradually test out how they feel.

• *Perception of the future* and the need to get on with the demands of living is a signal that recovery has started, some trust in the world and hope returns; certain survivors become more aware of what matters to them and have a greater insight into their coping resources (see Raphael, 1986).

As mentioned earlier, care for workers and helpers is an important component of any treatment approaches. Psychological debriefing to lessen the stress of encounters with death and devastation prevents illness which can arise out of feelings of depression at not being able to do more. Lack of preparation for the role, whether through lack of training or shock, may mean that those involved require support. Many of the helpers in the Liverpool/Hillsborough teams found that they had to relearn counselling skills so that they could empathise with large numbers of people unloading all their grief and anger upon them. Support groups are useful, especially because they do not make the helpers feel that they have failed or that they are themselves somehow being psychoanalysed. Group processes, as we shall see in Chapter 10, help members to explore their reactions, reviewing positive and negative aspects in order to integrate them – that is, to be able to look at a distance and retrospectively at what was learned for oneself, for others and for the future.

Case example

Tom, aged thirty-two and living at home with his family, was referred to a specialist service dealing with post-traumatic stress disorders. He had served some years before in the Falklands war where massive confrontation with the deaths of others and disfiguring injuries had not been integrated: these kinds of experiences do not easily go away and do not fade readily from mind. Tom felt that he had encountered hell on earth. Stressors such as words or places brought back all the intensity of the violence. For example, Sheffield was associated for Tom with the loss of friends and colleagues who served on HMS Sheffield, which was blown up in the conflict. He had recurrent dreams of the events, was hyper-alert and gradually became irritable and aggressive with his family.

When he had first returned home everyone was elated that he had survived. He too was only too glad to join in the celebration and forget what he had gone through; after several weeks his family expected him to get on with living and to 'put it all behind him'. Unfortunately, Tom could not do this: he had endured terrible smells, sounds and seen the mutilation of others; encountering violent death for the first time in his life he was preoccupied with death and the war which, after a time, no one wanted to listen to. He buried the intrusive images of his experiences and tried to get on with his life.

What was worse, Tom had actually shut out the fact that he had been exposed to the killing of his closest comrade. Both had been under fire when his friend was killed at his side. Tom had carried on in the battle as if it had never happened. So effective was his denial that he joined with the other soldiers to rejoice when the battle was won; this psychic numbness helped him through, protecting him from what is dreadful about war – that killing may be necessary for personal survival. It stopped him feeling, not only then, but for some years. As some Vietnam veterans complained, 'I can't feel for people like I used to'. Thus, on discharge, he continued to protect his ego, his defence against death anxiety and guilt. His family became tired of his inability to 'pull himself together' and, believing that 'the Falklands' were a thing of the past, did not want to listen to his accounts. He therefore became isolated, depressed and withdrawn and was referred to mental health workers skilled in treating post-traumatic stress disorder.

Usually, treatment methods include individual, family and group approaches, using behavioural techniques and counselling. The client was helped in abreactive sessions to try to remember the blur of events on the day that his friend was killed. In groups, other survivors and he drew on their anger and their pain in order to externalise their feelings. After some weeks, Tom was helped to face the detail of what had happened on the day of loss, what he had been doing and so on in detail.

A breakthrough occurred when he at last was able to shed tears for the first time. Like other people who want to give testimony to what the experience meant and how others may gain from it, Tom wrote about his recovery. His account begins:

I think now that at last the war is over for me, though it will always be there for me for the rest of my days. Looking back I have come to realise that we fight our battles on two fronts; one against the enemy in our sights, the other against the enemy within ourselves.

6

Task-centred Practice

Task-centred practice, also known as brief therapy, short-term or contract work has had a significant impact on both social work practice and the organisation of services. As the various names suggest, it is focused work which is time-limited and offers approaches to problem-solving which take into account the needs of individuals to bring about change in their situations, and the requirements of agencies that work is targeted and effective. As we will see in the account of the development of the method, its introduction challenged some of the principles of casework. In doing this it recognised that the person with the problems also had the means to resolve them, and that social work intervention should become more of a partnership. In this way task-centred casework can be seen to be at the beginning of attempts to empower users of social work services. It offers an optimistic approach which moves the focus away from the person as the problem, to practical and positive ways of dealing with difficult situations.

Just as importantly it led to a change in the way that services were delivered. The most common organisation of services now includes some kind of referral or intake point, where people can present their problems and receive short-term help to alleviate immediate pressures. If appropriate, they can then be referred on to other agencies or to other long-term service provision within the agency. This organisation grew out of the adoption of methods of task-centred casework by many social work agencies.

In this chapter, we explore how emphasis on substantive factors and concrete problems has been developed into a well-specified set of procedures. Discussion of some of the research into the effectiveness of task-centred casework will help to highlight the main ideas. How it differs from crisis intervention will be briefly explored. Again a framework for understanding is offered, summarising the components of task-centred work, while case examples illustrate the method in action.

How the task-centred approach developed

It seems hard to believe, in this era of short-term work, contracts with clients and setting up evaluations of projects, that for many years between 1920 and the 1960s practitioners tended to concentrate less on problem-solving processes and more on in-depth assessment and the client–worker relationship. Models of practice therefore tended to involve long-term work, exploration of clients' feelings, a tendency to talk about rather than take action on difficulties, and an interest in underlying rather than presenting problems. Consequently, some clients received help for years and compulsive care-giving by helpers often resulted in the difficulties becoming the responsibility and 'property' of the worker (Buckle, 1981).

This model meant cases were kept open for years: visiting was done on a friendly but aimless basis; providing pre-care or after-care services was the global aim but there were few specific goals to accomplish, with or without the clients' agreement. This was what Davies (1985) referred to in calling social workers 'maintenance mechanics': he said that this is a key social work role and suggested that craving for change is textbook idealism. However, proponents of task-centred practice would disagree. They would propose that social work should be a focused activity and, owing a debt to Perlman (1957), should educate clients to become good at problem-solving. Furthermore, with today's emphasis on efficiency, effectiveness and economy, we are having to justify our services and prove to those who fund us that social work works. This is not an easy statement to prove, although the quasi-experimental work done in Kent and Gateshead by Challis and his team (see Challis and Davies, 1989; Davies and Knapp, 1988) actually proved that change was possible with frail older people, whose quality of life improved with goal-directed resources aimed at keeping them where they chose to be – in their own homes.

So, how did we reach this position of being able to show the relationship between inputs and outcomes? In North America, in 1969, a four-year study into brief versus extended casework was published (Reid and Shyne, 1969). Clients in a large voluntary agency dealing with family welfare were offered two contrasting 'packages' of social work intervention: one was an experimental brief service of planned short-term treatment (PSTT), consisting of eight interviews; the other was the usual practice in the agency of long-term service lasting up to eighteen months. To everyone's surprise, the clients in the short-term group improved more than those given the continued service. In fact the latter tended to deteriorate! The authors hypothesised that a law of diminishing returns was operating. Once help is extended beyond a certain point, clients may lose confidence in their own ability to cope (as intimated in crisis intervention) and become dependent on the worker or the agency with whom they may develop a kind of negative attachment.

In addition, when improvement or change does occur, the study revealed that this is likely to occur early on in 'treatment', regardless of the worker's implicit long-term goals.

This research was taken up in Britain by researchers at the National Institute for Social Work and elsewhere in the 1970s and 1980s, which we shall come to in a moment. The vital elements in the initial Reid and Shyne experiment appeared to be that *brief periods of service, concentrating on limited goals chosen by the client*, were often more effective and more durable than open-ended work. It seemed that setting a time limit led to the expectation that rapid change would occur, thus increasing the motivation and energy of all the participants. The North American projects in the 1960s concentrated on advice-giving and active exploration of problems. They aimed for unambitious, specified goals; moreover, their performance was committed and hopeful. (These might have been placebo effects, adding to the success. But, in any case, consumer satisfaction studies always mention worker qualities as important (Sainsbury, 1986).)

The first book describing 'task-centred practice' as such appeared in 1972 (Reid and Epstein) translating the results of the tests into the elements of the approach which seemed to be linked to its success. By that time, an even more systematic and goal-directed framework had been produced which suggested that there should be a maximum of twelve interviews within three months, again focusing on limited, achievable goals which are chosen by the client. From then on, social workers who tried out the idea were instrumental in helping to further refine the model (Reid and Epstein, 1977).

Currently, task-centred practice deals with *eight problem areas* (which cover most of the referrals met with by practitioners). They are:

- Interpersonal conflict
- Dissatisfaction in social relations
- Problems with formal organisations
- Difficulties in role performance
- Problems of social transition
- Reactive emotional distress
- Inadequate resources
- Behavioural problems

(Reid, 1978; Reid and Hanrahan, 1981)

There are definite steps to be taken in the process of problem-solving, that is *five phases* in helping clients to achieve their own modest goals:

1. *Problem exploration* when clients' concerns are elicited, clarified and defined in explicit, behavioural terms and ranked in order of importance to the client.
2. *Agreement* is reached with the client on the target for change, which is then classified by the worker under the previous eight categories.
3. *Formulating an objective* which has been decided jointly. Agreement is reached on the frequency and duration of the contract. (In respect of contracts which are written, it is as well to clarify the traditions of certain social classes and minority ethnic groups, as the 'legal' concept may be misunderstood. Of course, such contracts in social work are not legally binding but simply clarify respective tasks and roles.)
4. *Achieving the task(s)*, for which no prescribed methods or techniques are proposed within task-centred literature.
5. *Termination* is built in from the beginning. When reviewing the achievements, the worker's efforts are examined, not merely those of the client or the other helping networks.

Throughout the development of this approach in North America, parallel research was being conducted in the UK by Matilda Goldberg and her colleagues (Goldberg *et al.*, 1977). They found that the model, used by a social service department area team in Buckinghamshire, applied to only a minority of clients, at least in its 'pure' form. Those with a need for practical resources who acknowledged that they had a problem fared best. Involuntary/unwilling clients or those who had chronic, complex problems were less amenable.

Having said this, there were positive gains for the workers in the project who improved their capacity for clearer thinking and forward planning. Tackling small, manageable objectives, rather than vague global ones, proved more realistic. For example, a contract set up by a student social worker with a fourteen-year-old boy to behave himself was breached when he committed offences. The contract stated that the goal would be to stop offending; not only is this a negative way of putting things (doing something positive is preferred), but the objective was too ambitious and stated in 'world-wide' terms. Far better to aim low, for instance a weekly contract that he will visit his 'gran' and try to keep out of trouble – for example not steal cars. Also, social workers in the project found themselves less guilty about being unable to sort out everything, the Utopian cure-all which we all foolishly try to cope with.

Subsequently, Goldberg's team set up three experimental projects using task-centred work in a probation department, in two intake teams, and in a hospital social work department (Goldberg *et al.*, 1985). As the findings and conclusions hold for all three settings and client groups they are worth summarising, plus they give us an up-to-date and rounded picture of where this model presently stands. Task-centred methods proved applicable to between one-half and two-thirds of all cases. The remaining groups largely ended the attempt to be task-centred after the problem-search (phase 1) resulted in no agreement about the target problem. On the other hand, most clients who completed all five phases were pleased with the approach and said that their problems were reduced. The clients who could not be helped included those we looked at in the last chapter whose life style centred around chronic 'cliff-hanging' episodes and those whose difficulties were deep-seated and longer term. Other groups who were not amenable to this approach are those who are not in touch with reality, therefore for the probation service clients who are involved in substance-abuse and mentally disordered offenders are not likely to respond to a task-centred approach.

The skills required of the workers included an ability to listen and grasp what the client was truly bothered about; to know when to use systematic communication styles and when to be responsive (this is analysed below); to have the ability to renegotiate the contract or agreement; to act as an empowering partner, not just a service provider; to be explicit about time limits, and to remind the client about ending the contact, without harping on this. Difficulties were encountered by social workers who recognised that it was not authentic to treat clients as equals when they have no control over resources or when people were under surveillance as part of statutory duties such as a probation order.

To take the last point a little further: while the task-centred approach and the notion of empowerment might be to move towards 'power-to-the-people', ultimately, as we can see from the sphere of practice in welfare bureaucracies, there has been a tendency to lean towards accountability towards other professionals rather than towards consumers. In addition, where there are perceived risks agencies are loath to adopt time limits. Of course, client self-determination and respect for persons are the accepted values of our profession (though hotly debated in the *British Journal of Social Work* – see Webb and McBeath, 1990). There nevertheless remain possibilities inherent in task-centred work of changing from service provision to service brokerage as community care plans show (Department of Health, 1989), and for the method to achieve some of the goals outlined in Chapter 3. For example, the accounts of creative problem-solving with elderly people (Challis *et al.*, 1990) would indicate that this method of practice might be appropriate within the process of care management.

Returning to the point about having to acquire the technique of simultaneously using two styles of communicating: it is specified in Reid and Epstein (1972) that communication be systematic and responsive, that is, keeping the client to the agreed task in hand so as to reach the target problem and remaining empathic to the client's messages, respecting their value. On occasion this feels to be something of a paradoxical expectation. The worker's responses should ensure that the client's problem-solving does not become diffuse, but clients have a tendency to wander from the point, discussing matters which are not part of the agreed focus. If, for instance, a client has a chosen objective to control their children's behaviour, and each time s/he meets with the social worker the discussion wanders on to marital circumstances, this might cause the worker a dilemma. Is communication becoming unsystematic or is the marital disharmony a more important problem? Or is it connected to the children's behaviour and therefore a central feature? There is always a possibility that the original problem-search and agreed target problems are no longer valid, that goals will have to be redefined. Of course, in practice, it is permissible to allow for some wider discussion and then, in view of the limited time available, to bring the client back to the task. Alternatively, it would be robot-like and unresponsive to cling to the contract and it might be necessary to say, 'We often seem to get around to talking about your marriage. Do you think we should look again at what we've decided to do?'. Of itself responsiveness will not bring about change; structuring the work may. Ensuring that we have really understood what a problem means to someone requires, as we have seen in earlier chapters, giving attention to the client's communications and not introducing ideas which are only of interest to the worker. Combining this with a structured use of time and planned strategies helps to accomplish change in a step-by-step fashion.

To give some idea how you can preserve both qualities, of systematic and responsive communications; you may convey that you understand that there are many other difficulties but that a start has to be made somewhere if the person does not want to become overwhelmed; an explanation could be given at the beginning of the process that each area selected by the client will eventually be discussed in detail. The point is to remain flexible; sometimes a passing remark seemingly unconnected to the task focus might be worth looking into rather than let it pass or change the subject. Thus, a woman who is worrying about her rent arrears may hint that her partner gets out of control when disciplining her children. Or, a client might say, 'I'm confused'. Such an incomplete sentence could hide many meanings which are worth bringing to the surface by asking, 'About what?' It is always useful to spot when clients and others translate, mediate or generalise their experiences using words such as nobody, never, always and so on. Having said that, it is important to remember that a fundamental principle is that the focus for the task-centred work is *agreed* by both client and worker, and not imposed by the worker's interpretation of 'what the real problem is'.

The benefits of using task-centred methods

Before going on to discuss when task-centred practice might be used and how the approach compares with crisis intervention, let us summarise the main benefits. First, and most importantly, task-centred does not mean simply assigning tasks, or setting 'homework' such as is common in behavioural and family therapies. It is a well-researched, feasible, and cost-effective method of working, which consumer feedback indicates is very helpful to the majority of parties (Butler *et al.*, 1978; Gibbons *et al.*, 1979). It offers a specific set of procedures where clients are helped to carry out problem-alleviating tasks within agreed periods of time. The client is the main change agent, helping the worker to assess and choose what the priorities for change ought to be (even if we have other ideas), and then agreeing who is going to do what.

Task-centred practice fitted well into intake teams (Buckle, 1981), and even though these may be disappearing in the light of community care reforms most social services departments will retain some kind of duty system and short-term projects. Interdisciplinary teams set up to establish community care may use a form of task-centred practice, basing their goals on what is worked out with service-users, in addition to having a pre-planned exit time. For example, one team worked with a 62-year-old, capable woman who spent over 50 years in a mental hospital; they allocated three months of their budget to assisting her to learn how to use a bus route and to settle in with her companions in a group-care sheltered housing scheme. A further task-centred set of goals will be worked out with her, if she wishes, once these early practical tasks are achieved.

Debate has taken place about the use of task-centred work in the probation service. Supervision is already time-limited in that it is defined by the sentence of the court. However, task-centred work is more than just working to a short time-scale. The possibility of using task-centred practice within the duration of a supervision order, and arguing for early discharge once the identified and agreed goals have been achieved, is obviously an option. However, the nature of the problems presented by offenders, in that they may be out of touch with reality by virtue of substance abuse or mental disorder, sometimes mean that this method is not appropriate.

Any practice which ensures that there is no misunderstanding about why contact is taking place is likely to be more successful – if only because it is more honest and does not build up false expectations. It also means that where the social worker is acting as an agent of social control, or is intent upon offering protection, there is no ambiguity about this. The use of task-centred ideas is welcomed also by black practitioners (Devore and Schlesinger, 1981) and by Solomon's (1976) black empowerment strategies, since the methods do not further oppress people by taking over their lives or implying that the worker knows best There is no mystery about what the worker is doing because she/he is as accountable as the client in carrying out agreed tasks. This lessens the sense of powerlessness when faced with 'authority' figures. Similarly, in women-centred practice, this method gives power to women clients to identify the source of problems, and some means of influencing them. In issues of child care this might mean that the focus is on finding a support group or network, rather than a critique of the woman's parenting skills.

Apart from the somewhat rigid time limits, which possibly ignore certain ethnic traditions which prefer slow entry into family and community relations, task-centred work is beneficial in that it:

1. Takes into account not only individual but also collective experiences during the stages of problem-search, agreement and setting tasks. The source of the problem is not presumed to reside in the client; as much attention is paid to external factors, such as welfare rights and housing, where there is scope for supplying 'power' resources such as information and knowledge (Hirayama and Cetingok, 1988). The role for the worker is one of resource consultant.

2. Like other approaches, such as the Psychosocial and Behavioural in Chapters 7 and 8, the focus can be on individuals, couples, families, groups and organisations. Practical advice on how to approach problems and systems can be rehearsed, modified and copied in groups; peers, as well as social workers, can act as teacher/ trainers in problem-solving (Northen, 1982).

3. Addresses the strengths of people and their networks. For instance, it is an antidote to the process of labelling which assumes that being black is a problem. There is scope to valorise black people's strengths and use the resources of black communities (Ahmad, 1990). One aim of the method is to enhance self-esteem as well as problem-solving.

4. Does not rely on the notion of self-disclosure via a one-way, vertical helping relationship, it tries to put worker and client on the same footing.

Obviously the practice does not always go as smoothly as the later case examples suggest, but nevertheless this approach has an over-arching usefulness; it does not require a search for 'suitable referrals' as even those which look as though they will not 'fit' may benefit from *task-centred assessments*. Here, the first two phases of problem exploration and classification can help everyone to see things more clearly and know what the work will entail. Similarly, some clients find it difficult to actually pinpoint the source of their distress or difficulty and again a partially task-centred approach could offer clearer definition, from whence they may choose not to go ahead or to be helped using an alternative method such as those found elsewhere in this book. It was mentioned earlier that it could be useful, too, in working with organisations; if you examine the management technology called Management by Objectives (MBO) you will see that it resembles task-centred practice, having agreed goals within a time-limited perspective (Coulshed, 1990): in relation to staff and student supervision, also, some practitioners find it valuable having agreed set tasks and in-built mechanisms for mutual evaluation.

Lastly, we should not overlook the use of time itself as a therapeutic agent; working within a time limit pushes forward the process. As one client expressed it, 'A good idea, can't depend on someone all my life' (Butler *et al.*, 1978, p. 407).

Comparison with crisis intervention

What are the differences between this approach and that of crisis intervention? Both encompass brief, focal work and may be used when clients are temporarily unable to sort out their own problems and are better able to then use help to improve coping in a time-limited framework. This is as far as the similarity goes. Some of the research into the effectiveness of task-centred practice seems to have been tried with people who were in a state of crisis. We recognised in the previous chapter that people often then cannot 'think straight', they cannot easily conceptualise their problems or the solutions without fairly heavy dependency on the worker in the initial and mid-way stages. Certainly, those in crisis are not ready for an energetic, problem-solving, equitable relationship with a worker, able to agree to a detailed contract which needs to be carefully thought through and planned. It may be that both methods handle significant social, emotional and practical difficulties – but these need not be crises in the accepted sense. We know that, even with some flexibility, the work under discussion in this chapter tends to be systematic, focusing on one task at a time; goals are behaviourally specified, the whole programme tightly scheduled to fit a maximum of twelve to fourteen interviews, the ending predetermined rather than dependent on the psychological recovery of the person in crisis. Turbulent change can occur in crises which call for worker responsiveness which is not necessarily goal-directed. In sum, clients in crisis are unlikely to be able to cope with the demands of a fully task-centred approach.

Some techniques in each of the five phases

Once again, these are not recipes for action, merely some notion of what is likely to crop up in the sequence of phases towards problem resolution.

Phases 1 and 2

In the initial contract, exploration and agreement phases (say between one and six contacts), if the client is not self-referred:

- find out what the referrer's goals are;
- negotiate specific goals and if these can be time-limited; and
- negotiate with the referrer what resources they will offer to achieve these goals.

If the client applies independently and voluntarily:

- encourage the client to articulate their problems;
- encourage ventilation of feelings about these;
- step in with immediate practical help if necessary;
- assist the person to take some action on their own, something small and achievable;
- elicit the array of problems with which the client is currently concerned;

- explain how the task-centred approach works, for example time limits, priority focus, schedule for interviews, anyone else who needs to be involved such as family members;
- define the stated problems in specific, behavioural terms;
- tentatively determine target problems with client;
- choose a maximum of three problems ranked for priority by the client;
- classify the problems under the eight categories; and
- list the problems in a contract, if used.

Phases 3 and 4

In formulating objectives and achieving the tasks (say between the fourth and tenth contact):

- make the task selection phase short; if the targeting of problems has been done carefully this will indicate what/who needs to change;
- get the client to think out her/his own tasks and what effects will be likely, helping if the client's assessment looks unrealistic, will make things worse or can not be achieved in the time;
- if other people are involved, get their agreement too;
- if need be, help the client to generate alternatives and identify what resources are around;
- support task performance by a variety of problem-solving means. For instance: refer to a specialised source if this is required (for example debt counselling, vocational guidance, classes to learn a language); demonstrate or use games/stimulations/video; re-hearse problem-solving; report back how it went; accompany client for moral support; discuss client's fears, plans, resources; regularly record the status of the problem; examine obstacles and failures in detail;
- if other areas of concern emerge, decide in collaboration with the client if these are worth pursuing;
- always ask about all the tasks in case failures are not mentioned;
- if the method has been modified as partially task-centred (for example for assessment only, or when time limits are not part of the contract) consider what follow-up or alternatives will be used.

Phase 5

In the termination phase (hard to predict how long the process takes in each situation but say the final two to three contacts):

- talk about what will be the effect of ending the contact;
- find ways of helping clients to cope with anxieties;
- review progress and give encouragement;
- help clients to identify further areas of work;
- extend time limits only if clients feel that they need extra time and have shown commitment to working on tasks;
- monitor only when mandated by agency or legal requirements or if part of a community care 'package';
- evaluate each person's inputs and record outcomes; and
- say goodbye sensitively.

For further information on task-centred processes, Epstein (1980) offers a detailed map of the model in action.

Case example

Mr Taylor was a 57 year-old widower who had spent his working life as a ship's captain. Travelling around the world had left him with no friends in his locality and his married son, who lived many miles away, could only visit him two or three times a year. Following a stroke six months previously the client had 'vegetated' in a facility for disabled people. Rehabilitation efforts had ceased: staff complained that Mr Taylor was uncooperative and aggressive; they even wondered if he was clinically depressed, as he slumped all day in a wheelchair, keeping himself to himself.

The social worker received a referral from the care staff to sort out the numerous debts which had accrued because the client had not claimed any benefits. She found that Mr Taylor, far from being hostile, was a gentle, shy man who was not used to discussing his private affairs. When he heard about the task-centred ideas, which would not pry into his background, he was pleased to talk about his problems. He defined these as 'problems with formal organisations' and 'inadequate resources'. The contract was agreed that they would meet weekly to work on two target problems:

1. To pay off rent, telephone and fuel bills within the following three months.
2. To claim outstanding benefits from social security, insurance companies and salary from previous employers.

General tasks, such as writing letters, listing the debts, making phone calls and deciding who would do what were dealt with in the first two meetings. A schedule was drawn up about the frequency and duration of the meetings (mornings and for 25 minutes as Mr Taylor tired easily). They agreed also to let the centre staff know what would happen.

Every Monday at the same time the social worker wheeled Mr Taylor to a pleasant spot where they discussed how the debts could be cleared and which were the most pressing. Responsibilities were allocated and each week they reviewed each other's task accomplishments. Sometimes the worker had to obtain necessary forms and give the client instructions on how to complete them, but no revision of the contract was needed. The client not only cleared his debts and claimed his allowances, but also began to talk about his past life as a ship's captain and to discuss how he might manage in the future.

Mr Taylor, in one of these discussions, confided to the worker his fear of returning home to live alone, and his loneliness at not knowing any neighbours. He talked about his shyness which had even stopped him getting to know anyone in the unit. Accepting that he had overcome his shyness with the worker, they examined ways in which to start a conversation, re-negotiating a further task-centred working agreement that:

1. He would start a conversation with one of his companions at lunch every day.
2. He would write to his son telling him how he had sorted out his finances, and ask if he would visit him some time.

Because the client's manner was so approachable, physiotherapy and occupational therapy were restarted, resulting in an ability to walk with a tripod. The son made a visit and offered his father a home. The unit's carers marvelled at the change, and, if there had been a multi-disciplinary team approach, all could have congratulated Mr Taylor for his own efforts.

Case example

This second situation was met with by a student on a four month community work placement. He was asked to make an assessment of the needs felt by the residents in one street which had achieved notoriety due to their 'criminal and irresponsible' behaviour. Intervention by police, social services, social security and housing officials seemed to have exacerbated the stigmatising and labelling of the tenants. Their council houses were almost derelict: empty homes all around were, in fact, devoid of roofs and floorboards (stolen, it was alleged, by the deviant street dwellers).

Having completed a community profile (for ways of going about this see the resource paper by Brewster, 1988) the student started to make contact with the residents asking them what they would like to see changed in the street. Perhaps not surprisingly, the majority of people wanted the professionals 'off their backs'; there were complaints about being viewed as undesirables, even though most tenants were coping with poverty and unemployment and yet still had time to help one another. They disliked the housing policy of putting temporary tenants in the empty houses, giving the whole place a temporary feel and a bad name. Although many in the street found it depressing, being rehoused was not on their list of priorities. They liked their close-knit networks.

The student found that one tenant had several daughters and their children living in the street; this woman had been an asset when a former community worker had tried to set up summer play-schemes. She told the student that most people were angry with the Housing Department who treated them as second-class citizens (whenever a temporary resident moved on the council workmen rushed to board-up the property as if to deter the street's 'criminal' element from stealing anything). As spokesperson, she believed that the major goal was to have a meeting with housing officials and confront them with these dissatisfactions.

Although this was not a fully task-centred project, in that the student did not have the time to list all the other problems found in the survey and the overstretched full-time community worker could not have carried on the work, the main objective, of having a meeting with a person of authority from the Housing Department did take place. It was a well-planned meeting, in the home of the above tenant, and attended by other residents in the street. Their concerns were heard sympathetically. Now, some years later, the area has been refurbished as part of a larger, long-term initiative between the public and private sectors.

It might have been useful in these examples, as with all task-centred programmes, to have explained to the network of other agencies involved how goal-oriented, short-term, client-directed methods work. As it is, many systems (sometimes even our own), believe that social work will go on for ever. Integrated community care services, involving health, social services, housing, voluntary and independent organisations, working together may help to give a more realistic focus, and planning in partnership might target care in a more systematic sense. In that we have said that task-centred work enables the client or user to be the change agent, it is possible to see how this method might well be employed by care managers working with users and carers to target different parts of the system in order to stimulate resources for a package of care. In this way the method is used not just to solve problems, but to meet needs which have been identified jointly.

This capacity to precipitate change and to identify circumstances which need to be changed makes it an effective method for probation officers when preparing some pre-sentence reports (PSRs). Obviously the timescale does not allow for the whole process to be worked through, but the report, in focusing on offending behaviour, might well identify tasks which can be undertaken to alleviate the pressure to offend. As such it becomes a task-centred assessment. If this work has started, and the offender is carrying out the agreed tasks, then a proposal for a community sentence with a clear explanation of the programme of supervision will be possible. Such an approach would be in line with NAPO's good practice guide (1995) for PSRs which acknowledges structural, social, economic, psychological and emotional causes of offending behaviour and argues that they 'need to stress that the solution to [these] causal problems does not lie in punishment but in addressing the possibilities for change constructively' (section 8).

Framework for understanding task-centred practice

To conclude this chapter, a framework for understanding task-centred practice is shown below:

- *Theories* which underlie the task-centred approach are really only concepts: they include the crisis notion that focused help given at the right time is as effective as long-term service. Also, task accomplishment is viewed as an essential process in human coping endeavours, the choice of tasks and success in tackling them motivating people towards improved problem-solving. Mastery of situations strengthens the ego, while success breeds success. Though no specific problem-oriented theory exists at this point, nevertheless the underlying values which guide this approach are that workers should state what they are trying to achieve and clients' self-esteem and independence is preserved when they are seen as experts of their own lives. The use of time-limits conveys the message that change is possible in the time agreed, and working to deadlines sometimes inspires commitment.

- *Problems* are psychosocial in nature and comprise eight categories which describe problem situations rather than client types.
- *Goals* are modest, achievable, specific and often framed in behavioural terms; they are chosen by the client in collaboration with the worker. Goals are inherent in each of the five phases, completion of which would qualify the approach as fully task-centred. However, a partially task-centred approach is possible when only some of these phases are reached: an example of this would be task-centred assessment.
- *The client's role* is to identify desirable and feasible goals and to specify tasks and sub-tasks, prioritised in a working agreement with the social worker.
- *The worker's role* is to make explicit the time-limits to the client and the agencies involved, and to assist in the problem-search, target and task-setting by which problems are reduced and some solutions found.
- *Techniques* are really activities, examples of which are:

   (a) *Problem specification*, for example 'When you try to get your son to go to school, what does he do; who helps you; how do you react; what happens then' and so on.
   (b) *Task planning*, which incorporates agreeing tasks, planning detailed implementation, generating alternative solutions and summarising, for example 'So what else could you try; could you do this before we meet next time; will you ask your husband to back you up; are we clear about what we've agreed?' and so on.

(c) *Analysing obstacles and failures* such as 'It sounds as though your husband says nothing when you try to get your son to go to school. What could we do to get him to help you more?'

(d) *Planning tasks*, the detail of 'Who will do what?'

(e) *Structuring interview time*, asking 'How long do you think we need?' and 'Our time is coming to an end, we have agreed.'

(f) *Reviewing and ending*, for example 'What did you think of the time limits; did they help or not in what you achieved?'

7

The Psychosocial Approach

In this chapter we explore some of the questions left by the earlier methods of practice. In reflecting on task-centred casework it is worth remembering that there are situations which are difficult to change, as well as people whose behaviour leaves even experienced workers puzzled and floundering. Assessment and intervention in such cases usually cannot be brief and straightforward. Methods of helping clients to be freer from their emotional problems have to be found because some people need to understand themselves and why they feel powerless to change. There are other clients for whom self-knowledge could be damaging or where such insight would seem to make no difference.

What can we offer people who show 'neurotic tendencies'; who cannot give 'good-enough' parenting; who seem to be insatiably dependent on others; who block out their emotions; and who 'act out' rather than talk through their difficulties, albeit that these are usually underlying rather than presenting problems. Such referrals are common to social work caseloads and are often the most demanding in terms of time, patience, practice wisdom and worker maturity. One treatment approach which provides a longer-term, sustaining and nurturing relationship, at the same time as reducing external stress, is the psychosocial approach which this chapter considers.

The psychosocial approach as a method of understanding

Everyone, and that includes social workers, has vulnerabilities; we sometimes do not know why certain events upset us or remind us of a part of the past which we would rather forget. As part of our duties, too, we could unconsciously slip into favouring one client group, for example children or women, over others, thereby risking the neglect of less 'attractive' clients on our workloads. This is why social workers need to attempt self-understanding and why, moreover, there is a need to try to understand others so that we may accurately understand the *person as well as the problem*. If we accept and are to take into account that people have inner worlds and outer realities, then we have to understand the 'person in-situation' whole (the psycho-social). Practice which automatically accepts that the presenting problem *is* the problem may, on some occasions, miss the point. If initial coping strategies or solutions do not seem to alleviate the distress, or in some cases seem to exacerbate the anxieties, then it may be worth taking time to explore other explanations.

The psychosocial approach helps us to develop a healthy questioning of the obvious. An open mind, imagination and a knowledge of personality functioning, human behaviour and emotional suffering are inherent in the ideas; they assist in reaching 'differential diagnoses and treatment plans'. This is another way of saying that clients interact with their environment in unique ways and if we are to give service which is accurately targeted then, when appropriate, we have to comprehend underlying feelings and motives which can block people from making optimum use of such help. An interesting example is offered by Spurling (1988) of Wendy, a woman who cooperated for a time in his efforts to help her feel less unsatisfied with her life and herself (we will comment later on what turned out to be a far from straightforward problem). After a couple of visits and missed appointments, the client wrote to say that she wanted to try on her own for a while; this was after her past had been mentioned. The letter ended that she would leave it up to him, showing maybe how she wanted help with her past life and was also terrified to do so.

The psychosocial model is usually linked to the writings of Florence Hollis (1964, 1970, 1991) though it is one of the oldest of the social work methods, going back as far as the 1930s and even beforehand, to Mary Richmond's (1922) then radical notion of formulating a 'social diagnosis' prior to deciding whether to give indirect treatment (that is, relieving environmental distress), or direct treatment (that is, influencing the thoughts and feelings of individuals). Later this became known as the Diagnostic School of social work. Throughout the 1950s and 1960s Freudian psychoanalytic ideas, particularly personality theory, began to feed into what became known as psychodynamic casework: added later were contributions from ego-psychology and object-relations theory known to social workers because of the work of people like John Bowlby. The 1970s and 1980s saw much emotional debate about this method of social work. In part, antagonism may have been justified inasmuch as the separate phases of study, diagnosis and treatment may have led to concentrating overmuch on the first two, at the expense of actually doing anything. As indicated in the previous chapter, workers sometimes relied on the client–worker relationship as an end in itself, spending a lot of time with people which research, published in 1976 (Fischer, 1976), suggested was ineffective. Many of the criticisms of psychodynamic casework need, however, to be cautiously analysed: the question of the effectiveness of any treatment process and its relation to change is far from easy.

It might be that, to some degree, the psychosocial approach is less a system of therapy and more an approach to understanding. There are treatment techniques, described by Hollis (1964), as we shall see. But even if we opt for other ways of intervening, if we have tried to make intelligible how people behave and feel, then there is a decreased likelihood of wasting time or dismissing someone as beyond help. As indicated, where we have tried to understand others and ourselves, we may then be able to see underlying reasons for actions – including our own. To return to the work undertaken by Spurling (1988): his persistence with the young woman Wendy became fruitful when eventually he was able to confront his own tentativeness about talking to her about the painful topic of her guilt, shame and anger at having been sexually abused by her father. The safety provided by the worker meant that, even though he was male, Wendy did not feel that it was 'interfering' when he helped her to tell the detail of what had happened. And, as the case study concludes, when something is spoken of for the first time in the presence of another, things can never be the same again.

Professionals have to want to hear; if they themselves lack self-awareness, are resistant to getting involved, or if there is fear of 'damaging' others by looking beneath the surface, they are more likely to make mistakes. Good supervision is invaluable in helping staff to unblock how they feel about clients and letting these feelings be used to guide actions. Bacon (1988) has shown, for instance, that professionals in child abuse case conferences may operate from a deep-seated, unconscious and collusive rejection of the family (and therefore the child). Social work has to live with the notion that in life there may be 'good' and 'bad'; we may unknowingly choose not to hear or talk about the latter because it is too threatening or because we want to be seen as 'helpful' rather than 'helpless'.

Finally, although caution was expressed in earlier chapters about an overuse of the question 'why?', in this approach it would be valid to ponder on why we and those we work with behave in ways which may seem irrational. Clients often ask, 'Why am I like this?' and, when indicated, helping people to remember traumatic incidents from the past or gain insight into the way they function might promote feeling more comfortable about themselves. Moreover, accurate plans for the future may depend on this: when the past is still in the present (Jacobs, 1986) it could prevent progress.

Assessing ego strengths

Basic to the psychosocial approach is a knowledge of psychosexual development (Howe, 1987, summarises these ideas in more detail). Freud emphasised the importance of early development, delineating several major stages: oral (first year of life), anal (ages one to three), phallic (ages three to six), latency (ages six to twelve) and genital (continuing from twelve for the rest of life). The origins of faulty personality development were thought to stem from childhood, adjustment problems resulting in unhealthy uses of *ego-defence mechanisms*. These are a further key feature of the psychosocial approach, since defences help individuals to cope with anxiety, thereby preventing the ego from being overwhelmed: they are normal behaviours but they can frustrate coping with reality. Common ego defences are repression, whereby painful thoughts and feelings are excluded from awareness; denial where again the person 'closes their eyes' to threatening actuality, but on a more conscious level than repression; and regression, where there is a return to behaviour which is immature. In order to assess how realistic and logical the person is in coping with problems and inner conflicts, that is to reveal which method of helping is indicated, we have to assess this element of personality structure.

According to the psychoanalytic view, the personality consists of three systems: the id, the ego, and the superego which dynamically interact. The impulses originating from the id are governed by the pleasure principle while the 'conscience', the superego, strives to inhibit these chaotic drives. The ego, in touch with outer reality, tries to mediate between instincts and the outer environment, thinking through ways of satisfying needs, anticipating consequences and rationally working out solutions. Thus, we can see that if we are to tailor our efforts to each individual's inner and outer needs we need to know if the ego can tolerate self-scrutiny, without being overwhelmed by anxiety; or, if probing into the past would not lead to change, what level of support the person requires in reducing the stressful demands of their external environment. Moyes (1988) describes a client whom she helped who some might have assessed as being too dependent, anxious and of low intellectual ability to make much use of the psychosocial approach to understanding. However, with verbal and non-verbal methods (board games and so on) the client did gain some insight into unmet childhood needs for security and dependence, and why these were preventing an ability to trust others, to engage in closer relationships and to develop autonomy.

When talking about ego strengths, we are not referring to a fixed condition but to an ever-changing capacity to cope with frustration, control impulses, make mature relationships and use defence mechanisms appropriately. In general, an individual's age, capacity to work through early traumas and the intensity of pressures all affect ego functioning: a truly mature person in this sense is someone who does not need to rely on others for positive self-esteem, and who has a deep understanding of who they are. Even if the social worker decides to work on reducing environmental change, as a way of giving hope and comfort to a person who does not desire self-awareness or could not cope with it, it is still useful to be able to gauge ego strengths to see how motivated or reluctant the person is likely to be and what kind of relationship is likely to develop. A fascinating account of working with marital problems in a social services department demonstrated how the two project workers (Mattinson and Sinclair, 1979) were able to sustain and nurture a group of clients whose problems – marital, financial and practical – were related to childhood fears of loss, abandonment and attachment. Drawing on psychodynamic theories, they were able to effect some change in the kinds of referrals which take up a vast amount of agency time, more so when workers do not make an assessment of ego functioning.

When helping adults who appear to have 'infantile' needs, or whose behaviour is baffling (for example those who intellectually understand what to do but who do not connect this to their feelings or actions), it might be useful to assess at what stage of psychosexual development they might be stuck. Especially when there has been a past trauma, for instance loss of a parent at a vulnerable age; then, when there is internal or external pressure, the client frequently regresses to the stage where these earlier issues were not resolved. This is why, in direct work with children, social workers who are skilled in the techniques of this method can help them to regress, revisit painful phases and start to build ego strengths undeveloped in the past. Specialists in this area find Bruno Bettelheim's *The Uses of Enchantment* (1988) a useful text. Fairy-tales are important in revealing children's anxieties and fantasies, and Bettelheim shows how they help to support and free the child.

Equally, those clients who seem totally unable to manage their lives (Kaufman, 1966) can be helped to gradually mature with a worker who feels comfortable in a nurturing, restitutive parent–child relationship, where dependency is accepted and worked through. Normally, these are the adults who antagonise agencies because of their neediness and their inability to care for anyone else (until they have been cared for). For example, there is the parent who forgets to have food in the house and who spends the money we give on cigarettes; the patient who is over-concerned with illness but whose numerous tests reveal no abnormality; the person who insists on seeing the social worker at all hours and then is aggressive when limits are imposed. Some time ago Wittenberg (1970) said that:

> The caseworker acts as a kind of mother who takes away the mess that the child produces and cleans it up and helps him to do so gradually himself. (p. 155)

With many clients who become stressed by even small matters, such as keeping to an arrangement, we often have to give material things; because verbal communications may have no meaning we have to *show* we care. Lives may have been marked by inconsistency, desertion, the intrusion of too many figures of authority or attacks on self-esteem, we have to provide understanding, holding and containment.

Before moving on to discuss how psychosocial methods have been criticised, it should be emphasised that ego strengths must be assessed before attempting any self-awareness and re-education; particularly when dealing with those who have been diagnosed psychotic or when working with the immature ego of the child, indiscriminate 'laying bare' of feelings can prove overwhelming to the personality, and interpretation and insight would probably be harmful. Indeed, the immature ego may need help to increase rather than decrease defences to prevent repressed (unconscious) material from threatening the fragile personality.

Criticisms of the psychosocial approach

In Britain, the psychosocial approach has been a controversial aspect of social work thought and practice for many years. In 1959, Barbara Wootton's *Social Science and Social Pathology* attacked social caseworkers for posing as miniature psychoanalysts. Wootton declared that, rather than search for underlying reasons for behaviour, the social worker would do better to 'look superficially on top', especially if practical help was sought. Consequently, a great deal of 'looking superficially on top' took place, workers were content to provide services and respond to problems as presented. This is frequently all clients want; but for those who had less 'common sense' and easy-to-understand difficulties, there began to be fewer and fewer workers trained to spot underlying problems. It has been argued that even when the goal is service provision, it is beneficial to think about the psychosocial person-in-situation so that resources are not wasted, should latent problems emerge.

The negative response to the psychosocial approach has a variety of explanations. One reason might be its clinical and obscure jargon; or its tendency to construe cause and effect, often simplistically blaming the past for the present; another the propensity to label clients as inadequate, manipulative or narcissistic whenever they failed to cooperate. Research found that clients were angry when workers, unable to give money, refocused their efforts towards intrusive exploration of their personal life (Mayer and Timms, 1970); and there was growing tension between critical sociologists and social work theorists, because the latter ostensibly favoured the status quo rather than struggle, through collective action, to change society.

When behavioural approaches began to be taught on training courses, the results of intervention with specific and overt behaviours could be witnessed and even tested for effectiveness. Comparison between the speed of change using psychosocial support versus behavioural techniques highlighted the utility of the latter (Hudson, 1975).

Furthermore, notions of a therapeutic relationship, self-disclosure, individualisation and self-awareness, plus the power of the worker to make the diagnosis, were antipathetic to the needs of black clients. Dominelli (1988) has suggested that casework 'pathologised' blackness and diverted workers' attention away from racist organisational policies. Middle-class social workers were criticised by radical sociologists and social policy analysts for concentrating on intrapsychic forces and 'insight giving' while ignoring the effects of harsh, competitive, capitalist systems (Bailey and Brake, 1975). Freud's theories were said to lack a materialist understanding of the individual (Corrigan and Leonard, 1978); so too, one of social work's most experienced practitioners/thinkers, still maintains that the psychosocial school aims to make people fit into a given environment (Jordan, 1987).

Feminist approaches to psychosocial counselling have been mixed. Critics such as Brook and Davis (1985) have suggested that its use by social workers pathologises women in the same way as it oppresses black people, often perceiving the cause of women's experiences and behaviour as being in themselves rather than in their economic and social circumstances. Other feminist writers (for example Eichenbaum and Orbach, 1983) have accepted some of the basic tenets of the psychosocial approach, and have used them to explore how women's experiences and socialisation may have led to them accepting negative ascriptions. They argue that psychosocial counselling can work with these negative views and help liberate women.

Behind the censure of the psychosocial approach and its base in psychoanalytic ideas may lie a presumption that the method is practised by authoritarian caseworkers, who are unable to reflect upon and question what they do. In the past, there may have been rigid believers who could not tolerate ambiguity, diversity and uncertainty about human behaviour, who failed to locate their practice in a socioeconomic or linguistic context. Nowadays, most social workers are very much aware that all forms of helping are really forms of power. There are, nevertheless, those who distinguish between 'good' collective struggles to change society and 'bad' individualised, 'conservative' approaches such as the one under discussion here.

False divisions between private and public worlds ignore the interaction between them. Many attempts have been made to integrate psychoanalysis with various sociological and political theories (see the valuable overview by Pearson *et al.*, 1988). Yelloly (1980), in one of the few books relating to social work and psychoanalysis, using the example of the early days of the women's movement, shows how personal predicaments reflect political existence: psychoanalysis offering insight into the psychological and social chains which keep human beings captive. The same point is made by the feminist psychoanalyst Juliet Mitchell (Mitchell, 1984) who is able to see the value and the drawbacks of a theory which, at one and the same time, implies the inferiority of women and the key to understanding women's psychology and their oppression under patriarchy; critics, moreover, need to realise that psychoanalysis does not begin and end with Freud – it is an active, evolving set of ideas, as Mitchell reminds us.

Nevertheless, it is as well to be mindful of the power of 'received ideas'. Rojek and his colleagues (1988) have alerted us to the hidden influence of the language of social work: although we use words such as caring and helping, is that what actually happens? Unless we develop self-criticism and self-awareness, we might unwittingly, by using the techniques which are described in the subsequent section, diminish and demean those we hoped would become 'beings-of-themselves'.

Some benefits and some techniques of the psychosocial approach

Practitioners may be surprised to find that they use some of the psychosocial methods all the time. Much of the 'bread and butter' of our job involves contemplating ideas such as loss, attachment, individual development, anxiety, transference and so on. We find it easy to accept as normal, for instance, regressed behaviour of those recently bereaved, who are afraid to be alone or who are convinced they have seen or heard their lost loved one. A knowledge of child personality development is a cornerstone for those involved in child care and child guidance work. It is commonplace, also, to meet clients who transfer feelings and attitudes on to us that derive from someone else, just as, in counter-transference, we unconsciously respond to the client 'as if' we were that person. For example, clients may relate to us as if we are the all-giving, all-powerful parent they need; if we live up to this fantasy we become unable to say no and to be honest about our limitations. A more subtle illustration of transference happened to a residential social worker who winked at one of the young boys in his unit when they were having a meal, and the child became hysterical. It transpired that this had reminded the boy of earlier sexual abuse from a swimming instructor.

Olive Stevenson wrote some time ago (1963) how she had applied understanding and skills derived from psychoanalysis to her practice when working with Jennifer, aged ten, who had suffered numerous upheavals in her first years of life. On being refused a chocolate by her foster mother who was ill in bed, Jennifer had destroyed a tray cloth which she had spent months embroidering for her foster parents. They were helped to make sense of what to them was nonsense, the worker explaining that Jennifer's early experience of giving and taking food and of being refused meant food had acquired emotional significance for her. The child experienced great anxiety when her carer was ill, displayed by infantile, primitive feelings of revenge. The understanding gained by the foster parents prevented possible disruption of the fostering.

Just when social workers think they are getting somewhere, they too might need assistance in supervision to 'stay with' someone who seems to be rejecting their help. Maximé (1986) talks about the confused self-concept and identity of black children reared in care (who have internalised images and feedback that 'black is bad'). These children express rage to others in their environment, especially black social workers, whom they view negatively. Self-rejection through self-destructiveness is another symptom of introjecting (taking in) negative external images of 'black is bad'. Maximé goes on to describe a five-stage process whereby a person can journey through to a secure and confident black identity:

1. The pre-encounter stage where the person's view is white-oriented, even denying to themselves that racism exists.

2. The encounter stage where the shattering experience of racism forces the individual to reinterpret their world.
3. Immersion–emersion where the old identity is shed and blackness is intensified, and sometimes deified.
4. Internalisation where the old and new self have separated.
5. Internalisation–commitment when a positive black identity advances so that people love and accept themselves as a black person who can become involved in black groups and black issues.

As hinted, another benefit of the psychosocial approach is that it can assist in supervision (Hawkins and Shohet, 1989); supervisor and supervisees need to understand jointly what is happening in a client–worker relationship. Besides helping the above social worker cope with rejection, there can be space to reflect on 'How does this client make me feel?'. Because it is not therapy, the boundaries have to be clearly drawn; but the session provides scope for the relationship 'out there' to be mirrored 'in here'. For instance, one student working in Relate yawned throughout supervision when talking about a couple who themselves were bored with their relationship and tired of the 'here we go again' rows they had (Mattinson, 1975, explores this further). On a broader front, psychodynamic concepts provide insights into the way that organisations and staff teams work. Simmonds (1988) analysed the defences set up by a group of residential child-care staff whose morale suffered when they could not follow up the young people who had left care to live independently: though this is a real-enough problem the principal issue was that the staff, not wanting to face the loss of the children, never discussed leaving with them and so everyone 'forgot' about the future or planned it somewhat unrealistically.

On this subject, Downes (1988) gives us another edifying case study: Neil, a newly-qualified worker who had been in an area team for four months, had been working for that length of time with a young girl and her baby deemed to be 'at risk'. Despite his colleagues thinking him unrealistic and a 'raw teenager' himself, he was determined to treat the client as a grown-up. The team preferred to be 'giving parents', thereby avoiding hostility. Neil and the client had a huge row when he refused to give in to her demands; the team thought him irresponsible, the motherly receptionist comforted the client who threatened suicide.

Downes analyses the splits between Neil and the client, between Neil and the team, and within Neil himself who struggles with himself as a 'sucker or a bastard'. What was missing was a team leader or other manager/supervisor who could have stayed on the boundaries of these dynamics.

Transactional analysis

Before moving on to consider some of the techniques which may be used in the psychosocial approach we will give some attention to a related form of intervention. The frequent comparison in accounts so far in this chapter of the worker/client (and indeed, worker/ worker) relationship with that of parent/child has been explored in the techniques of *Transactional Analysis* (usually referred to as TA). While there are significant differences in approach between TA and other psychosocial approaches, the common ground is the recognition of ego states. Developed out of the work of Eric Berne (1961), TA accepts a Freudian notion of ego states, where the ego is the conscious part of the personality, and the id and the superego are largely unconscious. However, Berne related these ego states to consistent patterns of behaviour which are labelled Parent, Adult and Child. These descriptions bear no relation to age or role, but are, according to Berne, structures of the human personality. The Child state carries thoughts, feelings and behaviours of childhood; the Parent holds all the messages, positive and negative, that are given by parents or other authority figures, and behaviours which provide models; while the Adult assesses situations and decides how to respond to information received. This initial description is further sub-divided by Berne into more descriptive sub-categories, for example Critical Parent and Nurturing Parent; Adapted Child and Free Child.

What is significant is that these ego states have observable behaviours attached to them, and recognizable inner feelings. In working with a TA model, workers will recognise behaviour and 'scripts' when clients are responding using a particular egostate. These responses lead to certain kinds of communication or transactions (a transaction being defined as a unit of social action). Berne argues that all transactions are designed to achieve 'strokes' or responses, and that primary need is for positive strokes (for being and doing), but if positive strokes are not forthcoming then negative strokes are better than no strokes at all. The two main types of transaction in ordinary conversations are:

- *Complementary*: this is where the transactional stimulus and the transactional response involve the same two ego states. This can be Adult to Adult, Parent to Child; the critical aspect is that the stimulus and the response are complementary.
- *Crossed*: this is where the stimulus and response may involve three or four ego states, and one person is responding in one ego state (Child) to the other's Adult communication.

Much more significant, for Berne, are those transactions which reflect what is going on under the surface and are revealed by incongruities of speech and behaviour. These are *Ulterior* transactions and are also described by Berne as 'games people play'. Games are ulterior transactions which are used repeatedly to achieve certain outcomes. Often the outcomes that are achieved are negative because the 'games' are not being played with the person, but with the parents or parental figures of childhood. Attempts to resolve past conflicts or misunderstandings are fruitless because the person in the current relationship does not comprehend, and may well respond in a way that is part of their own earlier transactions. The only way to resolve left-over transactions is to deal with them oneself, or with help from someone who does not engage with them.

An example of an ulterior transaction is where a client will constantly present problems, however minor, for the worker to resolve. This might be construed as attention-seeking behaviour, but often can lead to frustration that the client is always complaining. Such a reaction could well replicate past parental responses; but what the client (or the Child part of the client) was seeking was a demonstration that the parental figure (the worker) cares enough to 'put things right'; this would constitute positive strokes. The frustration could be construed as negative strokes, but even that is better than being ignored. It is important to emphasise that the client is not being childish, but the Child part of their personality is operating in the transaction.

TA differs from other psychosocial techniques in that it is an educational therapy where the desired outcome is behavioural change, the focus is on behaviour and not feelings or therapeutic insights. In this way TA has some things in common with behaviour modification which we discuss in the next chapter. The difference is that TA requires an understanding of ego states and defence mechanisms in order to bring about changes in behaviour. These can be utilised in exercises, games and structured fantasies, as well as straightforward interviews, to bring about understandings of the way that past transactions influence behaviour in the 'here and now'. The way that people use different scripts in their daily lives is written up in an amusing way by Berne in his *Games People Play* (1968). However, at times this might seem to trivialise some very significant transactions. For example, some of the marital 'games' that are described are often ways of avoiding, or may even contribute to, situations of domestic violence. However, an important outcome of Berne's work is the way that all of us in our day-to-day transactions can have crossed communications.

Psychosocial techniques

The goal of more-mainstream psychosocial techniques is to assist the person, the situation or both by reducing internal and/or external conflict. Therefore while the focus may be on the behaviour, some attempt is made to understand and resolve inner conflicts. Two main procedures are used – sustaining and modifying (see Hollis, 1964).

Sustaining procedures

These are techniques familiar to practitioners who talk about 'offering support' or 'building a relationship.' They include:

- *Ventilation* – this unburdening of feelings and thoughts allows the overwhelmed ego to concentrate on problem-solving.
- *Realistic reassurance* – by keeping the person in touch with actuality, not promising what cannot be done, keeping an appraisal of external facts to the forefront and so on, the ego's capacity for reality testing is strengthened.
- *Acceptance* in the relationship allows the superego to 'soften'; 'bad' feelings need not be defended against; the person lessens self-criticism, overwork, rigidity, shame at having a problem, and so on.

- *Logical discussion* gives the worker scope to assess someone's ability to reason and confront reality without needing to retreat into fantasy, symptoms of physical illness, pessimism and so on.
- *Demonstrating behaviour* whereby the worker models coping; he/she can be trusted and depended upon being able to tolerate frustration, set limits, keep perspective and to reason – ego strengths a client may need to 'borrow', that is copy or internalise, for a time.
- *Giving information* increases the motivation of the ego to handle problem-solving, for instance because it sustains hope, separates the facts of what is 'inside' the person and 'outside' in relation to facts and resources, and prevents magical expectations.
- *Offering advice and guidance*, in psychosocial terms, enlarges understanding, sustaining the client's own efforts to keep control; reducing doubt and fear of the unknown introduces hope and assists ego capacity for reflection, adaptation and readiness to cope.
- *Environmental manipulation*, for example in helping with rehousing, money or advocacy. Obtaining needed resources, the worker shares the burden of handling practical problems. Reducing anxiety increases self-confidence. (Deprivation produces irrational feelings of shame and guilt; or anger becomes explosive using up needed, productive mental energy.)

Modifying procedures

These also aim to reduce outer pressures while increasing ego awareness of previously unrecognised aspects of personality dynamics. In social work terms this would be the client gaining insight. Providing that the diagnosis of ego strengths has confirmed that self-scrutiny can be tolerated, techniques include:

- *Reflective communications* to enlarge clients' self-understanding. Within this is a set of methods which involve sustaining the person while they consider in a new light their opinions, attitudes, behaviour, present feelings, past traumas, early life experiences, using the relationship with the worker as a *corrective emotional experience*.
- *Confrontation* techniques include pointing out patterns of thinking, feeling and doing; for instance, a client who was anxious and

trying to come to terms with his homosexuality was confronted with the interpretation that his superego was torturing his ego when the worker suggested, 'It is as if one part of you is persecuting the other'. The client replied, 'That's how it feels'. He was then able to express his sexuality, but recognise where his conflicts were coming from. Confrontation may show clients how they respond in stereotyped ways in their relationships, using an example of the client–worker relationship itself. For example, a person who has had bad experience of dependency could find difficulty accepting anything that the worker says.

- *Clarification* techniques similarly include the use of interpretations to point out, for example, when a person's use of defence mechanisms is getting in the way of change, making them resistant. For example, 'Whenever we get around to talking about your father you change the topic'. Or, the past may inappropriately be influencing the present; for instance, a successful doctor felt very guilty because his father, a car worker, had always been ambitious for another son who became a manual worker, the GP felt he had betrayed his father who had always said 'You'll go nowhere, like me.'

- *Interpretation*, as implied, is a major procedure; usually it comprises an observation which helps the person to link their present circumstances in their lives 'out there' to the feelings that they have 'in here' – that is, the relationship with the helper to what went on 'back there', the past (Jacobs, 1986). This forms a 'triangle of conflict', an example of which would be a person unable to stay in any job without becoming resentful and challenging towards female managers: the worker might interpret it, 'You say you get anxious with women in authority. I remember you saying your mother was the boss at home. I wonder if you feel worried now because I am a woman who seems to be telling you what to do?' Similarly, interpretations might be necessary when symptoms are used as a diversion away from painful conflicts in life and in an individual's inner world: thus, those who treat eating disorders such as anorexia and bulimia interpret these as fear of feeling emotionally empty or wanting to get rid of one's badness; they offer, in one-to-one and self-help group relationships, the chance to talk about these 'baby' needs (see Dana and Lawrence, 1988).

While there is some doubt about the effectiveness of this kind
of interpretation (insight does not necessarily lead to change),
you can see that these methods are often no more than a reflective
discussion helping to answer 'why am I like this?'

The techniques do not aim to elucidate unconscious motives,
restructure personalities or use skills such as the analysis of dreams,
free association and the rest. We do not have the time, the training
or clients' permission to do this. 'Archaeological digging' into the
past is not necessary either, since all we are hoping for is that the
person might see things a little differently and feel that they have
more control over their problems in the present.

A framework for understanding the psychosocial approach

The theoretical base is that of Freudian personality theory, with an
emphasis on the ego's capacity for adaptation and problem-solving.
Building on this, Erikson (1965) has analysed human growth and
development bringing in the importance of psychosocial transitions
('Eight Stages of Man' [*sic*]), whereby he integrates social factors
with intrapsychic ones throughout the human life-span. Hollis
(1970) suggests that the interplay between the 'psycho' and the
social aspects would merit calling this a systems approach, Important concepts include defence mechanisms, personality structure,
transference and counter transference, resistance and early trauma.

Problems are either intrapsychic, interpersonal or environmental
ones. They relate to meeting basic needs, for example love, trust,
dependence, separateness and autonomy. Problems can be unconscious in origin; the 'cause' of a problem, the 'why?' is seen as
important.

Goals are to understand and change the person, the situation or
both; that is, direct and indirect intervention. Specific, proximate
goals help people with focused aspects of their lives, while ultimate
goals might be more vague and relate to self-understanding.

The client's role is somewhat passive, a patient role almost. Where
indicated, the person talks about thoughts and feelings, and by
bringing them into the open or into conscious awareness, begins to
understand themselves better.

The worker's role is to study, diagnose and treat the 'person-in-situation' whole; the worker may or may not share the assessment with the client, dependent on the client's ego capacity for self-understanding (This can be viewed as professional omnipotence, since we can never know all there is to know about someone's history or the workings of their mind.) Treatment processes include establishing a relationship, building ego support via the client's identification with the worker's strengths, helping the client to grow in terms of identity and self-awareness, and working through previously unsettled inner conflicts. A major contribution is obtaining needed practical resources and advocating with others to reduce pressure such that personality change may occur.

As for *techniques*, two main procedures are used, sustaining and modifying. The former sustains the ego via techniques such as demonstrating coping behaviour and listening (to encourage ventilation). The latter is used with sustaining procedures and involves the use of confrontation, clarification and interpretation.

Case example

A female probation officer was the third person to be assigned to supervise Joan who, for a first offence (stealing a social security cheque), had been placed on supervision. Previous probation officers had assessed Joan as a 'soft touch' for everyone in her street who used her as an unpaid baby-sitter and general dog's-body.

Joan was nineteen, unemployed and the eldest of a large, working-class family living in poverty. Following her mother's death when she was eleven, Joan's father had remarried and had five more children. Joan and her stepmother were not close; the latter frequently borrowed and did not repay money lent by her step-daughter. The client had stolen the cheque on behalf of an older woman friend and had not gained personally from the crime.

Joan seemed to have a low opinion of herself; her appearance was unkempt and she looked about thirteen years old. The probation officer, rather than encourage the woman to leave home as previous workers had done, decided instead to see what she could do to raise the client's self-esteem and relieve her feelings of depression. It was important to realise that Joan's social circumstances, not simply her personality in terms of ego functioning, had contributed to the offence: also, Joan, at that time, wanted to stay near to her father since, in some respects, he provided stability in her life. The psychosocial diagnosis thus incorporated an assessment, not merely of the client's possible immaturity (probably exacerbated by a lack of opportunity to get work and achieve what Erikson (1965) calls 'industry' versus 'inferiority'), but also her status as a woman, the somewhat sexist approach of the organisation in pushing her to leave home, the culture of the community in which many deprived people lived, and the ego support provided by her father.

The worker's efforts, accordingly, were both direct intervention and indirect intervention in the community. A home visit confirmed father's backing, although Joan's stepmother, needing help with the rearing of five young children, tended to compete with Joan for father's attention. He seemed to be something of a 'pig-in-the-middle', not knowing whose side to take whenever Joan and his wife argued. The probation officer planned to ask for an early discharge of the probation order and to raise in a team meeting the department's approach to female clients, which sometimes stereotyped them as irresponsible and inadequate.

In her direct work with Joan she explored the client's preconceptions of what the contact would entail. Having been controlled to some extent previously, and not wanting to depend on the worker who was perceived as a strong person, Joan eventually admitted that these were her fears. All her life she had been pushed around and she expected this from the probation officer; in any case, she had been compelled into the relationship and had negative feelings about it. Ventilation of these feelings brought them into the open where they seemed less threatening and also they could be talked about from a reality, rather than fantasy basis.

The probation officer spent some time in subsequent meetings giving information about services and benefits and clarifying with the client what should be their aims. These discussions increased Joan's motivation to see her needs as important as anyone else's and to realise that the worker was not the 'fount of wisdom' since Joan knew more than she about welfare systems, job opportunities and the like. Deliberate ego building on the part of the worker, who described Joan's helpfulness towards others as 'good and bad' and not merely a symptom of not being assertive enough, let Joan reconsider her own behaviour in a less rigid light. She had always swallowed others' opinions that she was a 'soft touch', lowering her self-regard. In actual fact she liked baby-sitting and looking after children, it was not just a case of being unable to say 'no'.

Nevertheless, a few weeks later, Joan was arrested for non-payment of the fine; she had entrusted this money to her stepmother who had spent it. She felt guilty about having to explain all this and reluctant to challenge her stepmother about it. With the worker's help this was sorted out, but in a way which modelled for Joan how it is not selfish to say what you want and yet that for women may be a harder thing to do.

At first, in the relationship, the worker accepted Joan's statement that she had got over her mother's death easily and that she had liked her father's new wife for a while. Later, however, Joan felt safe enough to admit to the worker (and to herself) how sad and angry she had actually felt. The lowering of these defence mechanisms in an atmosphere of acceptance released pent-up thoughts and feelings of loss, abandonment, jealousy and rage, which the probation officer was able to contain; they discussed how natural these child-like fears were, even though on occasion Joan's anger was directed towards her, especially when there was a need to reinforce the statutory requirements of the probation order.

The worker consciously used herself as a role model, being a woman and coming from the same sort of social background. At this stage Joan began to identify with her helper, talking and dressing like her. This apparent dependency did not worry the probation officer who anticipated the later stage of 'separation-individuation'; like the child who moves away from the parent but likes to go back for approval and comfort, in some ways we all retain traces of childhood needs. It was agreed that Joan would help the probation officer at a camp for youngsters, since Joan eventually wanted to work with children and this was a chance to get some experience. This helped her to gain a firmer sense of her own identity as the teenagers enjoyed her company.

As the ending phase loomed, Joan's father bought her a record player to replace one that had been stolen. This prompted his daughter to reflect with the worker, in a mature fashion, how awkward it must be for him and her stepmother to cope with their income and how he might feel torn between the needs of his daughter and his wife. The relationship with the worker at times resembled Joan's split between her anger at her stepmother and her admiration for her mother, being at times aggressive and at others cooperative towards the helper. This could have been confusing for both parties if some insight and understanding had not been gained. By the time the supervision order was discharged Joan had a much clearer idea of who she was; she rediscovered her sense of humour, which, living in an area of increasing unemployment, she would probably have to hang on to. She turned down the worker's offer of a place in a women's group she was planning, preferring to help herself.

8

Behavioural Social Work

Why is it that behaviour therapy programmes (formerly known as behaviour modification), which usually aim to change overt behaviours, are couched in difficult language? Given the simplicity of the basic tenet of this approach, that behaviour is learned and unlearned, we have to grapple with words such as modelling, observation, learning, imitation, social learning and vicarious learning – all of which appear to mean the same thing! Educators such as Sheldon and Hudson, whose work is referred to here, have helped to make the concepts relevant and accessible to social work. Learning theory, on which behavioural principles are based, is a vast, well-researched field. Also, behaviourism has influenced social work practice in a number of ways. In working with people with learning difficulties the principles of 'normalisation' or age appropriate behaviour involve the basic principles of learning theory. Programmes working with offenders, especially those who are dependent upon substances such as drugs or alcohol, involve cognitive behaviour therapy, as do those working with people experiencing depression. In some ways, there are similarities between behavioural approaches and the task-centred practice, in that both focus on a particular problem, follow specific procedures and impose time limits. Finally, when we discuss groupwork, we will see that aspects of learning theory operate in group situations. The objectives of this chapter therefore will be to explore four types of learning, describing some techniques and procedures, and, because it is of growing interest to social workers, taking the cognitive-behaviour therapy perspective and examining it in some detail.

Social workers who base their practice on aspects contained in the previous chapter would say that behaviour, thoughts and attitudes and feelings are influenced largely by the past and by internal conflict. As we saw, even transactional analysis wth its focus on behaviour, sees the roots of that behaviour in past experiences. The theorist responsible for developing behaviourism, B. F. Skinner, who died in 1990, would have contested this saying that behaviour and personality are determined mainly by current events in the external environment.

The behavioural approach to therapy grew rapidly in the 1950s and 1960s, partly to get away from the dominance of the psychoanalytic perspective. It was imported from social psychology and is an example of the way in which social work can adopt theories from other disciplines and apply them in practice to formulate different ways of helping people.

One of the early texts describing *Learning Theory and Social Work* was written in 1967 by Derek Jehu. His final chapter discusses ethical issues raised by approaches which seek to change people's behaviour, and points out that to encourage people to behave in certain ways or to attempt to extinguish behaviour which is deemed to be inappropriate or maladaptive presents many dilemmas. The debates about the term 'normalisation' in working with people with learning difficulties highlights some of these. It is assumed that there are 'normal' ways of behaving, which are common to us all and should be used as some sort of yardstick for deciding whether someone is ready to live in the community. Whatever group of people we are working with, unless the definition of normal reflects the wide variety of behaviours demonstrated by those of us who are not subject to social work intervention, it may be that social workers are at risk of wielding too much power and influence, and of setting inappropriate standards. The alternative term for normalisation – age appropriate behaviour – begs all sorts of questions and unless the notion of 'appropriate' reflects differences based on, for example, class, race, ethnic background and gender, social workers may be seen to be creating a brave new world in which everyone is expected to behave in the same way.

Jehu argues that social workers influence their clients in all sorts of subtle ways, and in discussions in earlier chapters about empowerment and user-involvement we have seen how policies and practices are attempting to diminish such influence. He points out the paradox that overt behaviour modification should present greater dilemmas than that which is more subtle and covert. Nevertheless, he recognises that behavioural models should help clarify the moral responsibility of the social worker, and that principles of client-involvement and consent can act as safeguards. Such principles are

intrinsic, for example, to the task-centred approach described in
Chapter 6. In working with offenders or those experiencing addictive behaviour, it is sometimes agued that informed consent can be
linked to principles of self-determination. If someone knows the
consequences of continuing to offend, or continuing to abuse
harmful substances, then they can actively choose to be involved
in a behavioural approach. However, if the alternative is the threat
of a custodial sentence, or continued incarceration in either a prison
or a mental hospital, then it is questionable how free such choices
are. These issues are raised at the beginning of the chapter to ensure
that due thought is given to them as the different approaches are
discussed.

Four types of learning

Psychologists have identified four types of learning which are basic
to an understanding of behavioural therapeutic approaches. *Respondent* (classical) and *operant* conditioning were developed in
work with animals. The former explained simple reflex behaviours
such as blinking when a light flashes, while the the latter model,
developed by Skinner (1938), examined non-reflexive, active, trial-
and-error learning. Experiments on *observational learning* showed
that we also learn by watching other people, while more recent
approaches recognise that that private self-talk and thoughts govern
our behaviour too and contribute to cognitive learning. Let us take
each of these four types of learning in turn.

Respondent conditioning

Howe (1987) gives an amusing set of examples which help to
illustrate how behaviour which is out of conscious control can
become controlled. He reminds us that Pavlov's dogs were taught
to salivate at the sound of a tuning fork just before food was
presented; thus the stimulus that evoked the response (fork sound)
became the conditioned stimulus and the saliva the conditioned
response. Textbooks represent this as S – R.
    The stimulus of a dog biting an unwary social worker will evoke a
fear response, resulting perhaps in the worker avoiding all the places

where dogs may lurk (in this event, the dog stimulus has widened and become *generalised* to a fear of all dogs). In other words, something happens and a specific *response* occurs. This gives a clue, moreover, to how the connection might be broken in therapy. Systematic desensitisation (also called reciprocal inhibition) is based on this principle of respondent conditioning. It is used primarily for anxiety and avoidance reactions. Having assessed the stimuli that provoke anxiety, relaxation techniques are taught and the client helped to establish an 'anxiety hierarchy'. So, for example, a person who is afraid to leave the house will be asked to rank which situations they find easy and which most difficult when trying to go outdoors. While the client relaxes, each situation, say from putting out the milk bottles to going to the shops, is imagined progressively up the 'ladder' of feeling. *In vivo*, that is real life experience, is probably one familiar to education social workers who may help a pupil to return to school by gradually getting used to the bus route, the playground, and finally the classroom with the other children.

Operant conditioning

This consists of actions that operate on the environment to produce consequences. The key feature is that behaviour is altered by its consequences. If the changes brought about by the behaviour are reinforcing (that is, bring about a reward or eliminate something unpleasant for the person), then there is more chance that that behaviour will occur again. Thus, operant behaviour therapy has been useful in returning long-stay hospital patients to the community, because token economy systems and verbal praise rewarded desired behaviour such as self-help and social skills and reduced unwanted, bizarre actions. Unlike insight-giving and the psychoanalytic approach, this method has been found appropriate for people who are diagnosed psychotic, since no interpretation of 'why' the behaviour occurs is necessary. (See Sheldon, 1984, for further examples of this method with those who are mentally ill.)

Positive reinforcement, known as the ABC of behaviour (Hudson and MacDonald, 1986), is most useful for social workers, especially those dealing with parents whose children misbehave. Parents find it fascinating to discover that they may inadvertently have been reinforcing the 'wrong' behaviour. Thus, the child screams and gets a sweet to keep him/her quiet: this behaviour is more likely to occur again because of the reward. To understand the sequence of events it is necessary to examine the Antecedents of the Behaviour and its Consequences (ABC). This is shown diagrammatically below.

Antecedents	Behaviour	Consequences
Mother, and Sweet Refusal	Child screams	Receives sweet

An important aspect of giving reinforcers, for example in encouraging young offenders in treatment centres to clear away their games, is that the reward, say a smile or thanks from the staff, should be given *immediately* and *consistently* by the whole team until such behaviour is occurring naturally and need not be so systematically commented upon (because the reward tends to lose some of its value over time). Here, 'correct' behaviour is rewarded and undesirable behaviour ignored. Using a visual aid to record positive gains such as 'star charts' can reward achievements. Randall (1990) used a similar device to boost an elderly person as she began to do household chores.

Chaining and backward chaining are operant procedures too; they can be used to teach new behaviours and have been successful in work with people with learning difficulties (Tsoi and Yule, 1982). Teaching self-help skills such as dressing or brushing one's teeth is not as simple as it sounds, though, because each successive step to achieve such behaviour has to be separately analysed and progressively tracked. As an example: backward chaining was used by foster parents to teach their foster son, who had a learning difficulty, to make his own bed. The foster mother performed all but the last link in the chain, then reinforced the child for carrying out the last step of tucking in the sheet. Then the last two links were left for him to master, and so on backwards. He needed a lengthy programme but eventually gained the satisfaction of fully completing the tasks himself.

The termination of something unpleasant is called negative reinforcement and is aimed at reinforcing wanted behaviour, so that children may keep quiet if only to avoid the pain of being shouted at. This is not to be confused with punishment, a confusion which has blighted recent social work practice when 'pin down' procedures have been adopted in residential homes as a means of changing behaviour. This strategy is not as welcome as a positive reward because it does little to increase new behaviour, and shouting can sometimes become rewarding when some attention is preferred to none. A combined strategy is preferred if the aim is to decrease or extinguish unacceptable behaviour; accordingly, when staff in a unit for disabled people wanted to stop a ten-year-old girl from whining, they collectively ignored her when she whined and played bubbles and gave her a much loved mirror when she was quiet.

'Time-out' (that is, from reinforcement), is an extinction procedure which, when used properly and ethically, can be successful. Some agencies mistakenly control aggressive behaviour by isolating people for lengthy periods – this is not time-out but dubious punishment. The procedure should follow within seconds of the misbehaviour, clear explanations should have been given in advance about what would happen and why, and the person should be taken to a time-out area, such as the corner of the room, where there are no pleasant distractions or harmful objects for between three and five minutes. When working with groups of parents whose children were 'driving them up the wall', Scott (1983) found it necessary to keep parents motivated by using humour (a relaxation technique, in essence), teaching them the 'when . . . then' technique ('When you have cleared away your toys, then you can watch television'), modelling the use of praise and time-out and, most importantly, warning that target behaviours usually get worse before they get better!

Observational learning

By copying what other people do we can learn something without having to go through a process of trial and error. Bandura (1977) says that there are three different effects of what is known as modelling: we can learn new skills or ideas; social skills can be imitated and practised; and fear responses can be inhibited, for example sitting next to someone on a plane who enjoys the experience. The main difference from the previous two types of learning is that reinforcement is not viewed as essential. Learning can be deliberate, such as the groups set up to teach social skills or assertiveness via role play and video films; or it can be unplanned when, for instance, clients copy the way workers talk to social security officials on the telephone. Imitative learning is even more likely when there is a good working relationship or where the model is perceived as competent and of high status. Black staff in nurseries for black children (see Morgan, 1986) are deliberately chosen to counter images of white people as superior; play materials which portray successful black people, music, art and literature provide positive symbolic models for the children.

Cognitive learning

Traditionally, learning theory has been concerned with outward behaviour, fixing people as passive beings whose behaviour can be altered by environmental controls. However, it has been recognised by cognitive behaviourists that we also feel and think, that we attach meaning to events. Bandura's work, mentioned above, paved the way inasmuch as some kind of internalisation of images can influence behaviour. Beck (1989) made a major contribution; working with depressed and emotionally disordered people he suggested that negative thoughts about themselves, their situation and their prospects brought about their emotional disorders. In the same way, Meichenbaum (1978) suggested that the way that we talk to ourselves, 'inner speech', affects our behaviour. Thus, if we keep telling ourselves that we will not cope, there is a likelihood that we will not.

However, in an excellent book on this topic Mike Scott (1989) reminds us that the idea that thought processes can have an impact on emotions and behaviour is not a new one. Readers may be familiar with Kelly's Personal Construct Theory (Kelly, 1955) which showed how people construct their own view of the world, and in Chapter 4 we considered briefly Ellis's (1962) Rational Emotive Therapy (RET) which maintains that we upset ourselves by our irrational thoughts – we are upset, not by events, but by the view we take of them. Modern cognitive-behaviour therapy incorporates ideas from Kelly and Ellis: as a social worker, Scott has found these theories to be appropriate when working with depression, anxiety, marital work and work with children. The processes used in the practice of cognitive-behaviour therapy will be explored in some detail towards the end of this chapter.

Some techniques and procedures

The different aproaches to learning mean that a variety of ways of
changing behaviour and increasing the number of response options
(that is new skills) are employed by those using a behavioural
approach. It is an action-oriented approach; people are helped to
take a specific action to change observable behaviour; goals are
spelled out in concrete terms, and the procedure is almost scienti-
fically evaluated by questioning what was done, how often, by
whom, for what specific problem and under which particular
circumstances. In the cognitive field, private or subjective meanings
are the key to a person learning to understand how their cognitions
(thoughts) have distorted reality and how, therefore, the individual
has the responsibility and the capacity to unravel disturbances,
regardless of their origin.

In comparison to the psychosocial approach, the client selects
goals, the relationship is seen as important but not sufficient to
achieve change, work is a joint effort, a written plan of action may
be signed, and the worker functions typically as a teacher who helps
the client to understand the method to perpetuate self-help. The past
is not seen as important; neither is the 'why', that is the 'cause' of the
problem pursued.

The initial stage of work is to do a behavioural assessment. This is
a detailed account of exactly what happens before, during and after
a problematic event. The client may keep a diary so that all the
factors which could affect outcomes are taken into account. Next,
the client says which behaviour is to be increased/decreased. The
worker clarifies who or what else in the environment could assist or
prevent the change effort (for instance, sometimes a partner might
subtly reinforce a woman's drinking pattern; slippery floors and
high toilets can deter frail elderly people from using the toilet). Each
goal is framed in behavioural terms: as with task-centred practice, it
is insufficient to say something like, 'John will do as his parents tell
him'. Far better to state that John will be home by 9 p.m. during the
week and 10 p.m. at weekends, what the reward will be and what
will happen if he arrives later.

A handout or explanatory leaflet may sustain the person's efforts.
For example, in challenging depressive thoughts a client may
complete a sheet recording thoughts; the emotions these aroused;
the automatic dysfunctional thought that accompanied this, such as

'I am worthless'; what rational thought response they tried, and the degree of success they achieved. Or it could be that the strategy is to increase a person's behavioural repertoire; for instance in helping to assert oneself with an authority figure, the techniques would follow the following steps:

1. Identify what behaviour is to be learned.
2. Instruct or demonstrate what this behaviour looks like.
3. Ask the person to role-play or copy the behaviour.
4. Provide feedback and reward desired responses.
5. Rehearse and practise again, modelling again if necessary.
6. Desired behaviour may need to be shaped gradually using praise.
7. Assign homework – 'practice makes perfect'.
8. Evaluate 'before and after' ratings of the behaviour.

At the beginning of the chapter the ethical dilemmas were highlighted and critics of this method argue that it is unethical to control or 'disrespect' people. Hudson and MacDonald (1986) argue that behavioural work is usually effective because it is prepared to measure what is achieved and engages the client on overt behaviour which they choose to change, not covert goals which the worker thinks would be 'good' for them. It could be argued that being prepared to share our skills with clients, teaching them what we do so that we are not indispensable avoids inappropriate dependence and gives clients more opportunities to achieve social acceptability. In this way behaviourism challenges the mystique of a psychosocial approach, but does little to move us away from a 'treatment' model.

The growth of cognitive-behaviour therapy

As stated earlier, the field of cognitive-behaviour therapy owes much to the work of the late George Kelly (1955). An interesting account of how personal constructs and personal change occur during social work training, using Kelly's ideas, is given by Tully (1976). The basic premiss is that we each bring 'theories' about the world, unique ways of anticipating events and relationships, which colour our cognitive processes. Similarly, Albert Ellis's (1962) work attempted to show that people's aberrations in thinking, such as self-defeating beliefs, create disturbances in the way we feel about things.

Ellis would propose that if someone is unhappy after a divorce, it is not the divorce itself which causes this but the person's *beliefs* about being a failure or losing a partner, or whatever. Beck's application of these ideas to treating depression (see Beck, 1989) in the 1970s, contributed significantly to the growth of the cognitive-therapy movement. By developing a system of psychotherapy which helped people to overcome their blocks and the way they reacted to situations, he educated them to understand their cognitive styles and underlying cognitive structures (or unconscious philosophies) which were activated by particular events.

Methods to correct erroneous beliefs included: an *intellectual* approach, which identified misconceptions, tested how valid these were and then substituted more appropriate concepts; an *experiential* approach, which motivated people to experience situations powerfully which could modify assumptions; and a *behavioural* approach which encouraged the development of new coping techniques, for instance the systematic desensitisation procedures described earlier. So, he worked not only on clients' thoughts but on outward behaviour and feelings. Most practitioners use the term cognitive–behavioural, nowadays, to illustrate that problem reduction involves a wide variety of modalities.

For a time, critics of such methods pointed out that workers seemed to ignore clients' stories and how they felt. Films of Albert Ellis show him humorously disputing clients' philosophies and crisply dismissing the importance of their early history and relentlessly repeating that, 'You feel bad because you *think* it's bad'. Although sensitivity and acceptance are seen as part of the therapeutic alliance, having identfed with someone a few goals, techniques could involve rapid-fire questioning which tries to reveal the absurdity and self-destructiveness of those irrational 'shoulds' and 'oughts' which block change. However, Beck (1989) warns against dogmatism and ignoring when clients disagree; he ensures that his interpretation is accepted saying, 'You've heard my view of the problem, what do you think of it?' If there are reservations the person is encouraged to offer other interpretations and consider the consequences of their ideas.

The stages which are followed in cognitive-behaviour therapy are:

1. *Engagement.* The client's expectations of help are explored in a leisurely fashion, conveying the message that there is time to

listen and that the worker cares. The use of open questions allows the person to talk freely.

2. *Problem focus.* Having identified some problems that could be targeted for exploration, the worker asks, 'Which problems do you most want help with?', that is prioritise.

3. *Problem assessment.* Here one specific example is examined in detail. The client is asked to describe an event, their underlying assumptions or inferences from it, their feelings, thoughts and behaviours towards the event and, 'In what ways would you like to feel, think and behave differently than you do now?', that is goals.

4. *Teach cognitive principles* and practices of the therapy and get the person to look at their own thoughts; for example, teach them to spot when they use the words 'should' and 'ought', 'I should (not) have done that' or 'I ought to feel guilty' and so on.

5. *Dispute and challenge* these target assumptions.

6. *Encourage client's self-disputing* through the use of questions. For instance, 'What evidence do you have? Is there another way of looking at this? Are your thoughts logical?'

7. *Set behavioural homework* to carry on this process and keep a diary of distorted inferences and self-evaluations.

8. *Ending.* Teach self-therapy to maintain improvement.

Currently, within the cognitive-behaviourist arena, there is acknowledgement that 'thought' is a much more complicated notion: the study of the relationship between thought and language has long been studied by Chomsky, a professor of philosophy and linguistics. Chomsky, in a critique of behavioural psychology, says that we are not a lump of clay, shaped by punishment and reward, otherwise how is it that very young children, without being taught deliberately, master the complexities of language (see Magee, 1982; Lyons, 1977)? In other words, there is probably an intimate relationship between the deep structure of language and the workings of the mind. We almost come full circle again to Kelly's theories of how we each construct our worlds.

In the probation service this interrelationship between thought and action has been the subject of much analysis in working with addictive forms of behaviour, especially alcohol addiction. Approaches to addictive behaviour have included counselling and alcohol education. Behavioural therapies originally depended upon the use of antabuse as a form of respondent conditioning. This involved administering a drug which created a nauseous reaction when alcohol was consumed. Ultimately the person addicted would associate the consumption of alcohol with nausea and would be deterred. More recently the research in the area of clinical psychology led to the development of treatments based on cognitive behavioural approaches.

The most widely-used approach is based on the work of Prochaska and Diclementi (*The Transtheoretical Approach: Crossing the Traditional Boundaries of Therapy*, 1984) where stages of change in the motivation of the person experiencing the addiction are identified and seen as forming the *motivational cycle*. When working with clients who are addicted to alcohol, probation officers organise their intervention around the stages of the cycle. The interventions involve work which is close to individual counselling, but also utilises some of the basic behavioural approaches outlined above.

The stages of the cycle are:

- *The precontemplative stage* where change is not necessarily desired by the client at a personal or psychological level, but their circumstances cause them to consider it. Often offenders who have been sentenced for alcohol-related offences, or who identify alcohol as contributing to their offending behaviour are at this stage.
- *The contemplation stage* involves an active structured evaluation with the worker of the pros and cons of changing and not changing.
- *The action stage* will be a conscious and planned attempt at controlling the addictive behaviour.
- *The maintenance stage* is when the drinking is under control, but behavioural and cognitive strategies are employed to resist pressure or temptation to drink, thus avoiding the
- *Relapse stage*, which is when there is a resumption of the addictive behaviour.

Those who are able to respond positively to the maintenance stage may move to a state where drinking is no longer seen as problematic behaviour to be consciously controlled. However many people move between stages of the cycle several times before they reach that outcome. In that there are no rules about the organisation of the cycle people may relapse to precontemplation or contemplation.

Acknowledging this enables the worker to see such relapses as a normal part of the change-cycle, and they will employ different forms of intervention at different stages, thus avoiding frustration and depression on the part of worker and client who might otherwise view relapses as failure. Techniques of *motivational interviewing* help the client move through the stages which involve a series of non-confrontational practices to help people recognise for themselves the need for change by identifying the positive and negative consequences of their drinking behaviour. Uncomfortable ambivalences revealed at this stage may be resolved by acting to change the drinking pattern. In this way the desire to change has been identified by the person themselves, which moves them from the pre-contemplative stage, although it can be revisited at different stages in the cycle.

Within motivational interviewing other techniques include *behavioural assessment methods*. These involve realistic appraisal of drinking patterns, consumption level and factors which precipitate drinking. Simple versions of drink diaries, or other reporting methods are used in the initial stages, but more complex recording methods can be adopted later. In discussing the use of motivational interviewing in a project with the probation service, Remington and Barron (1991) describe another specific technique – a *constructional approach to social casework*. This emphasises the need to reinforce positive motivation as well as eliminate negative behaviour. In working with the client on their strengths and abilities, treatment decisions are made and goals to be achieved identified, taking into account the function of the drinking in the person's life and trying to find other means of fulfilling that function. These techniques and the way they have been used effectively by probation officers are described comprehensively in Remington and Barron's article in *Probation Journal* which concludes by arguing that the general principles of this composite approach are relevant to a whole range of what they call 'appetite' problems, which include gambling, eating disorders, sex-related offending and the use of illegal drugs.

Apart from the positive outcomes of such approaches outlined in evaluations, a method (or collection of methods) which focus on both the behaviour, and the person's understanding of the behaviour gives some responsibility to the individual for wanting to change, and understanding the effects of that change, both positive and negative. In this way the individual is participating throughout the process, and can make informed choices about their participation, rather than having to conform to a set of behaviours imposed by the worker. Of course, the consequences of not changing may be that they commit further offences, or fail to comply with the probation order, but these outcomes become part of the considerations which either do or do not motivate the person to change their behaviour.

A framework for understanding behavioural approaches

- *Theoretical base* is learning theory, which includes respondent and operant conditioning, observational and cognitive learning.
- *Problems* which respond well to this approach include phobias, habits, anxiety, depression and obsessive-compulsive disorders (perhaps with drug treatment in tandem). Also, behavioural deficits, such as social skills, are treated through behavioural regimes.
- *Goals* are specific, observable (or self-reported in the case of something like a sexual difficulty). Goals must be stated in behavioural terms.
- *The client's role.* The person helps to measure the baseline behaviour, its frequency, intensity, duration and the context within which it occurs (see Sheldon, 1983). Diaries and other records may be kept. The client's view of what is a reward for them is vital, as are their goals for change. The person usually must be motivated or helped to be motivated. Where a child is the client, the carer or other change agent needs to be motivated.
- *The worker's role* is to help with the behavioural assessment and to mobilise any necessary resources. A contract may be drawn up. Strategies must be capable of being evaluated and measured for effectiveness. A concerned, genuine and hopeful relationship is necessary, if not sufficient, for change. The worker is active, sometimes directive and challenging, and an educator.
- *Techniques* include systematic desensitisation, extinction procedures and positive reinforcement, teaching self-control and thought-stopping techniques, motivating through positive construction, disputing irrational thoughts and giving information to other agents such as teachers, parents and colleagues involved in the programme.

Case example using cognitive-behaviour therapy

The following referral was dealt with by a student on placement in a psychiatric day hospital. The student, who shall be called Jim, had studied behavioural ideas and was trying some of the procedures used in cognitive-behaviour therapy for the first time.

Mr Lin was a fifty-year-old, happily married man with grown-up children. He was twice made redundant from his factory jobs and, just as he was about to return to employment, became increasingly depressed. Eventually, he was admitted to the day hospital where a multidisciplinary assessment revealed that he had been experiencing an array of problems – behavioural, cognitive, affective and physical. His symptoms included depression, feelings of unreality, fears of dying and loss of confidence. The multidisciplinary team, being an open and creative one, agreed that Jim could take a key part in the treatment regime.

Mr Lin agreed to see the student who explained about anxiety management techniques (Meichenbaum, 1978) and Beck's approach to cognitive therapy. They agreed to meet weekly for the duration of the placement and follow what these programmes suggested, with Mr Lin completing homework tasks in between. He had to learn to relax using an audiotape, keep a record of his upsetting thoughts, and measure how much success he had in replacing these with more realistic ones. Because depressed people find it hard to do anything active or pleasurable, Mr Lin was reassured that any change was for the good, so even filling in the thought record was a huge achievement, which would also break the monotony of his routine. Scott (1989) tells his clients that depression is like the mind hanging out a sign that it is 'temporarily out of order' or, 'the mind going on strike for better pay and conditions'.

The multidisciplinary assessment had not revealed a history of suicide attempts or impulsivity, and so the student introduced anxiety-provoking role-play situations in some sessions, restoring the client's loss of confidence in getting on a bus. Together they read out aloud leaflets on coping with depression; they practised the techniques of relaxation together. Other anxiety management techniques included reminding Mr Lin that his feelings of faintness and palpitations did not mean he was about to have a heart attack, as the medical report had ruled out organic disorders. He began to recognise that they are the body's normal reactions to stress and tension and are not dangerous in themselves. When encouraged to visualise a feared event and become tense, he felt how his body tensed; he was taught to wait for the fear to pass, not to fight or give way to it, to just 'accept it'. Mr Lin realised that his fear faded if he stopped adding to it with the fear of fear itself.

Regular practice at home speeded up recovery; he looked more hopeful with each week that passed. But the student gave him advice to 'go slow' and to expect setbacks, recommending these as an extra chance to practise. The word 'practise' was used deliberately rather than that of 'test' as the latter is daunting and can result in clients brooding on failure, rather than accepting that life is made up of good days and bad days, that recovery is 'two steps forward and one back'.

To show Mr Lin that he might be upsetting himself because of self-defeating thought patterns, Jim gave him a list to keep of the ten most common negative thoughts:

1. All or nothing thinking – seeing everything in extremes and polarised.
2. Overgeneralisation – one bad experience leads to constant bad luck.
3. Mental filter – dwelling on the bad and filtering out the positive.
4. Automatic discounting – brushing aside compliments, 'He's just being nice'.
5. Jumping to conclusions – such as mind-reading and fortune-telling; 'I know he doesn't like me; the future holds nothing'.
6. Magnification and minimisation – the binocular trick of blowing things up or shrinking them out of proportion.
7. Emotional reasoning – 'I feel guilty therefore I must have done something bad'.
8. Should statements – 'I should do this' or 'I must', produces guilt rather than motivation.
9. Labelling and mislabelling – of *oneself* as a failure rather than what you *did* as a failure.
10. Personalisation – whatever happens, assuming it is your fault.

Mr Lin could identify himself in these statements. As an example of 'picking on himself', he remembered doing some carpentry in the day hospital workshop which turned out unsatisfactory but which he magnified as 'disastrous'. Low self-worth is often central in depression; therapists using this approach often use the following challenge: when Mr Lin would describe himself as worthless, the worker would query this saying, 'If one of your family got depressed would you think they were worthless?' 'Definitely not', the client would reply to which the worker would respond, 'So is there a law for you and another one for other people?' Mr Lin eventually recovered. Therapies such as these have been positively evaluated (Scott and Stradling, 1990) and doubtless will feature regularly in community-based care in mental health settings in the future.

9

Working with Families

Working with children and families is a high priority for social services departments, and was reinforced by the introduction of the Children Act of 1989. Many direct referrals are for practical help or are part of statutory work aimed at protecting and controlling this client group (see Jones, 1983). Sometimes such referrals turn up difficulties rooted in unsatisfactory family relationships. Additionally, when undertaking assessments for community care it is apparent that in many cases workers will have to consider family relationships, and the dynamics of these relationships influence the outcomes of such assessments. It is not suggested that workers undertaking the assessments involve themselves in family work, but that they should have an understanding of the frameworks for considering family dynamics, and these may inform their assessments. Care managers, however, or provider agencies who are offering support and oversight of care packages which involve family members in caring for older people or those with mental health problems, may well have to become involved in some family work using their understanding of family dynamics and specialist interventions. Probation officers working with offenders of all ages frequently have to assess both the influence of the family on patterns of offending, and the impact of the offending on family dynamics. It is for this reason that this chapter focuses on the family as the site of intervention. For the same reasons, while only a minority of referrals are said to be 'marital' ones, that is conflicting partners, on close examination such interpersonal problems lie at the heart of many other difficulties (Mattinson and Sinclair, 1979). This is a compelling reason for promoting working with couples as well.

As has been indicated, work with families can occur in many different situations and for many different reasons, and the social work interventions already described can be used in family situations. However, this chapter looks in more detail at the skills that are used when the family is specifically the focus of the intervention. For some years this form of social work with families was known as 'family casework' (Jordan, 1972) and, if ever the whole family was seen together, this was intended to better the welfare of one of its members. In the past thirty years, 'family therapy' has become an accepted approach: this is more than doing 'casework with more people in the room', it is used when the whole family is the client and the target for change. When one or more family members are having difficulties this is thought to be a cause and a consequence of interaction.

People affect and are affected by one another and so it is necessary to see how people get along with each other and, more fundamentally, how the family solves its problems. This is an important part of the assessment, giving an indication also how dysfunction might be prevented. Although there has been dismay at calling these methods of practice 'marital and family therapy', with connotations of clinical work and learning 'tricks of the trade' (Whan, 1983), they will be referred to as such, merely for convenience. Parading skills or using the family as entertainment, which was the style of a few early 'followers' of this movement, is not an appropriate rationale for, or outcome of, family work. Down-to-earth workers have shown that the ideas can be used practically and in a range of settings (Treacher and Carpenter, 1984). Strategies for change which are employed with humanity and humility (Walrond-Skinner, 1979) can help families and couples to draw on their own problem-solving solutions and strengths.

Understanding family dynamics

Family trends in the 1990s and the diversity of family life from a race and class perspective make it impossible to advise what is a 'conventional family': quoting research from the Family Policy Studies Centre, Jervis (1990) shows that cohabitation, children born outside of marriage, lone-parent families, stepfamilies and dual-working couples are increasingly becoming the norm. Each family differs in the way members communicate, their values and their structural relationships. Although we all have a picture of how families behave and their composition, this stems very much from our experiences in our family of origin. When trying to understand family dynamics there is a danger that, if we are from the same ethnic group or class, we assume we have a lot in common. Trying to replicate our own family style with client families is another trap for the unwary. For example, O'Brian (1990) gives the following account of trying to engage a Bangladeshi family whose fifteen-year-old daughter had not attended school because her father objected to the school and to the need for her to have any formal education. Being from the same minority ethnic group, O'Brian said, 'Look Mr M. I know what it is like living in this country and having to accept its rules and regulations. We are both foreigners here and I understand what it is like for you'. Mr M replied, 'Sir, with the greatest respect you are not the same as us.' The girl's father went on to say that it had nothing to do with different religions either – it was that the social worker was in a position of authority. Another social worker, one of three brothers, was working with a family of the same composition. Despite having many years experience in family therapy, he began to behave as if he were one of the brothers. In work with families there is a danger that workers attempt to recreate a mirror image of their own family's functioning. (Bowen, 1978, believes that, before working intensively with other people's families, we should sort out our own!) Thus, it is as well not to generalise but to try to understand: 'How does *this* family work?'

Trying to understand a family is like jumping on to a moving bus: you have the disadvantage of being a temporary passenger on their journey through a stage in their life, with people leaving and joining along the way. Like individuals who cope with transitions and life crises, as we saw in Chapter 5, families go through a life-cycle. But it is a much more awkward business, because at each phase in their development the whole group has to reshuffle while at the same time providing stability and continuity for its members. Gorell Barnes (1984) deals with this concept of the family life-cycle, explaining what happens when we leave home, achieve independence, become half of a couple, have children, face an 'empty nest', become dependent and so on.

Such changes are made all the more demanding as each member is probably struggling with their individual life stages at the same time: a woman who has launched children and achieved independence may be faced with her mother who is having to adjust to dependence, perhaps on this same daughter. All the time, families are losing members and gaining members, making space for maybe competing needs, renegotiating the numerous patterns of relationship between people – this is why referrals often have life-cycle changes at the nub of what is going wrong.

According to Gorell Barnes (1984), families can be placed at one of three possible points on a spectrum from flexibility, through rigidity to chaos. Years ago, Jordan (1972) illuminatingly described families which were difficult to break free from as 'integrative', and those whose members were segregated and went their separate ways as 'centrifugal': Minuchin later (1974) termed these patterns of closeness and distance 'enmeshed' and 'disengaged'. These ideas may help us to assess if a family can 'bend' with its changing membership and processes (for instance, if there is adaptability of rules when a child enters adolescence): also, albeit that there are different cultural norms, to enquire if a family is able to regulate their boundaries and can tolerate closeness and distance, dependence and independence.

Another useful concept which helps us to understand how families act is to see it as a system, a set of interacting parts with a particular purpose. Families may have subsystems which comprise the marital subsystem, the children subsystem, the sibling subsystem, mother–daughter and father–son subsystems, and so on. The family's relationship to outside, wider systems, that is the suprasystem, is as important to understand as their internal dynamics. The case example of Paula in Chapter 3 revealed a woman who was struggling to bring up two children in a disadvantaged environment; other families in the street were so used to social workers entering and defining their lives that they were viewed as 'one of the family'; workers often found families outside in the street sorting out one another's problems until 'their' social worker arrived. With limited understanding, an assessment could be made which inferred that Paula and families such as this had 'boundary' problems, that is, allowed external systems to overly influence their internal dynamics. But, unfortunately, that is the reality for some. (When working with children to prepare them for new families, Redgrave (1987) often found the social worker painted in as part of the family group.)

In the same way, O'Brian (1990) points out that the suprasystem cannot be ignored when working with black families – racism affects every aspect of their lives. It helps, therefore, to see the family as an open system in transformation, constantly changing in relation to internal and external forces. Occasionally families 'get stuck', maybe as the result of coping with their own internal crises or because the agencies with which they interact over-react (Coulshed and Abdullah-Zadeh, 1985). When this happens, solutions become part of a problem spiral. For example, services sometimes are dependent on someone being given a label, such as 'a violent family'; in one family the education service managed to gain the attention of the social services by labelling an unhappy boy as an 'arsonist', although the actual event was a fire in a waste-paper basket.

Environmental circumstances are a large part of the assessment of family dynamics, if only to ensure that all efforts are not unravelled once a person returns to the context in which difficulties arose. In one agency, every member of a family had received individual programmes of help for over twenty years. Each time anyone returned to the fold, from residential assessment or care, their problems returned with them.

A tool which can assist in understanding family dynamics and which has been used with adoptive and foster families is the genogram, otherwise known as the family tree. It depicts relationship patterns and events over generations. Births, deaths, divorce, crises and other significant life events can be recorded briefly, and several pages of social history can be condensed into a diagram.

Typical symbols are shown in Figure 9.1, while Figure 9.2 illustrates a family whose eldest son, aged fourteen has committed offences. He has been brought up mainly by his mother, now widowed. The boy has a brother aged ten and a sister aged eight. Prior to their father dying, the children's parents were separated. Maternal grandfather died before the grandchildren were born, though his divorced wife, the maternal grandmother, is still alive.

Figure 9.1 *Genogram symbols*

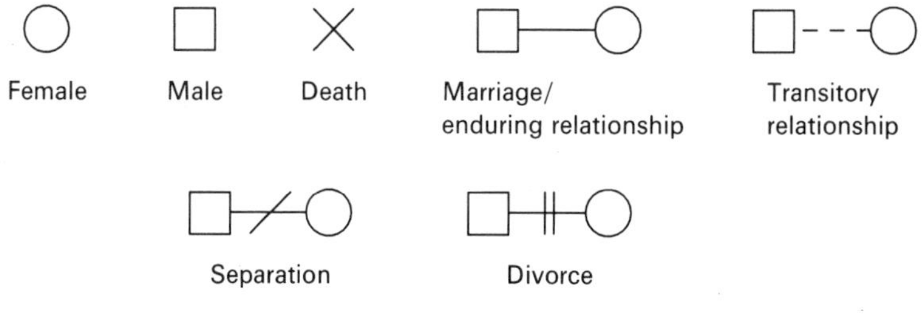

◯	◻	✕	◻—◯	◻- -◯
Female	Male	Death	Marriage/ enduring relationship	Transitory relationship

◻⟋◯	◻╫◯
Separation	Divorce

Figure **9.2** *Illustrative genogram*

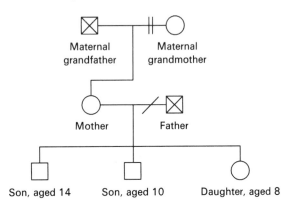

Burnham (1986) gives more examples of less-easy-to-draw family trees, such as those with multiple relationships, step-relationships and transitory contacts. Genograms can become a useful talking-point for families who, while they are helping the worker to complete them, begin to uncover their family's unwritten rules, myths, secrets and taboos. This map of family relationships can reveal, too, how patterns might get repeated across generations. Thus, the family, represented in Figure 9.2 had marital breakdown, death and children reared single-handedly by their mother as repetitive themes.

If we view the family as a small organisation (but with a shared history and future), then we may see that it has a hierarchy, communication systems, values, controls, decision-making, conflict-resolution, norms of behaviour and ways of coping with change. Just like an organisation, a family has an invisible set of rules for how people interact with each other and how homeostasis (stability) is maintained. In order to protect themselves, families develop ways of managing interactions between themselves and with outsiders. Sometimes, as we have said, these sequences and habits get in the way of moving on – they do not mean that the family is ignorant or rigid; indeed, none of us is prepared to accept change unless we know the advantages and disadvantages of this. What used to be termed 'resistance to change' has fortunately been rethought (Carpenter and Treacher, 1989), and we shall therefore look at some of the latest developments later in the chapter. Likewise, there has been criticism of the notion of 'circular causality', the idea that behaviour does not have a simple, linear cause; for instance, in domestic violence a 'systemic' analysis would hesitate to look for a 'cause' or someone to blame. Again we shall return to this. Possibly, it is only when we join an organisation that we learn how it really works. The same is true of families. Only if we achieve an alliance (throughout the process, not just at the beginning) together with an attitude that they are 'okay', will we ever have any inkling of what is going on.

This is not the same as saying that we approve of everything they do; in fact, as Dale and his colleagues at the NSPCC propose (Dale *et al.*, 1986), professionals can act dangerously if they trust the family too much or have too much optimism that things will improve. What it does mean is that taking time to listen to every member's point of view, being courteous, not taking sides and not confronting them with what you see as the 'truth' of their difficulties, is more likely to encourage discussion and sharing in which the worker is free to engage and disengage when the need arises. Further aspects of the therapeutic alliance will be signalled when we look at techniques of practice.

Finally, to improve the assessment of family dynamics some writers have devised assessment scales; these aim to help practitioners to objectively evaluate strengths and risks, for instance with incestuous families (Orten and Rich, 1988). The format focuses on behavioural rather than psychodynamic factors such that realistic plans may be formulated. So that, with father–daughter incest, if the parent denies the abuse, blames the victim and is mainly concerned about the consequences for self these are negative indications for the assessment of future risk. Though such instruments are not infallible they may prevent us working harder and harder to get families to care for their children when, at times, they may be telling us that they are unable to do so.

Four theoretical viewpoints in family therapy

Based on an understanding of family dynamics there are a range of interventions, spanning psychoanalytic to behavioural approaches, available to the worker. We shall examine the central tenets of four of these; psychoanalytic, structural, strategic and behavioural. All of them, in recent times, have been used in combination with systems ideas, outlined in Chapter 3.

Psychoanalytic models

Such models (see Box *et al.*, 1981) emphasise historical factors, uncovering unresolved conflicts from the past which continue to attach themselves to individual members of the family and their current situation. Names of therapists associated with this approach include Nathan Ackerman, Robin Skynner and Christopher Dare. The last, interviewing a family whose son stole his mother's tights and lipsticks whenever she went into hospital, explored the mother's relationship with her father in order to help the whole family gain insight into transgenerational family patterns.

The role of the therapist is to make interpretations of individual and family patterns and focus on how members feel about each other. In addition, there is an attempt to reduce interlocking pathologies; examples of these are when children are drawn in to act as 'marital distance regulators' (Byng-Hall and Campbell, 1981) or when symptoms such as children soiling are part of projected marital conflicts (Mainprice, 1974). Some of the tools used include the genogram and sculpting (using a *tableau vivant* to express emotional ties). With one family whose teenage son had taken on his father's role following divorce, a sculpt showed the family how little space was left for father to fit in again, once the spouses agreed to remarry.

Structural models

These models 'start where the family is', centring on present transactions, though the influence of what habits and role assignments have been learned earlier may be part of the assessment. People associated with this approach include Salavadore Minuchin and, in the UK, Andy Treacher and John Carpenter. Change in the way that a family's members deal with each other 'here-and-now', in the session, is the focus of the change effort. The worker joins the system to see how it works; to avoid being unable to withdraw from time to time, strategies have been devised to prevent getting too drawn in. These might be having a co-worker in the room or linked by audio/video facilities; physically withdrawing at intervals helps, as does leaving fairly long intervals of two or three weeks between interviews. The goal is to restructure the family's organisation so as to change unhelpful patterns of relating to one another. For instance, films produced showing Minuchin working with families show him asking a child who is carrying parental responsibility to keep out of problem-solving while an overlooked parental figure tries on this role; in another family a child was closer to her mother because her father was either pushed out or pulled himself out of family transactions – the direction given was for mother to encourage father there-and-then to talk with his daughter for a time. Some of the specific techniques include working with different sets of subsystems; changing boundaries, for example by seating arrangements or task-setting as above; 'tracking' which approves of family functioning by mirroring it, commenting on it and sharing information about one's own family; encouraging people to interact and then stage-directing them to try a different pattern in the session and at home.

Strategic models

These keep the time-focus on the present. The hypothesis is that current problems or symptoms are being maintained by ongoing, repetitive sequences of interaction between family members. Rather than historical events or unconscious conflicts determining behaviour, particular family 'truths', solutions to problems, communication mechanisms and mental constructs are given as explanations for the persistence of difficulties. There is nothing inherently 'wrong' with the family; in their efforts to sort out a solution they have redoubled their efforts producing a 'more of the same' rut. Theorists associated with this viewpoint are Jay Haley, Mara Selvini-Palazzoli and Milton Erickson. Usually, the methods of helping are active, time-limited, focused on the attempted solution, planned ahead of the session and directed at problem-solving. This might involve a team approach, using techniques such as circular questioning (mentioned in Chapter 3), neutrality, and delivery of a prescription given at the end of a session on how the family should proceed. Because some of these prescriptions are paradoxical in nature (for instance, suggesting no change in the family in order to stop them struggling with the same, ineffective strategies trying more of the same) some of the techniques have been decried as manipulative and disrespectful. Families were thought to resist change because the presenting problem was needed by them to serve a function in their system. Thus, a family with a member suffering from schizophrenic illness might unknowingly resist attempts at change, fearing that the removal of the disorder in one person could unbalance family homeostasis. In other words, another relationship sequence more feared might be triggered by the change. In one family, a twelve-year-old girl had become 'paralysed' for some time, despite no organic cause being found. All kinds of systems had been found by the family to cope with this symptom (what are known as 'redundant' behaviour sequences): these might be viewed as metaphors for the family saying that they could not move on through their life-cycle. Interventions might encompass 'reframing', that is implying that this was a positive solution, for example in bringing them closer together.

Workers in this way are using the family's language – to the above family the paralysis might not be talked of as an illogical feature of family life. However, as we noted earlier, some of the theories about resistance are being rethought. In their clear text, which offers an alternative to the somewhat adversarial strategic approaches, Carpenter and Treacher (1989) note that families who come to our agencies do so because of change, either one that has taken place or is in prospect. What families need is a worker who *expects* change, seeing it not only as possible, but inevitable. Noting strengths and family cooperation is preferred to noting the pathology of resistance. Indeed, we ourselves may be what is producing the resistance, failing to match what the family need with what we have to offer.

Behavioural models

These models again emphasise what is happening in the present, focusing on interpersonal/environmental factors which are 'rewarding', that is maintaining behaviour patterns. Generally, marital therapists working with the relationship of a couple rather than on individual 'failings' favour the methods; thus couples are taught to improve their communication skills, sexual satisfaction, assertiveness and negotiation skills, practising in-between interviews with homework tasks. Behaviour might be viewed as faulty learning or copying from one's own parents. Directing a couple to try out different behaviours in the session itself is common, with the worker operating as a trainer, model or contract negotiator. Therapists such as John Gottman (see Gottman *et al.*, 1977), R. Liberman and Michael Crowe (1982) are usually associated with this viewpoint. The latter therapist, like others, is beginning to integrate common elements from the four 'schools' of thought so that he uses structural and strategic techniques to extend his behavioural marital therapy.

*　　*　　*

Before outlining ways of beginning to work with families, it is important to briefly pursue a few of the criticisms of the concept of circular causality alluded to earlier. Family therapists who base their practice on systemic thinking suggest that while some events can be described in a linear, cause and effect way (that *A* causes *B* which has no feedback effect on *A*), this does not account for complex human interactions. To take one situation; can it be said that a husband drinks because his wife gets depressed without considering that both are involved in the sequence? Another valid explanation could be that his drinking causes the depression. Seeing events in this 'whole' or systems way reveals that each person is part of a circular system of action and reaction which can begin and end at any point and therefore there is little point in asking, 'Who started it?' However, one big problem with this circular view of events is that it ignores the unequal distribution of power. Where power is an obvious factor, such as the use of violence in marriage against women in the main, then this idea of complementarity, that behaviours fit together, is questionable (see, for example, Perelberg and Miller, 1990).

Feminist critiques of family therapy's systems framework have pointed out that this approach treats the family as an autonomous entity, denying or ignoring the socio-political context (see Beecher in Marchant and Wearing, 1986). The family is, after all, a subsystem of a much larger system if we accept this approach. The consequences of a narrow view which focuses on the family system ignores critiques of the family. These critiques include:

- That it preserves conventional male and female relationships.
- How women clients are told what to do to be 'good wives and mothers', mirroring society's expectations.
- Its preoccupation with the nuclear and immediate family, ignoring the fact that many women get a lot of emotional support from other women.
- The family as a primary arena where women suffer injustice because of their sex (which is why so many institutions are required to ensure its continued existence).
- The functional assumption that achieving balance in the family system is a common goal for each individual; whereas, say for women experiencing domestic violence, there is inherent conflict when one person has more power than another.
- The pathologising of women's emotions or the labelling of someone as 'unfeminine' who does not enjoy childrearing or housework.
- The minutiae of techniques which, as O'Brian (1990) points out in relation to racism, confine work to the family system rather than its links to the social structure.

To present feminist thought merely as a set of criticisms of existing theory is negative and contributes to the marginalisation of feminist theory (McNay, 1992). Feminist approaches to family therapy are more than a critique, they provides a framework for working with women and with significant others in their lives, therefore offering perspectives for working with men too. Positive approaches to working with women are offered by Hanmer and Statham and to working with women and men by Dominelli and McLeod (1989). As McNay points out, these are based on ways of exploring, challenging and changing power differentials within relationships.

If Carpenter and Treacher's (1989) analysis is accepted, that in every organisation including families and marriages there are winners and losers, then in general it is the loser who seeks help to restore their position. The winner has the least to gain by seeking help and is therefore a reluctant customer. Interventions which focus on power differentials are therefore crucial. Hence some writers affirm that it is possible to be a family therapist and a feminist (Pilalis and Anderton, 1986). Indeed, it could be an ideal position from which to challenge a family's's assumptions and routines. Just as those in community work have helped to raise consciousness, social workers in family situations and in marital work, without imposing their values, might address the issue of power using their advocacy, negotiation and education skills. Arrangements for intervening in families, including male and female co-working which can role model strong female leadership in partnerships, and techniques such as circular questioning which allows different perceptions of the relationship to be articulated, can contribute to the restructuring of oppressive power relationships within families. In this context therapists could facilitate women in establishing their own boundaries within family structures and in response to family demands. In doing so the family's interaction patterns which reflect societal expectations of gender roles could be made more explicit, and therefore more open to challenge.

Domestic violence

This discussion of power balances within partnerships, and the need to both make overt and challenge stereotypical assumptions about gender roles which may oppress women within family work, raises other issues about the position of women within families. There have been references above to situations of domestic violence, and before going on to discuss the different frameworks for intervening in families and the techniques which might be employed it is important to spend time considering the implications of domestic violence for working with families and couples.

In recognising that abuse takes many forms (physical, sexual and emotional), Mullender (1996) is clear that it is physical abuse, or the anticipation of it, which keeps all other forms of abuse in place, and that the aim of such physical abuse is power and control of men over women. When considering contraindications for working with families, it seems obvious to make links between the position of women with the need to protect children from the various forms of abuse. However, the situation is more complicated than this. Children need to be protected from abuse by men, but they are also subject to abuse by women (see Wise, 1990, for a discussion of the implications of this for practice). Also, studies have shown that children are witnesses to, or are aware of, the violence between their parents and this has adverse affects which are manifested in many different ways (Mullender and Morley, 1994). To make these claims is not to blame women for their failure to protect children, but to highlight that before any work with families is contemplated the workers need to be clear that they are not colluding with, or contributing to, abuse of women and/or children. Also, throughout work with families and couples there needs to be an awareness that symptoms of abuse or direct revelations of abuse may be an outcome. Workers need to be prepared to face such revelations, and to terminate the family work.

It might seem to be stating the obvious to say that family work or work with couples should not be contemplated when abuse is known to be taking place, but in Chapter 7 of *Rethinking Domestic Violence*, Audrey Mullender (1996) documents clearly why such statements are necessary. She reiterates and reinforces the guidelines given by Canadian writer Sinclair that:

> Marriage counselling is a viable option only after the following conditions have been met:
>
> • The offender has accepted full responsibility for his violent behaviour and has made concerted efforts to change that behaviour.
> • The victim is clearly able to protect herself, measured by her understanding and willingness to assume responsibility for her protection.
> • The potential for future abuse is minimal (there is never a guarantee).
> • The degree of intimidation and fear felt by the victim is significantly reduced, so as not to interfere with open discussion of marital issues. Make sure she does not think the issues she raises during the session will be used as an excuse by her husband to assault her after the session.
> • The goals of the couple are mutually agreed upon and couple work is entered into freely by both partners. Make sure he has not instructed her to remain silent on contentious issues.
>
> (Quoted in Mullender, 1996 p. 179)

This is not to say that all work should be abandoned if there are obvious signals, or even suspicions, that abuse has taken, or is taking place. The arguments for, and the implications of, working with men are outlined in a number of places (Perrott, 1994;

Mullender, 1996; Cavanagh and Cree, 1996). What is being said here is that before working with families and couples it is a prerequisite that consideration should be given to such checklists to ensure the safety of women and children. Only when these conditions can be met should decisions be made about working with families and couples along the lines discussed below.

Beginning to work with families

Gorell Barnes (1984) and Burnham (1986) provide us with examples of 'selling lines' and letters to attract families so that we have people to work with! However, it is well-known that when the concrete needs of families are met in the initial stages of helping, it is more likely that they will stay with us to carry on helping them to solve their other difficulties. So, practical needs may have to be dealt with first. Similarly, O'Brian (1990) offers the following guidelines for planning work with black families:

- Be clear about who is asking for your involvement; if it is an agency, what do the family feel about this?
- Is the referral discriminatory, for example have the services failed the family? (He gives an example of a school who referred a pupil because 'West Indian parents are not interested in education'.)
- If the above is the case, should you deal with the referring system first? (They could be informed that usually parents are concerned and if need be invited to the first meeting, held in the school.)
- Beware cultural stereotyping by oneself.
- Should direct work with the family be done by someone who shares their experience of racism?

With all referrals, as was stated in Chapter 2 on assessment, the referring person is a key figure and, occasionally, is the problem.

Before the first meeting with the family it will be necessary to explain why the whole family need to be involved, saying for instance, 'If there's a problem in the family it's bound to affect everyone' or 'It helps to get everyone's ideas about what could help'. Even then, as we have seen, families who have a history of being on 'the books' of a variety of agencies naturally resent intrusion and what they see as victimisation by professionals. Strategies for

engaging families with many problems might start by acknowledging their loyalty to each other and how difficult their problems
must be to cope with. Underlying dilemmas can be confronted too,
how raising some issues is hard on them but yet they may have tried
to change without success. Where numerous organisations are
involved, the use of a network meeting to prevent overlap and
duplication can reduce pressure on the family, as can home visits
when families are short of money.

Families who have received a lot of help are sometimes isolated –
they also may need connecting to a support network of friends,
relatives and sympathetic neighbours. It is vital to respect people
and their cultural values, confirming too that they are still in charge
of any changes which they choose to make. Many family therapists
help the group to weigh the pros and cons of change, slowing down
hasty decisions, confirming the family's's underlying need for stability.

Haley (1976) helpfully divides the interview into four stages; a
social stage, problem stage, interaction stage and ending stage.
Taking each in turn:

1. The *social stage* is worth taking time over. Being courteous,
    getting to know everyone, asking them to sit where they wish if
    it is away from their home, introducing oneself, carefully trying
    to remember everyone's name and interests, checking if anyone
    is missing, noting the mood and how they deal with you and
    each other are some starting points. When someone is absent
    this could be a sign of non-cooperation; on the other hand, there
    may be genuine practical problems or, sometimes individuals
    may want to be seen without other family members. The reasons
    for this should be ascertained and respected. Home visits can be
    less stigmatising and less threatening for the family, but it may
    mean the worker being active in asking for a barking dog to be
    removed or a television set switched off. Preventing a headlong
    discussion of the problem is necessary as this can result in
    certain members being neglected. Clarify what you know of
    their situation and why you wanted them all to be there.
2. The *problem stage* starts by asking what is the problem or how
    you can help or what changes they want. Listen to everyone's
    views without making interpretations, offering advice or trying
    to get them to see the problem your way. Find out the detail of

who does what to whom and how the problem affects individuals, using circular questioning when appropriate. It may *not* be appropriate when the worker and the clients are from different ethnic backgrounds: for example, saying that everyone is different, allowing children to have a voice, objecting to older children looking after younger ones and so on could lead to disagreements (Liverpool, 1986). A therapeutic alliance relies on us checking our attitudes and assumptions and increasing our knowledge of other cultures (see Lau, 1984). Still, as O'Brian (1990) reminds us,

> *Black people do mistreat their children. Elderly black people are not always cared for by their families. Black women are subjected to domestic violence.* (p. 8)

3. In the *interaction stage* involve everyone with each other; often this happens anyway as members begin to talk to one another. This is probably how they solve their problems so you may be less active, watching the speakers and the listeners, only directing when the focus on problem-solving appears to drift.

    Bearing in mind differences in culture mentioned above, you may ask certain members to talk to one another rather than you keep the attention on their suggestions and solutions. You have to strive to maintain an alliance with the family, supporting strengths, perhaps putting yourself in the one-down position but being persistent, recognising their fears and sometimes addressing these. The family may try to deter you with the dog or the television, or by denying the problem, blaming others or drawing you into their viewpoint, showing how helpless they are: when the time is right you can talk generally about taking change slowly and aiming for very limited goals of their choosing, so as to engage them and take their fears seriously.

4. The *ending stage* should see some agreement on a simple goal, arrangements for future meetings, any tasks to be achieved in-between and time limits sorted out. With some families it may have been the only planned meeting with the whole group; where families turn down family therapy as an approach, they may accept just one meeting of this kind for assessment purposes. Who is to attend in the future may be planned, though working hardest with the least committed person can sometimes get them to come back.

Case example

Sue, thirteen, had not been to school for a year. The school social worker had never seen her as Sue refused to come downstairs during home visits. A psychiatric assessment was planned but the family, which included three older sisters who had all left home, agreed instead to work as a group. Co-workers, one male and one female, from an area social services team saw the family at home in the evenings on four occasions. Prior to contact, the workers hypothesised from the family life-cycle stage and the family tree that Sue might be struggling with adolescent challenges while her parents faced re-forming as a couple, preparing for the prospect of their last child leaving home.

The workers knew from the education social worker that father was a long-distance lorry driver, who had never been interviewed, and that mother and daughter were very close. There was some suggestion of marital violence throughout the marriage, plus some strict disciplining of the three other sisters. The workers hypothesised that the women needed to ally themselves against father's physical power; in family therapy terms this would cross hierarchical and generational boundaries. Also, when men are temporarily absent from the family and return at intervals from their jobs, this increases strain on the couple who have to continually re-negotiate space, decision-making and roles.

On each visit, timed to coincide with father's trips home, the workers often had to wait for him to arrive. Though there was some pressure to begin without him this was resisted because this would have been no different from previous problem-solving which had not produced change. The workers had to demonstrate to the family that they were 'with them', but at the same time objectively trying to help them sort out Sue's non-attendance at school. So, the meetings were kept informal until father arrived.

Father was a largely built man and quite intimidating to look at but the workers treated him as if he were cooperative, asking him to plug in our audiotape which he happily complied with. (The reason for this and returning the tapes to the family on completion had been discussed.) Sometimes, just as in network assemblies, the mere bringing together of a whole family is powerful enough to unblock communications or prevent them being diverted through something or someone else. Thus it was with this family; although Sue never spoke, she listened intently as the women bravely confronted her father's over-zealous disciplining. He confessed he was ashamed of once having tipped one of them out of bed and looked astonished when his wife said that she intended leaving him once Sue had left school. She planned to get a full-time job and establish her independence. Sue had never been hit by her father; she looked young and boyish with jeans and a short haircut, but kept her head bowed throughout most of our meetings. Mother was asked if she would take Sue with her when she left and she said that she had not decided. The workers addressed what seemed to be connected themes of growing up and leaving home, using the co-therapy relationship to model problem-solving and respect for each other's views. Tentatively they suggested, 'Perhaps Sue is sacrificing her growing up to save the family from splitting up?'

The use of circular questioning revealed different viewpoints, introducing new information about how each third-party saw relationships in the family in regard to the specific problem but also because the family's reality was that marital conflict was an issue. For example, the workers asked, 'When your mother rows with your father what does Sue do?' and, 'When your mother leaves home, who will be most and who will be least upset?.

In many ways the sessions provided a channel for the family talking about something which had been simmering for some time but which all were afraid to confront. Since the older girls had ideas about growing up and managing school it was decided to draw on their expertise. Working with the sibling subsystem on their own for a time in the front room, the older sisters were set tasks to confide in Sue what their teenage years had been like. Their parents agreed that no-one would enquire about these get-togethers. After six weeks, during which the sisters met each other for these talks, which all enjoyed, Sue returned to school where she subsequently did extremely well. The married couple believed that they would carry on sorting out their plans for their relationship; neither wanted help with this and, some time later, they are still married.

Working with couples

Prior to drawing up a framework for this approach we will consider some observations on marital or couples work. While the theoretical viewpoints remain the same, in that there are psychoanalytic, structural, strategic and behavioural forms of work usually based on systems thinking, other points are important to mention. One is that social work students and practitioners seem to be reluctant to engage in marital work. Maybe it is 'too close to home'; most of us have experienced marriage at close quarters and some have experienced the trauma of marital breakdown. The agencies, outside of specialist ones like Relate, also appear to sustain this defence against working with anxiety-provoking, intimate material, preferring to work with one of the couple and then mainly in terms of resource-giving.

For those who have decided to work with marital difficulties, James and Wilson (1986) give a useful breakdown of how to proceed; when to work with the marital system or one partner, whether the goal is enriching the relationship or freeing from it. These authors also have a useful chapter in their book on working with couples from minority ethnic groups, again recommending that we look beyond cultural stereotypes of, for instance, the subordination of South Asian women or the issue of arranged marriages. This is a useful reminder that working with couples can include various arrangements for partnership which do not have to involve either legal or religious marriage ceremonies. It is the dynamic of the couple relationship and the emotional commitment to being a couple which is the focus of the intervention.

What one might find in the initial assessment of a couple whose relationship is fundamentally stable is that they have sought help with a transitional crisis: often expectations of marriage or partnership are too high and they are unaware that there is no partnership without conflict. Those in couple relationships sometimes project the unwanted part of themselves on to the other so that there is a great deal of blaming and attempts to make the social worker an ally of one partner. However, referrals, especially to statutory agencies, often come in the guise of problems with parental roles, attacks from the family of origin, continual threats of separation and eviction which stem from ambivalent marital bonds (see Mattinson and Sinclair, 1979). These are marriages and partnerships characterised by instability, where there is difficulty in trusting each other and making attachments, related to a deep-seated longing for love and security. Because of this there may be a lot of work to be done with the individuals on their own as well as on their relationship.

Incidentally, although therapists prefer to work conjointly (with both partners) there is no objection to seeing only one; Carpenter and Treacher (1989) place an empty chair in the room and say something like, 'If John were here what would he say?', as well as giving (usually a woman) support to get the other person to accept help. Also, as was indicated in the discussions about domestic violence, there are some situations when to insist on conjoint work might put the woman and/or the children at risk, and would be totally inappropriate. (For discussion of the implications of, for example, mediation work in cases involving domestic violence see Hester and Radford, 1996.)

Where problems are sexual ones, generally, as we have seen, behavioural methods are preferred, although a deeper understanding may be required if these have little effect. For instance, some couples dread differentiation; they keep negative feelings and differences out of their marriage or partnership, thereby frustrating adult sexual roles. (Books by the Institute of Marital Studies, for example *The Marital Relationship as a Focus for Casework*, are valuable in exploring psychodynamic factors in marriage.) Many of the underlying problems for couples, whatever their composition or legal status, are about intimacy and distance, sameness and difference or how each person gets their needs met, 'how often each can be allowed to be the baby' (Clulow and Mattinson, 1989, p. 56).

A framework for understanding family and couples work

- *Theoretical base* is systems theory used in combination with psychodynamic, structural, strategic and behavioural ideas. Important concepts include the question of causality, boundaries, hierarchy, homeostasis and interactions inside the family and with the suprasystem, that is external systems.
- *Problems* are those of family transactions; family problem-solving patterns and communications which become blocked, distorted or displaced through one member. Myths, secrets and taboos carried over from previous generations might also hinder problem solving. A number of problems arise as a response to life-cycle transitions when there is a need to flexibly adapt and re-align relationships. Some solutions could become the problem.
- *Goals* are minimal, often aimed at changing overt behaviour, though some methods aim at insight as well. The family are helped to choose limited, specific goals, usually within a brief time frame. Workers aim to join the family or couple, inasmuch as they offer support while attempts are made at restructuring relationship patterns and behavioural sequences.
- *The client's role.* In this approach, the couple or the family is the client. They may also be the target for change and the team which

works alongside the therapeutic team to change transactional patterns within or outside their system.

- *The worker's role.* There may be two workers as co-therapists, or a therapeutic team, who hypothesise how the system of family transactions relate to the problem presented. Work with external systems could be just as important, especially when numerous agencies are involved who unwittingly mirror family dynamics. It is vital to sustain the couple's or the family's attempt at problem-solving; to not take sides or blame; to not perpetuate power inequalities but to raise awareness of these, and to offer a positive redefinition of their difficulties to help those who have become stuck trying 'more of the same'.

- *Techniques* are numerous. This is why caution is advised against being bewitched by technique at the expense of helping the family in an authentic, non-adversarial way. Joining and restructuring operations include tracking communications and themes about family life (sticking to detail helps; mundane themes often reveal the typical ways in which people manage each other); intensity around the specific problem might be necessary in order to break out of 'redundant' problem-solving routines; observation is as important as listening, so that process and content, how the family behave and what is said, are clues to helping; and being careful not to undermine family competence but to confirm their strengths. Other methods involve use of the family tree and genogram; creating physical space and shifting relationship boundaries; setting tasks; taking time out of the interview to check with colleagues what is happening; or using 'live' super-vision with the supervisor in the room to ensure effectiveness and objectivity. More 'advanced' techniques, aimed at exceptionally chronic difficulties, might be the use of paradoxical prescriptions (advising no change) and the (possibly gifted) use of metaphor, stories and anecdotes. Self-disclosure, in a self-aware worker, can be used on occasion to talk about one's own family life.

10

Working with Groups

It is probably true to say that every method discussed so far could be used when working with groups. Much of the early literature on groupwork arose from group analytic methods, however there is growing interest in the effectiveness of cognitive therapy with groups. Some writers view family therapy as groupwork (Zastrow, 1985). However, because family therapy uses such different methods, despite many concepts being the same, it is probably better not to consider it as groupwork. Community work also uses groupwork as a major form of intervention (see Twelvetrees, 1991). Having said that, it might be assumed that groupwork involves using any method of intervention, but with more than two people. Groupwork is more than this, and this chapter will explore some of the theories which support groupwork as a separate, and some argue, more effective method of intervention, as well as looking at different stages of groupwork intervention. It introduces some of the types and purposes of groups, comments on the tasks for the worker, discusses how to handle particular difficulties, and recommends literature which is most accessible to students and workers. What follows is particularly relevant to staff teams developing community social work: groupwork can be used effectively to extend the networks of carers and service-users, to promote self-directed groups, and to develop new resources such as parent and toddler groups. Also the principles of groupwork are important when developing consultation processes, setting up user and carer fora and chairing meetings.

What is different about groupwork?

One definition of a group is a collection of people who spend some time together, who see themselves as members and who are identified by outsiders as members of a group (Preston-Shoot, 1987). However, group membership extends beyond the time that the members spend together, it involves a commitment and loyalty which arises out of the individual's interaction with group members and the group leader(s)/group facilitator.

It is an interesting exercise to list the number of groups of which you are or have been a member. Such an exercise helps to clarify what we think we mean by a group, but also illustrates the number of different groups any one person belongs to. Both of these points are important for some of the basic theories of groupwork. For example, when we join a new work team we might not immediately feel part of the group, indeed we might feel quite excluded. What is it that eventually makes us feel that we are a member, that we have 'arrived', and why is it that some people never feel accepted, they experience exclusion? Being part of many groups causes conflicts of loyalties and confusions about behaviour. When we join a new work team we discover that tasks are done differently, systems might be better, or worse. Part of being accepted involves negotiating that fine line between holding on to the positives of our past experiences and working practices while accepting that there are things to be learnt in the new situation.

These experiences help us to begin to understand the complexity of group dynamics, and give some indication why we need to consider the literature and gain experience before undertaking groupwork. The leadership of groups involves a set of skills which may only be learned by doing. Opportunities for students and workers new to groupwork to acquire supervised groupwork practice are expanding. Sometimes students will act as co-worker with an experienced groupworker, or there may be opportunities to be a participant observer. Also, there is a growing amount of literature including some skills manuals which involve groupwork exercises.

At the core of groupwork theory is the capacity of groups to bring about change. Peter Smith (1980) considers processes of social influence to demonstrate that groups bring about more lasting change than individual work because groups provide influence both by feedback, and access to coping skills. More importantly, the range of participants in a group includes those who have similar experiences, difficulties or goals which increases the repertoire of the individual. The three types of social influence are:

- *Compliance*, which occurs when a group member behaves in a way that s/he thinks is acceptable to, or desired by, the group. Such change might be relatively minor and short-lived. It can also occur in individual interviews, especially as compliance occurs when one person is seen to have more control over another. In groups, individuals are often initially compliant to the leader's wishes.

- *Identification*, which occurs when one person is attractive to another, and the second adopts the behaviour and attitudes of the first in order to sustain a positive relationship. In that groups involve a number of participants, they provide more opportunities for identification to occur. (There are risks here, as those working with offenders are aware. If the attractive person displays anti-social or criminal behaviour then the risk of 'contagion' occurs.);

- *Internalisation* which is seen as the most important element in group learning and occurs when a group member makes changes because they observe the behaviour of someone who is attractive to them and the behaviour works for them in their own situation. Again groups provide a number of opportunities to observe and test out different coping strategies.

The process of modelling is not the only process that is enhanced by participation in a group, rather than individual work. In all interactions we reveal something of ourselves, and as we get to know people we reveal more of ourselves. This process of *disclosure* happens in individual interactions, but obviously is multiplied in groups where we reveal different aspects of ourselves to different people, and in different circumstances. When we disclose aspects of ourselves, we receive *feedback* from others. Sometimes that is direct feedback, people tell us they agree or disagree, or indirectly by their behaviour and attitudes we discern that they do or do not like what we say or do. The process of feedback has been discussed in Chapter 4, and all the principles outlined there apply to groups. When we receive feedback from individuals we can ignore it, or perceive it as a difficulty (or a benefit!) of our relationship with that individual. In groups, feedback which is received from more than one source is more difficult to ignore. Also, as group participants individuals are more likely to give feedback in the knowledge that their views or perceptions will be supported by other group members.

The Johari window (Figure 10.1) devised by Joseph Luft and Harry Bumberg (Golembieuski and Blumberg, 1970) illustrates how this interaction of feedback and disclosure contribute to an understanding of ourselves. Either through defensiveness, lack of insight or not having been in situations before, there are aspects of our behaviour which are not apparent to us. The process of feedback, handled appropriately, helps us to understand how our behaviour impacts on others, and group situations give us the opportunity to test out how much that is a particular response from one individual, or is a more general repsonse to our own behaviour. The experience of being in a group, of disclosing parts of ourselves and receiving feedback, is therefore likely to reduce the unknown or unconscious area and contribute to insight.

Smith's notion of social influence and the processes of feedback/ disclosure in the Johari window both involve change, and this change is brought about by challenge and confrontation, not in the sense of open argument and disagreement, but by individuals becoming aware of aspects of their behaviour and that of others and having to deal with it. It is the potential for this change which makes groups both an effective method of intervention, but also the source of anxiety for both participants and groupworkers. This potential is

Figure 10.1   *The Johari window*

DISCLOSURE

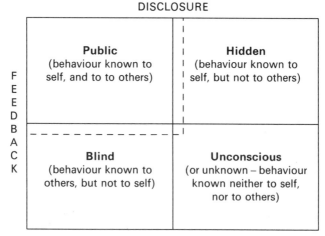

Public (behaviour known to self, and to to others)	**Hidden** (behaviour known to self, but not to others)
Blind (behaviour known to others, but not to self)	**Unconscious** (or unknown – behaviour known neither to self, nor to others)

(FEEDBACK — vertical label on left)

Source: Golembieuski and Blumberg (1970).

present whatever the focus or purpose of the group, because it is the interaction between a number of different participants which provides the opportunities for feedback and insight.

As Mullender and Ward (1991) point out, even in their model of self-directed groupwork, which sets out with the prime aim of raising awareness and assisting users to set their own agendas for change, personal change occurred within the group's members. This was most positive in that it enabled members to be more confident and take on more public roles.

Types and purposes of groups

It helps to understand that group aims usually prescribe the type and methods to use. Different purposes are those broadly categorised by Papell and Rothman (1966) – remedial, reciprocal and social-goals models. In detail, Preston-Shoot (1987) distinguishes social or recreational groups; group psychotherapy; group counselling; educational groups; social treatment groups (for example sex offenders groups); discussion groups; self-help groups; social action groups (for example welfare rights); and self-directed groups (for example campaigning or other objectives decided by the members).

The reason why groups fail to 'get going' might be related to how they are formed, composed and led, but also a failure to be clear about purposes. While during its lifetime a group may change its purposes, for instance from discussion to campaigning, unless it is openly stated at the outset what the purposes are groups can 'lose their way' and become very puzzling for their members. One group, supposedly a recreational one for single mothers, had a hidden agenda aimed at getting the women to improve their parenting skills. So it was doomed from the start. Whitaker (1975) shows how a group could be retrieved by bearing in mind four issues:

1. Success is more likely if other people in the agency support the group purpose and procedures. Sabotage is also less likely.
2. A group is more likely to be effective if a consensus can be established within the group about aims and methods.
3. Structural factors such as size, duration, composition, constancy of membership, and ratio of staff to members influence effectiveness.

4. A group which has lost its purpose should be reconstituted with a different mandate or terminated.

The only reason for using groupwork as opposed to any other practice method is that it is the best way of helping the people concerned, not because the workers want to try it. Indeed, groups have their disadvantages, not least that some individuals are frightened of them. This fear is linked to a sense of ambivalence; of wanting to belong to the group but being afraid that the group might demand the giving up of autonomy, asking members to do or think something with which they do not agree. As we have seen in the beginning of the chapter, this might not be an unrealistic fear. On the other hand, groups provide what Yalom (1970) terms 'curative factors' not available through individual approaches. They can be a source of power for clients pressing for social change; mutual support, exchange of information and motivating hope also stem from group processes. The use of groups in the probation service also demonstrates how groups can be used for education (for example alcohol awareness and impaired drivers courses), confronting unacceptable behaviour (for example anger management and offending behaviour groups). Groups therefore offer the opportunity to learn and test interpersonal and other social skills; they offer a sense of belonging and 'being in the same boat' which is reassuring. There is scope to use the leader or other members as role models and to get feedback about coping attempts. Perhaps, most significantly, there is a chance to help as well as be helped.

Planning the group

Having decided on the type and broad aims of the group, a major task is planning and preparation. Questions to be answered comprise:

• *Who*? The composition of a group may already be determined, such as those in hospital wards, residential and day centres and neighbourhoods. Where the group can be formed, an ideal balance suggested by Redl (1951) is: 'homogeneous enough to ensure stability and heterogeneous to ensure vitality'. Racial homogeneity might be necessary where this is preferred by minority ethnic groups (see Sheik, 1986); similarly, sameness of gender may best meet the purposes of the group (see Reed and Garvin, 1983). While, overall, perhaps the best guide is commonality of needs, it is necessary to be aware of the balance of composition. So, for example, it would not be helpful to have only one black person, one woman or one man in a group.

- *How many?* The question of group size depends on the aims of the group, but usually there needs to be more than three and less than fourteen people, what Brown (1992) suggests is 'large enough for stimulation, small enough for participation and recognition'.

- *How long?* Open-ended or time-limited, this question also needs to incorporate a decision whether or not to have open or closed membership (in settings such as hospitals or prisons there is often little choice, as the movement of patients, prisoners and staff on shift systems dictates membership).The length of each session needs to be considered too, for instance work with children or older people who are frail (see Cornish, 1983) requires short sessions with rest breaks.

- *Which methods?* The methods must suit the members, skills of the leader(s) and the stated aims. It may be that it is only when the group has met that final decisions can be taken. Then there are a variety of games, discussions, activities, experiential exercises and entertainments available (the *Annual Handbook for Group Facilitators* is a worthwhile source). Boyce and Anderson (1990) use drama therapy, video and written exercises in their groupwork with adolescent girls who have been sexually abused. In the probation service methods might be dictated by agency policy, or by the specification of the court, as in the case of a violent offender who receives a community supervision sentence which involves attending an anger management group.

- *What resources?* There are a number of practical issues to be addressed such as, is there a meeting place; is transport available if necessary; will refreshments be provided; what equipment is needed, and so on? For groups with special needs, appropriate accommodation and support systems will be required. For example, some people with disabilities are accompanied by helpers who will assist with practical tasks; some older people with hearing difficulties may need someone to sit with them to ensure they hear all that is going on. Resources have to be mediated with the agency which may want a breakdown of costs in terms of time spent, staffing by one leader or two, if an outside consultant is to be used, what recording systems will be used, and if workers in the whole team can make referrals, for instance from their current workloads.

Stages of group development and the worker's tasks

Groups evolve through stages when their behaviour, the leader's interventions and the accomplishment of tasks or activities are affected. Following individual 'screening' (for client and worker!) you have to be confident that you can follow the energy of the group through trust, openness, interdependence and finally independence. At different stages the worker has to be central, pivotal, peripheral and central once again. Accordingly, the worker is in tune with the stages of group development known as forming, storming, norming, performing and adjourning (Tuckman and Jensen, 1977).

Other groupwork theorists name these stages differently, but all agree the phenomena to be observed at each: Yalom (1970) describes orientation, conflict, and then cohesiveness; Schutz (1966) outlined cycles when the group is concerned with inclusion, control and affection, while Whitaker (1985) talks about formative, established and termination phases.

Quickly, in the forming stages, members move from orientation and exploration, in which there is parallel communication aimed at the worker, to more communications with each other. The group and the worker are tested to see if trust can be established. The tasks for the practitioner are to help people to get involved, to link people and their common concerns and to encourage the development of a group bond. When any of us join a group we want to know if the sacrifice of our individual wants will be compensated by joining the group, so the worker takes any opportunity to point out how they, sharing similar interests and problems, are in a position to understand and thereby help one another. To summarise the skills and tasks of the leader in the early meetings:

- give a short presentation of yourself;
- ask members to do the same;
- review information given to members prior to joining;
- amend any aim and agreements;

- acknowledge initial uncertainties;
- get each person to say what they hope to get out of the group;
- summarise issues as presented;
- establish norms for listening and accepting;
- facilitate interaction, 'Does anybody else feel the same?';
- play the absent member role, putting into words what people may want to say but are not yet ready to risk;
- show concern for each individual;
- balance answering questions with 'Does anyone else know the answer to that?' (Northen, 1969; Heap, 1985).

During the storming stage, subgroups and pairing may have formed (later, these relationships extend to include the whole group). It is a stage characterised by the replacement of 'Do I belong?' with, 'Do I have any influence?' Struggles for power and control underlie communications and there is a tendency for members to polarise around certain issues. Further exploring and testing takes place: the group is quite fragile and may not continue if the leadership does not provide enough security while individuals query if they are going to get what they came for. This stage can be draining. Some skills and tasks are:

- keep calm in the face of member–member, member–leader conflicts;
- do not retaliate when your authority is challenged; it may stem from ambivalence about membership or maybe a transference reaction;
- model acceptance and openly recognise that people are different;
- do not pick out isolated or difficult members for attention;
- try to pace and time when to facilitate and when to be quiet;
- begin to release responsibilities to the membership.

The norming stage indicates that group cohesion is established; intimate and personal opinions may be expressed by members to each other. People start to look for 'affection', that is signs that they are accepted by the wider circle. Cooperation, sharing information and decision making by consensus promote synergistic (the extra power of combined action) outcomes. People identify with the group and its future: a 'we' feeling develops, a growing *esprit de corps*. A norm of high attendance, ritual ownership of seats, and some exclusivity is likely to make it difficult for new members to join. A lack of conformity to group norms can lead to scapegoating or group pressure to conform. New leadership from within the group may result in altering basic group norms. For the worker, the tasks are to:

• let people help each other by stepping out of a directing role into a listening, following one;
• be pivotal when observing and commenting on what seems to be happening, asking the group what their perceptions are as well as offering ideas of your own;
• be more aware of process as well as content; it helps to ask oneself (and perhaps the group), 'What is going on here? What is this issue really all about?' in order to help people to express feelings and challenge comments.

When performing occurs, this means that the group has developed a culture of acting together to solve problems: it is no longer the leader's group, rather the worker becomes peripheral as the members perceive that 'This is our group'. Individual and group goals are tackled, meaning that members model coping mechanisms and values for each other. A high-status or charismatic member may further enhance a group's willingness to let individuals 'try on' different roles, thus preparing for eventual differentiation and independence from the group. In one group a member who could be relied on as the 'competent and responsible' one acted as a facilitator for the rest and bravely pointed out that sometimes he did not feel confident and would prefer sometimes to take a break from feeling responsible. The worker:

• observes how the group members handle each other and the tasks;
• gives ideas when these are sought;
• shows interest and expresses praise and appreciation of efforts; and
• continues to model in relation to confidence, attitudes and problem-solving.

The ending or adjourning stage usually follows the achievement of the task and requires disengagement from relationships. All groups have to end sometime otherwise they risk stagnation or low pro-ductivity. Imposed time-limits can prevent the worker from hanging on to a group merely because he or she feels guilty or uncertain about 'letting go'. There will be a sense of loss and maybe rejection and attempts to continue the group, despite agreed parameters, but with good leadership there will ultimately be acceptance and a sense of achievement. The worker, more active again, can:

- set goals for the time left in partnership with the group;
- review experiences, emphasising gains as well as feelings of loss;
- reinforce interests outside the group;
- help the group to return to the planning stage if they want to continue but with some other purpose; and
- evaluate the sessions and ask for feedback.

Handling difficulties in groups

Describing group development through the above phases might suggest that all is straightforward and predictable when, in reality, stages only represent tendencies from which any group can veer. Furthermore, there is a great deal of what Heap (1985) calls 'latent' communication in groups which demands greater diagnostic under-standing and groupwork skill. Often there are recurring themes, for instance when a group seems preoccupied with a particular, appar-ently irrelevant, topic. This might be mistakenly ignored instead of associated with something people cannot talk about directly. Lit-erature in groupwork refers to this as a common group tension or focal conflict. Heap (1985) gives an example of a group of prospec-tive adoptive parents, who, while waiting for a child, were brought together for general discussions about child development and adop-tive experiences. One day the worker found the group heatedly discussing legislation giving shopkeepers the right to open and close when they chose. The group was angry and resentful at being at the whims of possessors of valued goods. An indirect communication was the group's anger with the adoption agency's powerful with-holding of children from them. Recognising the deeper meaning of content and managing the processes around focal conflicts takes sensitivity and advanced skills.

Beyond symbolic communication difficulties, workers fantasise about the possibility that a group will simply take no notice of the leader or that strong emotions will result in chaos and damaged individuals. Books which suggest techniques, such as that by Corey *et al.* (1982) can inspire some confidence until more experience is gained. But even experienced workers are anxious when a group member is isolated, scapegoated, speaks too much or too little. Generally, many of these difficulties can be put back to the group for their resolution; otherwise individual counselling might help or it may be that the behaviour is needed by the group for some reason and should be explored.

In addressing the scapegoat phenomenon, for instance, Shulman (1979) suggests that the worker first observes the pattern, tunes into her/his own feelings about this, avoids siding with or against the scapegoat, and asks the group to comment on what is happening. Then, if the scapegoat does not need protection or mediation, the worker attempts to reduce guilt, fear or whatever feelings the group is suppressing and projecting on to one member by talking about such feelings in a general way. For example, in student groups one person may be aggressive and outspoken; the rest hide their feelings so as not to be different or unpopular. It is possible to point out that what the outspoken student is saying is felt by a lot of people even though they may not admit it. Then one can go on to reflect on how social workers may fear conflict and yet it is an issue every day in practice; having the courage to confront it is what matters.

If the leader does not handle the monopoliser in the group, Yalom (1970) warns that members will start to be absent or explode! The problem with allowing someone to dominate a group is that this stops others with useful things to say from contributing. So intervention has to take place early on to prevent group structure hardening, and while the leader still has patience. For example, in a group of carers one man went on at length about his experience. As this was the first meeting he might have overwhelmed other participants with his knowledge and so, having thanked him for prompting the group to explore a range of ideas, the worker indicated clearly that she would like to hear everyone's point of view. Stimulating silent members counteracts monopolisers as well as making the group structure a more functional one. If a person stays silent, some groups resent this believing that the person is quietly judging them or not sharing. Teasing silent members or saying 'We haven't heard from you, Mrs Smith' is not helpful, whereas something like, 'I remember you said something about this once, Mrs Smith. Could you remind us about your suggestion as I think it would help'. Conveying an interest in hearing from people and modelling respect can also be done non-verbally with a touch, gesture or eye contact – swivelling one's eyes around a student group will usually catch a reticent person who might speak if encouraged with a nod.

Obviously there cannot be prescriptions for handling all the problems that arise, but Whitaker's book (1985) details usable interventions for the newly-fledged and the experienced practitioner.

Just a few final words on recording group sessions and the use of co-leading are needed before we proceed to the case example. In relation to recording, some groupworkers keep a register showing standard information such as date; session number; members and leaders present/absent; plan for the session; diagram of seating arrangements; what happened (that is content and process); an evaluation of what went well and what did not (Brown, 1992). Others draw a series of circles representing each member: the circles are divided into three portions indicating the beginning, middle and end of the session, noting atmosphere, influence, participation, tasks and decision-making at each time-stage in the 'interaction chrono-gram'. These methods give an account of the group process and are useful for the worker and co-worker to reflect on the session, prepare for the next, and make appropriate interventions related to specific group members. However, where groups involve members who are on the caseloads of other workers, systems have to be agreed for giving feedback to colleagues which does not breach any confidentiality agreements the group may have agreed. Also, there should be agreement in advance as to what arrangements there will be for contacting individuals who have indicated specific problems which have not been, or cannot be, dealt with in the group.

As far as co-leading or co-facilitating goes, Preston-Shoot (1987) indicates that the advantages might be evident in large groups (though not always); for continuity when one leader is absent; when members might get out of control or express strong emotions such as co-work in Young Offenders Groups and work with people who are mentally ill; and when work will be done in subgroups. Planning, selecting and presenting a co-leader to the group should include consideration of gender and race combinations. Groupwork is demanding, and few of us are able to concentrate all the time. Co-working allows for the responsibility for taking the initiative to be shared. It also enables the other person to observe and reflect on the group processes as they occur. This dynamic can provide valuable feedback to the group itself while it is in process, and to the co-worker in the post-group discussions or 'wash-up'.the disadvantages could be where the co-workers hold widely differing views on goals and styles and where the sole worker already has the resources required. Such disadvantages can be overcome by careful selection of co-workers, and appropriate supervision of the groupwork intervention

---

Case example: prisoners' wives group

This case example is chosen as an illustration of a form of groupwork which used to be undertaken by statutory agencies, in this case the probation service. With changing policies in the statutory sector the opportunities for such groupwork have diminished. This coincides with a recognition that the way to empower certain users of services is to hand over responsibility to them, and encourage confidence and skills-development to move them towards self-directed groupwork (Mullender and Ward, 1991). The brief description reflects the different stages of group development, and the lessons that are learnt are equally valid where workers or agencies set up groups for the purpose of the agency without careful investigation of the needs and expectations of service-users.

The group was originally established by a probation officer who had responsibility for working with men sentenced to imprisonment. The agency felt that if partners of such men were supported during the sentence, they would provide a stable influence both while the man was in prison and on his release. Within this policy there was recognition that the partners of those in prison faced a number of difficulties; economic, social and emotional. The original aim was to provide a weekly group which would provide regular support, give information and practical advice and encourage the women to talk about their experiences. The image was that with this support, they would be waiting at the prison gate with open arms at the end of the sentence, and thus contribute to the man's rehabilitation.

In the light of this aim the group was open-ended; women could join at the point of their partner's sentence and would be expected to leave when he was released. A creche was provided by volunteers for children, to give the women some respite, and transport was provided to overcome some of the practical hurdles of attending the group. Referrals could come from any probation officer working in the geographical area; the woman would not necessarily have access to a probation officer in their own right.

The meetings involved a mixture of approaches including talks by representatives from housing and benefit agencies as well as unstructured meetings where women talked about issues relevant to themselves. It was hoped that the members would identify topics they wanted to discuss and suggest or arrange speakers, but in the early stages they were very passive, dependent upon the worker to 'lead' and to arrange a programme. This was frustrating for the worker who had envisaged that once the group was set up it would be possible to hand over the responsibility for running it to the women themselves.

Although confidentiality was discussed and encouraged, it became apparent that the women talked about the group to their partners on prison visits. Other probation officers were then receiving views about the group via a circuitous route and wanted more information from the worker. It was agreed that the only information that could be shared was whether a woman attended. If there were obvious problems, the woman would be encouraged to contact the relevant probation officer.

After the initial stage of getting to know each other, a pattern emerged in the groups. Women who joined were expected to give their 'credentials' for membership by giving information about their partner's offending behaviour, and his current sentence. The early forming was soon challenged by one or two women who began to articulate understandable dissatisfaction with their situation, and with the men who had contributed to it. They would dominate the discussions and the worker had difficulty allowing this exploration of sets of feelings, while being aware that it was unsettling for other group members who did not share these feelings, or if they did they were not ready to express them. Some women began to miss the group to avoid being part of discussions which tended to focus on how to get a divorce, rather than how to manage home and family. The eventual decision of one or two of the group members to commence divorce proceedings caused consternation among probation officers, men in prison who saw the group as contributing to the breakup of marriages, and the women themselves. The fact that they were divorcing their partner meant they no longer qualified for membership of the group, despite the fact that they still had need for support.

The group worker had to recognise that the original aim might have been inappropriate. She had to raise this possibility with the group. The criteria for membership were reaffirmed. There were discussions about the confusing and conflicting feelings experienced by all the women in the group and the different ways they coped with them. Those women who continued agreed to take a more active role in arranging meetings. There was some discussion about another group, for women when their partners came out of prison, but it was agreed this would have to be set up by women themselves.

The group continued on this model for some two years, but when the original worker left the area the probation service was no longer able to commit the resources. However, in view of the history of the group and the strength that some women had gained from it they were able to make representations to a voluntary agency and to set up another group, independent from the probation service and led by two women whose partners were in prison. This group provided weekly support, but was also able to take on a more active campaigning role demanding different approaches from the probation and prison services The original aims had therefore been met in the long run.

11

Community Work

In this chapter it is almost as if we come full circle. The text started with a consideration of the principles of care management which were introduced as a result of government policy on care in the community. That policy, however, has been subject to all sorts of criticism, namely that it is care by the community, not in the community. The implication of this is that statutory organisations have been relieved of the responsibility (and the cost) of caring for people in need, and that relatives, friends, volunteer organisations and individual volunteers will take on the caring responsibilities. As we saw in Chapters 2 and 3, these policy changes have created changes in the roles and tasks of statutory social workers who are becoming commissioners of services provided by individuals and groups. Much of this activity has been framed in terms of 'market' activity, but as was argued in *Care Management* (Orme and Glastonbury, 1993) for care management to operate properly there needs to be a whole set of activities around ensuring not only that needs are understood, but also that individuals, groups and organisations within communities are prepared and able to provide the facilities.

Community care therefore uses a notion of community which is to do with location but not in the usual sense of an actual place. It is used in a negative sense to identify that people are cared for in places other than state-funded residential establishments such as elder-care homes, or mental hospitals. This notion of community is also used in the criminal justice sysem to describe community service or community sentences. During the 1980s there were debates about whether community service orders would actually require offenders to do services *for* the community. In recent years the policy has been clear, community simply means an alternative to custody. With electronic tagging and other surveillance methods there is no suggestion that there will be any reparation to 'the community' (although offender mediation schemes are addressing this at an individual level), nor is there any suggestion that communities will take responsibility for offenders.

However, community care and community approaches to crime do carry other expectations. As members of communities, individuals in their capacity as family members, friends, neighbours or willing volunteers are expected to provide informal care for those with identified needs. Also, individuals are invited to join neighbourhood-watch schemes or become volunteer or part-time constables to protect thir community from crime.

The origins of community work are complex and pre-date the policy initiatives in community care. While there is a strong tradition within the voluntary sector for community action, community work is also a significant aspect of statutory social work. This chapter seeks to provide some definitions of community work and to explore developments which have led to distinctions between, for example, community work and community social work. It will look at skills, interventions and implications for practice.

As in the previous two chapters we are looking at a particular setting – the community. But already we have identified that definitions, understandings and uses of the term are complex, and sometimes contradictory. As with families and groupwork it is possible to use many skills and interventions in work with communities, not least because they are made up of individuals and families. Skills in interviewing and counselling are appropriate, as are groupwork skills. Also communities may be in a state of crisis, as we saw in Chapter 5 when we thought about disasters such as Lockerbie and Dunblane. Community work need not be something different from social work with individuals, it is both informed and influenced by individual work, and equally informs and influences in its own right, as we have noted in different parts of this text.

This position is not held by all, and debates about the 'holy trinity' of casework, groupwork and community work have littered social work texts. Some have argued that community work must be regarded as a distinct form of practice which calls upon a theoretical and knowledge base which is more sociological and less psychological than individual work and groupwork (Payne, 1991). However, the radical approach to social work recognised the importance of using community approaches as part of social work and welcomed the change of emphasis that it represented. By working with individuals within their context, problems were seen to have many dimensions, and responses could be more flexible. Howe (1992) identifies collective action as forming part of the methods of socialist welfare work (alongside fighting for rights and entitlements, and arguing that social problems are the consequences of a capitalist economy). Feminist writers, while critiquing developments in community work, point out that mobilising strengths and resources in collectivities arose out of the women's movement, but recognising and responding to individual need was not abandoned (Dominelli and McLeod, 1989). Such analyses require that whatever the method of intervention, personal problems are seen as political issues. It is this perspective, and the opportunity to use skills differently, which has been the major contribution of community work to social work practice.

'Community'

Before going further it is necessary to clarify what we mean when we talk about community. Many attempts have been made to define communities, most of which include notions of size and place – for example 'the smallest territorial group that can embrace all aspects of human life . . . the smallest local group that can be, and often is, a complete society' (Davis, 1961). This might be a very large group indeed, and each term within the definition can be subject to interpretation. Locality can include street, town or city boundaries, while societies can be regional, national and international, as reflected in the title the of the European *Community*.

For these reasons, the notion of community is the most contested within sociological literature, and while there are often common elements in definitions (locality, attachment, shared interests) there is little agreement of the relative significance of any of these elements (Allan, 1991). For further discussion and a review of the literature *Readings in Community Work* edited by Paul Henderson and David Thomas (1981) is a useful anthology.

At a very basic level there are two distinctions made which highlight the complexities of defining community:

1. *Community as locality*: sometimes called community of residence, where place is both synonymous with community and influences those who live in the community. The individual is expected to share things in common with others living in the

same geographical area, and to feel some loyalty to that area and its inhabitants. Relationships develop (some positive some antagonistic), and to some extent the lifestyle adopted by those living in the community will be influenced by the views of others in that locality. The individual will be part of many networks of relationships whose focus is on the local area. It is these local networks of formal and informal relationships together with their capacity to mobilise individual and collective responses that constitute a sense of community.

2. *Community of interest*: or functional communities, exist because individuals will also have a number of relationships with people and institutions outside a circumscribed geographical area. They might share a common interest based on leisure or work, and these networks ·of relationships might extend even beyond national boundaries. For example, international associations of social workers constitute a community with a shared interest in the profession of social work. Shared interests might also arise out of a particular social disadvantage, hence the Disability Rights Movement constitutes a community of interest which has a national context, as does the Women's Aid Federation. Both have links with groups experiencing similar disadvantage in other countries.

Over time, these distinctions have been challenged. Mobility of individuals and families due to economic changes have meant that networks were maintained in a variety of ways. Clubs and activities for people based on their place of origin, be that Ireland, Scotland or the West Indies, allowed for a celebration of characteristics related to place in a quite different geographic location. Advances in communication have led to enormous increases in communities of interest, not least those who have a shared interest in the use technology for enhancing communication. This might suggest that we either abandon the notion of community, or widen the definition. For the purposes of working with communities a useful definition focuses on the conditions necessary for effective interventions for, and by, communities in order to bring about change, or 'realise' the community. In this approach a community is:

• a unit large enough to be a political force and small enough to account for, and relate to, the individual person;

- an optimal location to develop alternative models of social (and economic) organisation;
- a point of mobilisation of people to effect social change which can be self-organised;
- a unit of people which can command sufficient resources to establish alternative institutional arrangements; and
- a unit for analysis which will identify the forces and material conditions determining social relations

(Provided by the Non-Violence Study Group
and quoted in Thomas, 1983)

From this definition it is understandable that Thomas argues that it is the concept of 'neighbourhood' which has most influenced community work. He argues that, based on geographical areas, neighbourhoods may contain 'different intensities of networks that express people's support, care, trust, responsibilities and obligations to one another. Neighbourhoods will vary in the presence or absence of these networks, and their function will vary in this respect over time and place' (Thomas, 1983 p. 173). While we will see that even this tentative notion of neighbourhood is questioned, uses of the term and understandings of 'networks' has become significant in the development of social work with communities. But this claim highlights another definitional conundrum, and that is the difference between community work and community social work.

Community work

In undertaking a review of the role and task of social workers, the Barclay committee defined both social work and community work and in doing so made a distinction between them. Community work they claimed embraced both direct work with community groups and work at the inter-organisational and planning level, and was concerned to:

> enable members collectively to overcome problems and enhance the common feeling, solidarity and competence in the community by direct working with groups and organisations within the community, or encouraging their formation. But community work also takes the form of involvement in planning and influencing policies. This work can be an element of social work, but it

does not include the whole of social work, nor does social work embrace the whole of community work. (Barclay, 1982, p. xiii)

This very positive statement counteracts perceptions of community work merely as activities which take place off the premises of statutory social work agencies; or as provided by voluntary agencies or volunteers – as opposed to professional workers (Jones, 1981). Such definitions merely describe characteristics associated with community work, rather than describing community work *in a social work context*. This latter phrase is significant because all sorts of people undertake forms of community work, run clubs or organise community-based movements, such as residents associations, but this is not necessarily happening in a social work context. This distinction between community work, community work undertaken by social workers and community social work, documents important historical movements.

For example, it has been argued that early initiatives such as the Charity Organisation Society and the Settlement Movement involved coordination of agencies in a way that is reminiscent of community work (Baldock, 1974). They were ultimately replaced by statutory social work, at a time when it was assumed that the emergence of the welfare state would eradicate poverty and need. Part of the welfare provision was in the area of housing, and the community work developments of the 1940s and 1950s were associated with the postwar development of public housing, usually in the form of community associations. These had their limitations because they did not represent organised forms of local social systems, but groups pursuing particular interests. At the same time the welfare state did not eradicate need, and social work was accused of explaining poverty and problems in terms of social pathology (Cooper, 1989).

Hence there was a marked interest in community development in the 1960s as a way of responding to poverty. The national Community Development Projects (CDP) were set up by the Home Office Children's Departments, and community development workers were employed who were independent of the newly-created social services departments. They were to be active mobilising resources within the community The focus was on organising local communities and improving coordination between welfare agencies. The work undertaken included:

- individual welfare rights;
- advocacy;
- surveys;
- campaigning; and
- community self-help projects (for example, advice centres, adventure playgrounds, women's refuges).

Historically, community action therefore involved workers dissociating themselves from statutory social work using a structuralist and collectivist approach and working in egalitarian ways with community groups. Community work tried to understand situations not only in terms of who holds the power, but also whose interests are served by a particular policy and practice. Community workers had to define goals for activity and change, and democratise the provision of resources. Although focusing on the community rather than the individual was seen to be a positive move away from casework approaches which had been criticised, there was a danger that the community itself was pathologised and experienced as the problem (Loney, 1983).

Baldock (1974) analyses the professional background of community workers and identifies that although the majority of community workers might have been employed in social work agencies, few of them had a social work qualification. The longest tradition of community workers has been in education, both in the more 'formal' settings of adult education, but also in the use of education skills to mobilise and equip communities to undertake campaigning and advocacy for themselves.

A further source of influence on community work was the establishment of Community Relations Councils (now called Race Equality Councils) introduced by the 1968 Race Relations Act. Although, or more accurately because, they are operating on behalf of racial groups, these Councils were involved in individual casework and education as well as community development and inter-agency liaison. The final source of community work was urban management where housing and planning authorities both developed community work approaches within their own statutory organisations and liaised with emerging voluntary groups who worked with local community groups, particularly in working-class areas to fight local authority planners. Definitional distinctions therefore emerged which separated community work, which was undertaken by those paid to do it, and community action was undertaken by those in conflict with authority. These distinctions led to debate in the 1970s about whether community workers should become a separate profession, and whether there was scope for radical activities by those undertaking community work in statutory agencies, including social work agencies.

From the beginning we can see that community work is used in a number of different ways. As well as being a form of intervention it is:

1. an *attitude* that defines a more participative and egalitarian set of relations;
2. associated with a *critique* of existing power and resources;
3. a *principle* of service delivery, making services local relevant, accessible and accountable to their users;
4. a *frame of reference* and identification of like minded people; and
5. a *work site* for those professionals who do their job 'in' the community (as opposed to an office).

(Thomas, 1983)

Whoever was involved in community work, whatever their professional background, what did community workers do? The Gulbenkian Study Group (the 'Gulbenkian Report' 1968) identified a common element among those engaged in various forms of community work, in that they were 'concerned with affecting the course of social change through the two processes of analysing social situation and forming relationships with different groups to bring about desirable change' (1968, p. 4). To bring about, or affect the course of change the focus for the work would be:

• community development;
• inter agency liaison; and
• research and development in all areas of social welfare.

One of the most widely accepted models of community organisation and intervention has been provided by Rothman (1968). His conceptualising of community organisation practice included social planning, locality development and social action, the latter two relating directly to definitions of community given earlier in this chapter.

- *Social planning* or community organisation operates at the macro-level of planning and policy-formulation, and involves the community worker in facilitating agency and inter-agency coordination and sustaining and promoting organisational groups.
- *Locality development* involves direct work with people and focuses on the total community, as bounded by geographical borders for example council estate, neighbourhood, village. The various power structures and organisations have to be included as a focus for the community practice, with members of the power structure being recruited as partners in a common venture. For Rothman, this means that community development is also undertaken within these total communities
- *Social action* is also about direct work with people and conceives the focus for action as some community sub-part or segment, that is those who are identified as having, or join together because of, mutual interests or oppressions. The power structure is assumed to lie outside the client system and is therefore an external target of action.

These distinctions between the where and the what as a focus for community work intervention are repeated in York's (1984) description of *community organisation* with social welfare agencies as the target for action; *community development* with neighbourhood residents as the target; and *community action* for and with disadvantaged groups using political methods. While there seems to be some agreement that there are different strands to community work intervention, York has criticised Rothman's focus on the difference between locality development and social action as being irrelevant to practitioners who do not necessarily experience the divisions as starkly as the theory suggests (York, 1984). Community workers,. according to York, see their focus for action as being both within and outside the communities they work with, whether these be local communities or communities of interests such as disability rights groups. He therefore offers a different framework for theorising community work, or community social work, as he calls it. He argues that 'conceptual continua' or dichotomies (York, 1984, p. 247) are more helpful to students and practitioners because they allow for differences to be made visible, but also emphasise similarities. He draws on the work of Batten (1967) to suggest that there is an over-arching dichotomy between *directive* and *non-directive intervention*, and that most other dichotomies of practice are included in this. The notion of directive and non-directive reflects the primary goals of the worker, what they want to achieve, rather than roles that they adopt at any one time in their work.

- *Directive intervention* involves the agency deciding, more or less specifically, what it thinks the clients need, what they ought to value or what they ought to do, and even at times how they ought to behave.

- In *non-directive intervention* the worker does not attempt to decide for people, or to lead, guide or persuade them to accept her/his specific conclusions about what is good for them, but works to get them to decide for themselves what their needs are. The worker's role is to provide favourable conditions for successful action by strengthening and stimulating incentive, providing information, and helping community members to analyse problems systematically.

According to York, all other dichotomies presented in community work can be subsumed into this directive/non-directive continuum, or that continuum is a better explanation of what community work involves in any given situation, or any one approach. An example of how different approaches would be viewed in this model are given below.

Directive intervention	*Non-directive intervention*
Task approach	Problem approach
Initiating roles	Enabling roles
Treatment	Reform

To emphasise that this is a continuum of activity, rather than a set of opposites, it has been suggested that there are various degrees of directiveness, associated with particular skills:

1. *Channelling* (strongly directive): the practitioner asserts a particular point of view with supporting arguments and documentation in a particular situation or negotiation. The thinking of all involved is channelled towards a particular goal, identified and framed by the worker.

2. *Funnelling* (considerably directive): the practitioner provides a range of choices, but funnels thinking towards a given area by asserting his or her preference and giving the rationale for that choice.

3. *Scanning* (mildly directive): the practitioner scans the range of possibilities related to solving a particular problem and presents them impartially. This provides orientation to goal-selection, setting out the boundaries within which possible rational goal-selection may take place.

(see Henderson and Thomas, 1981)

Yet another way of analysing community work intervention is to identify the different arenas in which community workers are involved, and in which they might use the methods discussed above. These arenas will involve negotiations with different people and and it is these negotiations which provide the focus for activity. For Henderson and Thomas (1981) these arenas include:

1. Transactions with local people, either as individuals or in group situations.
2. Transactions between the group and other systems in its environment.
3. Transactions about the group within the worker's own agencies.

The directiveness/non-directiveness model is seen as relevant in the transactions with local people with questioning as central to a non-directive approach. Drawing on group processes, Henderson and Thomas identify seven types of interventions/discussions that exemplify non-directive approaches in community work. Although functions which need to be performed in community work with local people (or neighbourhood work), these can be undertaken by different people in the group and the community worker needs to ensure that the relevant processes occur. They include:

- Galvanising;
- Focusing;
- Clarifying;
- Summarising;
- Gate keeping;
- Mediating; and
- Informing.

When working at the interface between local people and more formal and established organisations the community worker also has to ensure that a number of functions are carried out which include: broker, mediator, advocate, negotiator, bargainer. Again these can be performed by different people, but thought has to be given to what role will be played by which individuals. A balance has to be struck between the appropriate activity for the paid worker who might be acting in some form of representative role for the group or community at, for example, town or city council meetings or interviews with local authority officers. Also where lead roles are taken by community members, the paid worker might have a set of facilitative functions which include: observer/recorder, delegate or plenipotentiary.

This notion of representative becomes more complex for a paid worker when having to manage transactions about the group or community within their own employing agency. Henderson and Thomas identify two functions for the worker, but emphasise the need to establish guidelines between the community and the worker to clarify the worker's status and ensure effective communication. The functions are:

1. Re-routing enquiries from the agency to the appropriate member of the local group.
2. Opportunistic interventions by the worker on behalf of the group within the agency.

Many of the skills that have been referred to have resonance with those described earlier in this text. Questioning, clarifying and summarising were dealt with in Chapter 4 where we discussed interviewing and counselling. Negotiating was seen to be an integral part of community care and was discussed in Chapter 3, and skills for networking are described at the end of this chapter. Meanwhile, we have to clarify a possible confusion. While we have plotted the developments of community work as parallel to, but independent of, statutory social work, we have drawn upon writers such as York who have been discussing community social work. While it is apparent that as a form of indirect action or because of different understandings of problems social workers in statutory agencies did adopt some of the principles of community work, community social work has a more specific context and this in some ways provides the link with current arrangements for community care.

Community social work

Critiques of community work as a separate activity, and the experiences of independant or outreach workers of being isolated and marginalised from colleagues in social work agencies, did not lead to changes of attitudes within social work towards community workers but to moves within social work to embrace some of the principles and practices of community work. While volunteer and independent community action has continued often supported by dedicated (in every sense) community workers, policy developments which incorporated the language of community, if not a full appreciation of the work, began to inform activities of statutory social workers in the late 1970s and 1980s and have been at the centre of initiatives for community care, albeit not in a way that many in social work would have hoped for.

The Seebohm report (1968) gave attention to, among other things, the rise of community care as a key statement of policy intent. Social services departments, which were created by the Seebohm report, would have smaller administrative units with area teams serving particular localities. It was envisaged that this would improve access to service provision and provide a greater sense of identification with the local area by social workers. Decentralised decision-making would be more responsive to local need.

More importantly, the area-based organisation should, it was argued, change the relationship between statutory social workers and the catchment areas in which the workers were operating. The departments were to encourage, support and promote voluntary effort and engage in 'assisting and encouraging the development of community identity' (Seebohm, 1968, para. 477). But this emphasis on arrangements for delivering social services did not address what community workers or social workers working with communities actually did.

Hence, while the basic notions of community social work were introduced by the Seebohm report, the terms and the principles were more fully explored by the Barclay committee who defined community social work as:

> formal social work which, starting from the problems affecting an individual or group and the responsibilities and resources of social services departments and voluntary organisations, seeks to tap

into, support, enable and underpin the local networks of formal and informal relationships which constitute our basic definition of community, and also the strengths of a client's communities of interest. (Barclay, 1982, p. xvii)

Community social work would therefore be one of the functions of statutory social workers. These arrangements were intended to provide an infrastructure for informal care in the community and formed the basis of policy initiatives which culminated in the National Health Service and Community Care Act 1990.

The Barclay committee argued that social work teams should operate in even smaller geographical units than those recommended by the Seebohm committee, they recommended that a 'patch' approach would enable workers to work with local resources to provide 'neighbour-hood clusters' of formal and informal care. This would involve personal social services in:

- working in close collaboration with informal caring networks;
- finding ways of developing partnerships between informal carers (including self-help groups), statutory services and voluntary agencies;
- ensuring ready access of caring networks to statutory and voluntary services; and
- offering those who give and receive services opportunities to share decisions which affect their lives

(Barclay, 1982, para. 13.13)

A minority report to the Barclay Report (Appendix A) argued that a community social work approach cannot be an 'add on' to existing methods and structures of social work practice, but requires social workers to develop a different approach. This approach drew on the 'patchwork' model which had been successfully developed in Normanton (Hadley and McGrath, 1984) and involved smaller, autonomous and accessible social work teams which had good liaison with local agencies and integrated field and domicilliary staff. Doubts that even such an approach would work were voiced by those who questioned the assumptions that there were readily existing informal networks of informal care (Allan, 1983). Barclay's main recommendations were seen to be based on a particular, rather romantic, reading of the traditional urban community studies of the

1950s and early 1960s. Allan identified some important considerations for statutory workers stimulating and working with informal networks to provide informal care:

1. In kinship relationships the burden of care falls on women.
2. Unlike previous studies of communities, the people who require care are often those who have not spent enough time in the area to build up relationships. Or as people who are homeless and rootless, they have no locality or community of interest.
3. Often the nature of the problem with which help is needed is exacerbated by a breakdown in family or kinship relationships, either at the point that help is needed, or at some time in the past. For example, in families where one person has a mental health problem, the partner may well have been providing 'informal care' without anyone being aware of it. The point that help is sought is the point when, for whatever reason, they can no longer care.
4. Sometimes the nature of the problem, or the way in which the person deals with the problem, means that they have not built up strong positive relationships with friends and neighbours in the community. Approaches are made to the statutory agencies because there is no alternative.

While these were important criticisms of the policy that the community should provide informal care resources, the notion of community social work as a community-oriented support for statutory social services had some support. It is clear from Allan's list that community social work would involve more than social workers 'doing community work', and different approaches identified by the authors of Appendix A involved changes in organisational features including localisation, integration (within social services, between social services and other agencies and with informal networks), wider roles and greater autonomy. The reorganisation of service delivery would allow for greater flexibility of approach, but also the skills required were identified as:

• working second-hand through lay people;
• 'the development task' which requires a range of supportive and entrepreneurial activities; and
• development of social planning.

(Barclay, 1981, p. 233)

This approach argued that although community care does not necessarily have any relation to the traditions of community work, it offers opportunities to develop skills and approaches which have been traditionally associated with community work. Hence Barclay argued that the skills required involved a focus on networks. Networks could be identified by:

- standing in the client's shoes and seeing the various people with whom that person is in touch;
- focusing on the actual or potential links which exist or could be fostered between people who either live in the same geographical area or in the same residential home or long-stay hospital, or attend the same day-centre; and
- keeping in mind the communities of interest which develop between people who share similar interests sometimes because they share similar problems.

In the various discussions about commnity social work, there seems to be a division between those who focus on giving useful advice or guidance for skills and those who concentrate on processes. However, in both approaches there is agreement that there needs to be a moving on from, or a separation from, what have been more traditional social work skills. This does not mean abandoning those skills, but using them in different contexts, or using different combinations of skills. More particularly this might involve recognising and validating skills and interventions from colleagues who are non-social workers and developing an informal style especially by:

- being flexible;
- being capable of responding in more than one way at the same time;
- not being bureaucratic;
- being clear and honest; and
- working as a member of a team.

(Hadley, Cooper, Dale and Stacy, 1987)

Although most of these requirements would seem to be good principles for any social work intervention the emphasis is on the cooperation with everyone, not just those who are designated social workers, and includes the participation of those who are tradition-ally users and carers. It is for this reason that Hadley and his colleagues see community work (or groupwork) not as an 'add on' casework but as a part of an integrated approach, with each of the methods of intervention interacting with each other. This notion of an integrated approach echoes the discussion of systems theory in Chapter 3, and it is no coincidence that the flexibility of approach argued by Hadley *et al.*, the involvement of others in responding to problems or needs, has direct implications for the discussions of user-involvement and empowerment.

A different critique is offered by Smale and his colleagues (1988) who see the approach represented by the Barclay report and Appendix A as reflecting the development of community social work as localisation. Other models, they argue, emphasise indirect service and local participation (Beresford and Croft, 1986). Smale *et al.* suggest that a shift in thinking is required away from identified clients to a focus on the relationships between people, and the patterns of these relationships. They take the notion of partnership and involvement outlined in Barclay and argue that through mana-ging change and innovation in the practice of social workers, community social work involves a process of working out aims and objectives through a review of needs and resources with a wide range of people:

> Community social work is essentially about the *processes* the workers engage in, the *relationships* they make and how they maintain and change them. These processes generate the specific aims and objectives of the workers and those they share the work with. (Smale *et al.*, 1988, p. 23)

In focusing on processes and relationships Smale *et al.* do not prescribe specific sets of skills, or methods which could or should be utilised in 'doing' community social work. The whole emphasis of the 'approach' is that methods, skills and actions will evolve from the focus of the team of social workers identifying both what resources they have available within themselves and the 'commu-nity', and what is required. However, they do list areas where more emphasis might be required in training social workers and other social work staff, either at basic level or as part of staff development activities. These include:

- Working across agency boundaries;
- Working on the margins of complex systems;
- Working in teams of peers and others;
- Working in ways open to public accountability;
- Working with devolved responsibilities and budgets;
- Working in networks of partnership; and
- Working to understand sequences of behaviour that perpetuate problems and intervening to change these patterns.

(Smale *et al.*, 1988)

While Smale *et al.* resist a prescriptive approach to skills for community social work, it is apparent that there are some recurring themes in this chapter which relate to both community work and community social work. We have already said that many of the skills utilised are those which social workers might use in work with individuals and groups. However, a recurring theme has been that social workers will need to work with networks, they will have to identify them, consult with them, and cynics might say they will have to create them. It is therefore important that we give some attention to the skills involved in working with networks.

Networking

All of the literature assumes that the understanding of community is based on:

> a network, or networks of informal relationships between people connected with each other by kinship, common interests, geographical proximity, friendship, occupation, or the giving and receiving of services – or various combinations of these.
>
> (Barclay, 1982, p. 199).

This understanding is expected to inform the work that is done within the community, especially to stimulate networks either to be part of collective action or to provide informal care services for community care. Consideration of networks is not exclusive to working with or in communities, they are relevant when focusing on work with individuals and families.

Three separate networking strategies include:

1. *Network therapy*: a therapeutic approach where network assemblies, using techniques drawn from large groupwork, help families in crisis by bringing together their network to act as the change agents; the case example is of a network assembly (see Rueveni, 1979).
2. *Problem-solving network meetings*: these bring together formal and informal carers; they are useful when unravelling noncomplementary professional networks in order to sort out who is doing what (see Dimmock and Dungworth, 1985).
3. *Network construction*: this method aims to sustain, change and build new networks. Used originally to help those with chronic schizophrenia whose institutionalisation had led to the loss of their networks, network building can be used, for example, to provide community care services for older people (Challis *et al.*, 1990) and to engage supporters for those with learning disabilities (Atkinson, 1986).

A network assembly

Bringing together a 'tribal' gathering to act as change agent for a family member in crisis was devised by Speck (1967). He recognised the loneliness of people who keep problems to themselves or receive help from large, impersonal organizations. Therefore, with an individual's permission, he invited the network to one or two 'healing ceremonies': any household members, active and passive relatives, friends and neighbours, contacts from work, leisure, places of worship and those who knew of the person were asked to contribute to working out ways of helping at a time of great need. These full-scale assemblies often resulted in up to fifty people attending. Partial network assemblies (Van der Velden *et al.*, 1984) have since simplified the procedure using fewer participants of about a dozen people.

The referral is taken by a team of three or four social workers who know and respect each other's work. A preliminary assessment interview with significant members ensures that an assembly is appropriate and that everyone understands what will happen. The family is asked to invite about twelve contacts to their home; they are coached in how to do this and how to explain that the purpose is to get the benefit of everyone's ideas. The balance of the group is important. Each core member needs to have one ally, someone as a supporter to prevent scapegoating and promote compassion. Representatives from the close and distant zones around the family's world allows peripheral people, who have no axe to grind, to provide different perspectives, a range of solutions and possibly increased energy to help with the emotional and practical issues which are raised. The skilled team hope to exploit the 'network effect', which is the result of simply bringing people together.

The stages of helping begin with convening the network, moving towards connecting members with one another ('retribalisation'), then shifting responsibility for solutions from the team to the natural group. Customarily, an introduction exercise is used to help people to relax. One social worker acts as the conductor while the rest act as group facilitators. Everyone listens as those central to the referral put their view of the problem.

Lists of complaints are transformed into goals for change, then the outsiders are asked for their solutions. Normally, polarised opinions and ideas emerge; the team use this energy to mobilise people towards alterations: activists within the group help to shift the meeting from depression at what seems unalterable towards breakthrough when solutions and offers of support develop. At this point of 'exhaustion/elation' the professional team leave.

These innovations have helped families facing bereavement, illness, suicide attempts, alcoholism and drug addiction and other 'hopeless' situations, reminding participants that others do care and that friends and neighbours still rally around in desperate times. Ballard and Rosser (1979) write about a family who were subject to violent attacks from their daughter Christine, aged eighteen. Following her discharge from a psychiatric hospital they met 35 members of the family's network: this was really a full-scale assembly needing the space of the local vicarage. Christine's network varied in their reactions to her 'crazy' behaviour, but after venting their anger they then became depressed that they had not helped more. Problem-solving in small groups, the assembly produced offers of assistance with accommodation, transport, employment and renewed contact with the family. At a follow-up meeting, no tangible support had been given but the family were less bothered about this aspect than their relief at being reconnected to their support network.

A problem solving network meeting

This form of networking is in essence, a straightforward negotiation session, developed by Garrison and Howe (1976). It can be used by professional networks who, in the process of helping, have become stuck and who need to clarify their respective roles and responsibilities. The meeting is a structured one, where each participant in turn might be asked, 'What is the problem?', 'What has been tried so far?', 'How can agency personnel help?' and 'What goal can everyone agree to work towards?' Thus, in this form of networking the purpose of the meeting and the time available for it need to be clearly stated. Everyone needs to have the opportunity to state their position and plan, then specific tasks are delegated. Usually a follow-up meeting is needed (about three weeks later) to ensure that agreements are working.

Carpenter and Treacher (1989) discuss 'agency triangles' when clients or agencies triangulate a spectrum of other agencies so that no-one is sure who is the 'customer' anymore. Disputes between inter-agency networks rage as much as they do in the referred problem; passing the buck and arguing about who 'should' do what unfortunately becoming a major issue for those involved in monitoring complex cases. The following example shows some of this.

Case example

John was a thirty-year-old man with learning disabilities. He lived with his brother and sister-in-law and attended the local Adult Training Centre where the rest of the trainees' needs were more involved than his own. John started stealing and according to the Training Centre manager this was due to the environment being insufficiently challenging. The client was put on probation and the officer duly arranged for him to attend a Life Skills course at a college in the town. John refused to attend and his family insisted that he return to the Adult Training Centre.

When the client, his family, the centre manager, probation officer and the case manager met to rethink the package of care, their meeting was chaired by a team leader who was independent of the case. It became clear that all the agencies were working on what they thought was good for John, without consulting him or his family about *their* choices It transpired that they were quite happy with the Training Centre; John, in particular, did not want to lose contact with his friends there, whom he had begun to miss. The network meeting revealed different viewpoints and some misunderstandings about the philosophies of each agency; the users of the service were given the chance to hear these views and put forward their own.

A network construction

This involves the social worker coaching someone in how to sustain, build or change their network. First, the person is helped to draw a network or ecomap (see Figure 11.1); a sheet with many circles is

Figure **11.1** *Network map*

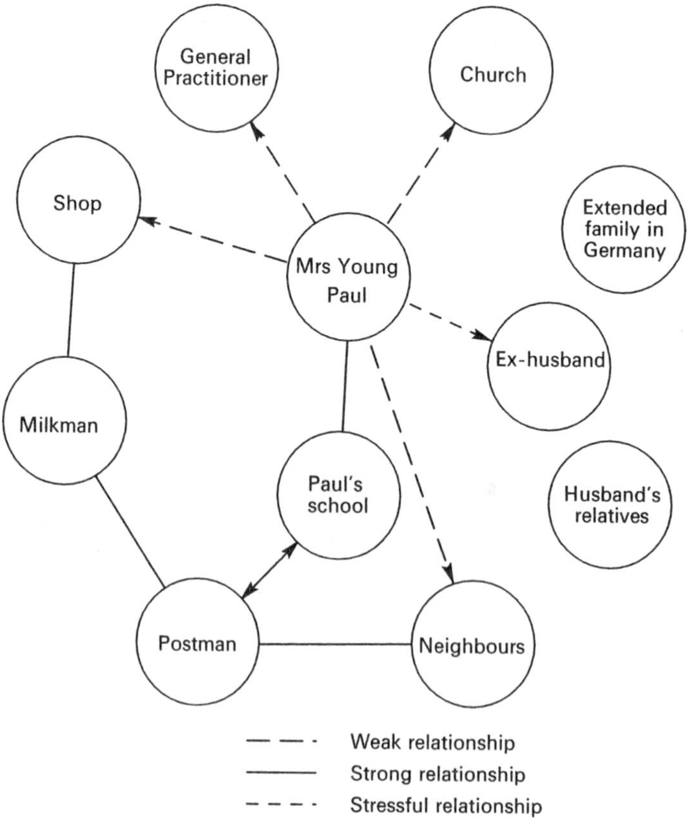

— — · Weak relationship
——— Strong relationship
— — — · Stressful relationship

used to represent the household itself, neighbours, general practitioner, school, clubs, shop, work and so on. The network map is filled in using the same colour to connect who knows whom: relationships between the client and others which are strong, weak or stressful are depicted by different symbols.

Secondly, the person is helped to assess from this the sources of interference and intimacy and, if appropriate, asked if they wish to lessen or strengthen these bonds. Thirdly, overlooked sources of help are examined, with the client and worker planning how these could be developed.

Case example

Mrs Young was a thirty-five-year-old woman with one son, Paul aged twelve years. She had recently divorced her husband who had access to his son at weekends. Mrs Young had come to the UK from Germany fifteen years previously and although living on a busy council estate knew very few people. She applied to the large Voluntary Society to become a foster parent to an older child. The worker from the placement team helped Mrs Young to map her network; as we can see from Figure 11.1 (and comparing it possibly to your own), the client had a small and not very active network to whom she could turn for support. Some members had strong ties but the client agreed that she was isolated and had wanted a companion for Paul. Mrs Young had stopped writing to her own family in Germany: the worker encouraged her to rebuild these links which she did, eventually being visited by them. Paul's school taught evening-classes in German where, in time, Mrs Young began to help students there. She withdrew her application to foster.

Network strategies can provide exciting solutions in community care schemes to sustain and nurture helpers. On the other hand, undoing the original support network, encouraging friends and relatives to withdraw when they are under severe stress, has been important too (Challis *et al.*, 1990). So-called 'toxic' networks, for example those of people involved in criminal activities, similarly may need to be loosened. These practices provide 'people muscle', unite and reunite networks, and give back the chance to show concern for others in a non-bureaucratic way.

Conclusion

It was this lack of bureaucracy, and the empowering functions of networking that stimulated writing about community social work in the 1980s. The Barclay report was seen to herald a reorganisation of service delivery of social services which was more responsive to need and less bureaucratic. As we saw in Chapters 2 and 3, the emergent community care policies were more about reducing statutory responsibility for service provision, based on a market approach to service delivery. Despite this change in the philosophy of welfare provision, or perhaps because of it, social workers need to be aware of and familiar with the principles, philosophies and practices of community work and community social work because, either as workers in purchaser or commissioning agencies trying to identify and stimulate resources to meet need, or as workers in the voluntary and independent provider agencies, they require the skills to facilitate users and carers to identify and express their needs. Also, to support users and carers and others in the community it will be necessary to develop appropriate services to meet those needs, whether these be self-help, pressure groups, support groups, counselling or other forms of intervention.

Conclusion

All social work efforts have to come to an end sometime. In fact as we noted in the introduction there are many endings in social work. Each time we end our contact with users, be it at the end of an interview, home visit or group session, important principles of preparing ourselves and the other person for the parting or ending have to be kept in mind. Also social work can be episodic. We can undertake a piece of work in our capacity of care manager or court officer, and then another worker may be involved. Although the contact with the agency might not end, the particular relationship between you as worker and the user does. Final termination or these transfers of work may be planned or unplanned, initiated by client or worker, mutually agreed or unilaterally decided. Closing 'cases' and ending relationships receives surprisingly little attention in the literature, though the topic of evaluation is stressed by policy-makers, researchers and managers (see Davies and Knapp, 1988; Coulshed, 1990). Good care management, as a system and as a practice, depends on showing that we have achieved planned goals in a cost-effective, accountable way. Assessment, monitoring and sustaining are held up as the main features of care management practice in the early literature (Challis and Davies, 1989) but identifying need, commissioning and purchasing help from other provider agencies highlight that the involvement of the social worker might be transitory. Endings are therefore an integral part of the commissioning or purchasing aspects of care management. In provider relationships where the contact may be more ongoing, ending only when there is a change of service because of the person's changing needs, or more distressingly through death; the need to prepare for these endings is equally important.

Ending social work intervention

Reasons for closure or transfer to another worker or agency are diverse. They include:

- agreed goals being achieved within a pre-set time;
- clients deciding they have been helped enough;

- workers leaving or clients moving from the district;
- the end of statutory requirements;
- agency policy on time limits;
- workload management and priority systems;
- resource limitations;
- lack of time and pressure of work;
- advice from supervisor;
- influence of other agencies; and
- death of the client.

We saw in the chapters on crisis intervention, task-centred practice and behavioural approaches how these models were developed to allow for built-in termination. It was viewed as a positive step, a way of motivating people by focusing efforts at specified goals. Equally, family and marital therapists tell us that we should recognise when enough is enough (Carpenter and Treacher, 1989), letting families and couples get on with their lives without us. In the previous chapter, it was recommended that groupworkers and community social workers take the process of termination seriously, learning to anticipate possible reactions of denial, backsliding into earlier difficulties, reminiscing and reviewing the worth of the experience. But, unfortunately, not all methods of helping or settings for practice lend themselves to a rational model which sets goals, assesses progress and then smoothly starts the process of withdrawing. For example, in a Barnardo's project to find foster families for adults with severe learning disabilities and challenging behaviour, a key worker found herself having to say goodbye to a man she had worked with intensively for nine years. He and she were devastated despite the new attachment to the foster family having been spread over a long period.

Though written some time ago, a couple of articles by Bywaters (1975) help us to understand why so many of our contacts end, not with a sense of achievement and neatness, but with feelings of loss, work not completed or not even begun. His research into social services revealed bureaucratic, theoretical and psychological drawbacks for clients and workers which affected both the decision to close or transfer as well as the process of achieving this. Coupled with the above organisational reasons for closing cases, he found that workers often felt that they could not control endings and neither were clients consulted about the decision. Social workers tended not to use the time-limited approaches; many were aiming for more extensive goals than clients were aware of, using open-ended casework methods. Practitioners often felt that they could do more, or that cases should be left open until a resource such as housing became available. Moreover, feelings of guilt, uncertainty and loss affected the process of handling endings. Thus, staff felt guilty knowing that time spent with one person was time not spent with another; uncertainty about their effectiveness plus the client's ability to cope in the future impeded a positive approach to endings; feeling lost and resentful after putting in a lot of work were other reactions.

Clients and workers may experience transfer or termination of work as a type of crisis (even if the attachment has been short-term) if each has invested a part of themselves. Students on placement report feelings of sadness and anxiety at 'abandoning' clients; the death of a client is especially distressing and might need reassurance that shedding tears is not unprofessional. Clients and workers may be reminded of earlier losses by the experience of closure. And yet, much in the same way that crisis prevention was possible with 'worry work' and preparation, clients and workers can anticipate endings in advance, enhancing their growth-promoting opportunities.

A good model of ending could incorporate the following:

1. A discussion in the first meeting that help will not go on for ever. Clients' feelings and perceptions of this are important and need to be sensitively handled. For instance, those in crisis might ask, 'How long will this take?' and, for some, it might be reassuring to know that help will not suddenly be withdrawn. For others, it may be a relief to know that a social worker will not always need to visit.

2. Using the experience of termination or transfer as a learning experience for the client rather than a painful, separating one. In groupwork it was noted that transitions are eased when people are helped to wean away from the experience – outside relationships and activities are rewarded. Confirming the client's self-confidence and self-reliance underlines what they have gained and how they have dealt with the experience of help coming to an end.

3. Where possible employing a fixed time limit purposefully, using time itself as a therapeutic agent.

4. Giving the client certain objectives to achieve in the ending phase.
5. Beforehand, exploring a person's feelings about the end of the relationship. (Anticipate possible setbacks, which provide opportunity for worry work.) Gradual withdrawal aids such as reducing the frequency of meetings, arranging for semi-independent living accommodation, progressively leaving longer time with future carers, and so on.
6. Introduce the new worker if there is to be one, and talk in that meeting about the fact that the client could well feel very angry about the arrangement. After one social worker did this, the client vented much resentment but then was free to build a fresh relationship with the incoming practitioner,
7. Help the person to construct a natural helping network in the community, mobilising practical resources if need be. Then do a follow-up visit.
8. Explore your own feelings; show the client that you will remember them; have confidence in their ability to manage without you but express the goodwill of the agency whose door is left open should they need to return for further help.
9. In some contexts a ritual or ceremonial ending with photographs, a party and a small farewell gift could mark the occasion.
10. Write a closing record, together, if appropriate.

Finally, it might help readers to suggest, as we have done at various points in this book, that developments are not always linear. We often need to reflect on, and to return to situations which have gone before in order to make sense of them with new information and new insights. This is not to say that there is nothing new under the sun, but that only by reflecting on how we have applied our learning can we ever be sure that we have understood. To this end this book marks merely a beginning of learning which can be enhanced by further reading and exploration, but more particularly by reflecting on every situation and every interaction with clients/ users, who teach us that in social work learning never ends.

References

Abrams, P. (1980) 'Social Change, Social Networks and Neighbourhod Care', *Social Work Service*, February, no. 22, pp. 12–23.

Adams, R. (1996) *Social Work and Empowerment*, Basingstoke BASW/ Macmillan.

Ahmad, A. (1990) *Practice with Care*, London, Race Equality Unit/ National Institute for Social Work.

Ahmad, B. (1990) *Black Perspectives in Social Work*, Birmingham, Venture Press.

Allan, G. (1983) 'Informal Networks of Care: Issues Raised by Barclay', *British Journal of Social Work*, 13, pp. 417–33.

Allan, G. (1991) 'Social Work, Community Care, and Informal Networks', in M. Davies (ed.), *Sociological Perspectives on Social Work*, London, Routledge.

Aros-Atolagbe, J. (1990) 'Soapbox', *Social Work Today*, vol. 21, no. 35, p. 36.

Atkinson, D. (1986) 'Engaging Competent Others: A Study of the Support Networks of People with Mental Handicap', *British Journal of Social Work*, vol. 16, Supplement, pp. 83–101.

Avison, D., Forbes, I., Glastonbury, B., Orme, J. and Waldman, J. (1995) *Havant and Petersfield Information System: A Model for Consulting Pre-users of Community Care Services for Older People*, Research report, Southampton University (unpublished).

Bacon, R. (1988) 'Counter-transference in a Case Conference: Resistance and Rejection in Work with Abusing Families and their Children', in Pearson, G., Treseder, J. and Yelloly, M. (eds), *Social Work and the Legacy of Freud: Psychoanalysis and its Uses*, Basingstoke, Macmillan.

Bailey, R. and Brake, M. (eds) (1975) *Radical Social Work*, London, Edward Arnold.

Baldock, J. and Ungerson, C. (1994) 'Becoming Consumers of Community Care: Households within the Mixed Economy of Welfare', York, Joseph Rowntree Foundation.

Baldock, P. (1974) *Community Work and Social Work*, London, Routledge & Kegan Paul.

Ballard, R. and Rosser, P. (1979) 'Social Network Assembly', in Brandon, D. and Jordan, B. (eds), *Creative Social Work*, Oxford, Basil Blackwell.

Bandura, A. (1977) *Social Learning Theory*, Englewood Cliffs, N.J., Prentice-Hall.

Bar-On, A. A. (1990) 'Organisational Resource Mobilisation: A Hidden Face of Social Work Practice', *British Journal of Social Work*, vol. 20, no. 2, pp. 133–49.

Barclay, P. (1982) *Social Workers: Their Role and Tasks,* London, Bedford Square Press.

Batten, T. R. (1967) *The Non-Directive Approach in Goup and Community Work*, London, Oxford University Press.

Bayley, M., Parker, P., Seyd, R. and Tennant, A. (1987) *Practising Community Care: Developing Locally-based Practice*, University of Sheffield, Joint Unit for Social Services Research.

Beck, A. T. (1989) *Cognitive Therapy and the Emotional Disorders*, Harmondsworth, Penguin.

Beecher, S. (1986) 'A Gender Critique of Family Therapy', H. Marcant and B. Wearing (eds), *Gender Reclaimed: Women and Social Work*, Sydney, Hale & Iremonger.

Benn, C. (1981) *Attacking Poverty Through Participation: A Community Approach*, Sydney, Pit Publishing.

Beresford, P. and Croft, S. (1986) *Whose Welfare? – Private Care or Public Services*, Brighton, Lewis Cohen Centre for Urban Studies at Brighton Polytechnic.

Berne, E. (1961) *Transactional Analysis in Psychotherapy*, New York, Grove.

Berne, E. (1968) *Games People Play*, Harmondsworth, Penguin.

Bettelheim, B. (1988) *The Uses of Enchantment: The Meaning and Importance of Fairy Tales*, Harmondsworth, Penguin.

Bhaduri, R. (1990) 'Counselling with Karma', *Social Work Today*, vol. 21, no. 33, p. 16.

Biehal, N. (1993) 'Changing Practice: Participation, Rights and Community Care', *British Journal of Social Work*, vol. 23, pp. 443–458.

Black, D. (1979) 'Early Help for the Bereaved Child Avoids Later Problems', *Modern Medicine*, 17 May, pp. 49–52.

Bornat, J., Pereira, C., Pilgrim, D. and Williams, F. (eds) (1993) *Community Care: A Reader*, Buckingham, Open University Press.

Bottoms, A. and Stelman, A. (1988) *Social Inquiry Reports*, Aldershot, Wildwood House.

Bottoms, A. E. and McWilliams, W. (1979) 'A Non-treatment Paradigm for Probation Practice', *British Journal of Social Work*, vol. 9, pp. 159–202.

Bowen, M. (1978) *Family Therapy in Clinical Practice*, New York, Jason Aronson.

Box, S., Copley, B., Magagna, J and Moustaki, E. (eds) (1981) *Psychotherapy with Families: Analytical Approach*, London, Routledge & Kegan Paul.

Boyce, L. and Anderson, S. (1990) 'A Common Bond', *Social Work Today*, vol. 21, no. 34, p. 38.

Brady, J. and Johnston, V. (1995) 'Consultation – Talk About Meeting Needs', *Research, Policy and Planning*, vol. 13, nos. 1, 2, pp. 19–24.

Braye, S., and Preston-Shoot, M. (1995) *Empowering Practice in Social Care*, Buckingham, Open Universty Press.

Brewster, B. (1988) *Supervision and Management in Social Work*, London, Central Council for Education and Training in Social Work.

Brook, E. and Davis, A. (eds) (1985) *Women, the Family and Social Work*, London, Tavistock.

Brown, A. (1992) *Groupwork*, London, Heinemann Educational.

Brown, R., Bute, S. and Ford, P. (1986) *Social Workers at Risk: The Prevention and Management of Violence*, Basingstoke, BASW/Macmillan.

Bryer, M. (1989) *Planning in Child Care: A Guide for Team Leaders and their Teams*, London, British Agencies for Adoption and Fostering.

Buchanan, A. (ed.) (1994) *Partnership in Practice: The Children Act 1989*, Avebury (in association with CEDR).

Buckle, J. (1981) *Intake Teams*, London, Tavistock.

Burnham, J. B. (1986) *Family Therapy: First Steps Towards a Systematic Approach*, London, Tavistock.

Butler, J, Bow, I and Gibbons, J. (1978) 'Task-centred Casework with Marital Problems', *British Journal of Social Work*, vol. 8, no. 4, pp. 393–409.

Butler, K. and Forrest, M. (1990) 'Citizen Advocacy for People with Learning Disabilities', in L. Winn (ed.), *Power to the People: The Key to Responsive Services in Health and Social Care*, London, King's Fund.

Byng-Hall, J. and Campbell, D. (1981) 'Resolving Conflicts in Family Distance Regulation: An Integrative Approach', *Journal of Marital and Family Therapy*, vol. 7, no. 3, pp. 321–30.

Bywaters, P. (1975) 'Ending Casework Relationships', *Social Work Today*, vol. 6, no. 10, pp. 301–4; and vol. 6, no. 11, pp. 336–8.

Caplan, G. (1964) *Principles of Preventive Psychiatry*, London, Tavistock.

Carlen, P. and Worrall, A. (1987) *Gender, Crime and Justice*, Milton Keynes, Open University Press.

Carpenter, J. and Treacher, A. (1989) *Problems and Solutions in Marital and Family Therapy*, Oxford, Basil Blackwell.

Cavanagh, K. and Cree, V. E (eds) (1996) *Working With Men: Feminism and Social Work*, London, Routledge.

CCETSW/IAMHW (1989) *Multidisciplinary Teamwork: Models of Good Practice*, London, Central Council for Education and Training in Social Work.

Challis, D. and Chesterman, J. (1985) 'A System of Monitoring Social Work Activity with the Frail Elderly', *British Journal of Social Work*, vol. 15, no. 2, pp. 115–32.

Challis, D. and Davies, B. (1989) *Case Management in Community Care*, Aldershot, Gower.

Challis, D., Chessum, R., Chesterman, J., Luckett, R. and Traske, K. (1990) *Case Management in Social and Health Care*, Canterbury, Personal Social Services Research Unit.

Chamberlin, J. (1988) *On Our Own*, London, MIND.

Clulow, C. and Mattinson, J. (1989) *Marriage Inside Out*, Harmondsworth, Penguin.

Commission for Racial Equality (1989) *Racial Equality in Social Sevices Departments: A Survey of Equal Opportunities Policies*, London, CRE.

Cooper, J. (1989) 'From Casework to Community Care: "The End is Where We Start From"', *British Journal of Social Work*, vol. 19, pp. 177–201.

Coote, A. (ed.) (1992) *The Welfare of Citizens*, London: Institute for Public Policy Research/Rivers Oram Press.

Corby, B. (1982) 'Theory and Practice in Long-Term Social Work: A Case Study of Practice with Social Service Department Clients', *British Journal of Social Work*, vol. 12, no. 6, pp. 619–38.

Corey, G. (1986) *Manual for Theory and Practice of Counselling and Psychotherapy*, 3rd edn, Monterey, Brooks/Cole.

Corey, G., Corey, M. S., Callanan, P. J. and Russell, J. M. (1982) *Group Techniques*, California, Brooks/Cole.

Cornish, P. M. (1983) *Activities for the Frail-Aged*, Bicester, Winslow Press.

Corrigan, P. and Leonard, P. (1978) *Social Work Practice Under Capitalism: A Marxist Approach*, Basingstoke, Macmillan.

Coulshed, V. (1990) *Management in Social Work*, Basingstoke, Macmillan.

Coulshed, V. (1991) *Social Work Practice: An Introduction*, Basingstoke, BASW/Macmillan.

Coulshed, V. and Abdullah-Zadeh, J. (1985) 'The Side Effects of Intervention', *British Journal of Social Work*, vol. 15, no. 5, pp. 479–86.

Croft, S. and Beresford, P. (1990) *From Paternalism to Participation: Involving People in Social Services*, London, Open Services project.

Crowe, M. (1982) 'The Treatment of Marital and Sexual Problems: A Behavioural Approach', in A. Bentovin, G. Gorrell-Barnes and A. Cocklin (eds), *Family Therapy, Complementary Frameworks of Theory and Practice*, London, Academic Press.

Dale, P., Davies, M., Morrison, T. and Waters, J. (1986) *Dangerous Families: Assessment and Treatment of Child Abuse*, London, Tavistock.

Dalrymple, J. and Burke, B. (1995) *Anti-Oppressive Practice: Social Care and the Law*, Buckingham, Open University Press.

Dana, M. and Lawrence, M. (1988) 'Understanding Bulimia: A Feminist, Psychoanalytic Account of Women's Eating Problems', in G. Pearson, J. Treseder and M. Yelloly (eds), *Social Work and the Legacy of Freud: Psychoanalysis and its Uses*, Basingstoke, Macmillan.

Dant, T. and Gearing, B. (1993) 'Key Workers for Elderly People in the Community' in J. Bornat, C. Pereira, D. Pilgrim and F. Williams (eds), *Community Care: A Reader*, Basingstoke: Macmillan/the Open University.

Davies, B. and Knapp, M. (eds) (1988) 'The Production of Welfare Approach: Evidence and Argument from the PSSRU', *British Journal of Social Work*, vol. 18, Supplement.

Davies, M. (1985) *The Essential Social Worker: A Guide to Positive Practice*, Aldershot, Wildwood House.

Davis, K. (1961) *Human Society*, New York, Macmillan.

Department of Health (1988) *Protecting Children: A Guide for Social Workers Undertaking a Comprehensive Assessment*, London, HMSO.

Department of Health (1994) *Implementing Caring for People: Care Management*, London, HMSO.

Department of Health Social Services/SSI and Scottish Office Social Work Services Group (1991) *Care Management and Assessment: Practitioner's Guide*, London, HMSO.

Department of Health, Cmnd. 849 (1989) *Caring for People: Community Care in the Next Decade and Beyond*, London, HMSO.

Department of Health/Social Services Inspectorate (1990) *Caring for Quality: Guidance on Standards for Residential Homes for Elderly People*, London, HMSO.

Department of Health/SSI (1989a) *Homes are for Living In*, London, HMSO.

Devore, W. and Schlesinger, E. C. (1981) *Ethnic-Sensitive Social Work Practice*, St Louis, C. V. Mosby Co.

Dillon, J. T. (1990) *The Practice of Questioning*, London, Routledge.

Dimmock, B and Dungworth, D. (1985) 'Beyond the Family: Using Network Meetings with Statutory Child Care Cases', *Journal of Family Therapy*, vol. 7, no. 1, pp. 45–68.

Dominelli, L. (1988) *Anti-Racist Social Work*, Basingstoke, Macmillan.

Dominelli, L. and McLeod, E. (1989) *Feminist Social Work*, Basingstoke, Macmillan.

Downes, C. (1988) 'A Psychodynamic Approach to the Work of an Area Team', in G. Pearson, J. Treseder and M. Yelloly (eds), *Social Work and the Legacy of Freud: Psychoanalysis and its Uses*, Basingstoke, Macmillan.

Doyal, L. (1991) *A Theory of Human Need*, Basingstoke, Macmillan.

Doyal, L. (1993) 'Human Need and the Moral Right to Optimal Community Care', in J. Bornat, C. Pereira, D. Pilgrim and F. Williams (eds), *Community Care: A Reader*, Basingstoke, Macmillan/Open University.

Dryden, W. (ed.) (1984) *Individual Therapy in Britain*, London, Harper & Row.

Egan, G. (1981) *The Skilled Helper: A Model for Systematic Helping and Interpersonal Relating*, California, Brooks/Cole.

Eichenbaum, L. and Orbach, S. (1983) *Understanding Women*, Harmondsworth, Penguin.

Ellis, A. (1962) *Reason and Emotion in Psychotherapy*, New York, Lyle Stuart.

England, H. (1986) *Social Work as Art: Making Sense for Good Practice*, London, Allen & Unwin.

Epstein, L. (1980) *Helping People: The Task-Centred Approach*, St Louis, C. V. Mosby.

Erikson, E. (1965) *Childhood and Society*, Harmondsworth, Penguin.

Evans, R. (1976) 'Some Implications of an Integrated Model for Social Work Theory and Practice', *British Journal of Social Work*, vol. 6 no. 2.

Fischer, J. (1976) *The Effectiveness of Social Casework*, New York, Charles C. Thomas.

Ford, P. and Hayes, P. (eds) (1996) *Educating for Social Work: Arguments for Optimism*, Aldershot, Avebury (in association with CEDR).

Forder, A. (1974) *Concepts in Social Administration: A Framework for Analysis*, London, Routledge & Kegan Paul.

Freed, A. O. (1988) 'Interviewing through an Interpreter', *Social Work*, vol. 33, no. 4, pp. 315–19.

Freire, P. (1972) *Pedagogy of the Oppressed*, Harmondsworth, Penguin.

Garrett, A. (1972) *Interviewing: Its Principles and Methods*, New York, Family Service Association of America.

Garrison, J. E. and Howe, J. (1976) 'Community Intervention with the Elderly: A Social Network Approach', *Journal of the American Geriatric Society*, vol. 24, pp. 329–33.

Gibbons, J. S., Bow, I., Butler, J. and Powell, J. (1979) 'Clients', Reaction to Task-Centred Casework: A Follow-up Study', *British Journal of Social Work*, vol. 9, no. 2, pp. 203–15.

Golan, N. (1978) *Treatment in Crisis Situations*, New York, The Free Press.

Goldberg, E. M., Gibbons, J. and Sinclair, I. (1985) *Problems, Tasks and Outcomes: The Evaluation of Task-centred Casework in Three Settings*, London, Allen & Unwin.

Goldberg, E. M., Walker, D. and Robinson, J. (1977) 'Exploring the Task-Centred Casework Method', *Social Work Today*, vol. 9, no. 2, pp. 9–14.

Goldstein, H. (1973) *Social Work Practice: A Unitary Approach*, Columbia, South Carolina: University of South Carolina Press.

Golembiewski, R. T. and Blumberg, A. (eds) (1970) *Sensitivity Training and the Laboratory Approach*, Itasca, Ill., F. E. Peacock.

Gorell Barnes, G. (1984) *Working with Families*, London, Macmillan.

Gottman, J., Notarius, C., Gonso, J. and Markman, H. (1977) *A Couple's Guide to Communication: Skills Teaching for Couples*, New York, Research Press.

Gulbenkian Foundation (1968) *Community Work and Social Change*, London, Longman.

Hadley, R. and McGrath, M. (1984) *When Services Are Local – The Normanton Experience*, London, Allen & Unwin.

Hadley, R., Cooper, M., Dale, P. and Stacy, G. (1987) *A Community Social Worker's Handbook*, London, Tavistock.

Haley, J. (1976) *Problem-Solving Therapy*, San Francisco, Jossey-Bass.

Hall, E. (1987) 'The Gender of the Therapist: Its Relevance to Practice and Training', in G. Horobin (ed.), *Sex, Gender and Care Work*, London, Jessica Kingsley.

Hanmer, J. and Statham, D. (1988) *Women and Social Work: Towards a Woman-Centred Practice*, Basingstoke, Macmillan.

Hardiker, P. and Barker, F. M. (eds) (1981) *Theories of Practice in Social Work*, London, Academic Press.

Hawkins, P. and Shohet, R. (1989) *Supervision in the Helping Professions*, Milton Keynes, Open University Press.

Heap, K. (1985) *The Practice of Social Work with Groups: A Systematic Approach*, London, Allen & Unwin.

Henderson, P. and Thomas, D. N. (1980) *Skills in Neighbourhood Work*, London, Allen & Unwin.

Henderson, P. and Thomas, D. N. (1981) *Readings in Community Work*, London, Allen & Unwin.

Hester, M. and Radford, J. (1996) 'Contradictions and Compromises: The Impact of the Children Act on Women and Children's Safety', in M. Hester, L. Kelley and J. Radford (eds), *Women, Violence and Male Power*, Buckingham, Open University Press.

Hirayama, H. and Cetingok, M. (1988) 'Empowerment: A Social Work Approach for Asian Immigrants', *Social Casework*, vol. 69, no. 1, pp. 41–7.

Hodgkinson, P. and Stewart, M. (1991) *Coping with Catastrophe: A Professional Handbook for Post-disaster Aftercare*, London, Routledge.

Hollis, F. (1964) *Casework: A Psychosocial Therapy*, New York, Random House.

Hollis, F. (1970) 'The Psychosocial Approach to the Practice of Casework', in R. W. Roberts and R. H. Nee (eds), *Theories of Social Casework*, University of Chicago Press.

Home Office. (1992) *National Standards for the Supervision of Offenders in the Community*, London, HMSO.

Howe, D. (1987) *An Introduction to Social Work Theory: Making Sense in Practice*, Aldershot, Wildwood House.

Howe, D. (1994) 'Modernity, Postmodernity and Social Work', *The British Journal of Social Work*, vol. 24 no 5, pp. 513–32.

Hoyes, L., and Lart, L. (1992) 'Taking Care', *Community Care*, 20 August, pp. 14–15.

Hudson, B. L. (1975) 'An Inadequate Personality', *Social Work Today*, vol. 6, no. 16, pp. 506–8.

Hudson, B. L. and Macdonald, G. M. (1986) *Behavioural Social Work: An Introduction*, London, Macmillan.

I.M.S. (1962) *The Marital Relationship as a Focus for Casework*, London, Institute of Marital Studies.

Jacobs, M. (1985) *Swift to Hear: Facilitating Skills in Listening and Responding*, London, SPCK.

Jacobs, M. (1986) *The Presenting Past: An Introduction to Practical Psychodynamic Counselling*, London, Harper & Row.

James, A. L. and Wilson, K. (1986) *Couples, Conflict and Change*, London, Tavistock.

Jehu, F. (1967) *Learning Theory and Social Work*, London, Routledge & Kegan Paul.

Jervis, M. (1990) 'Family Fortunes', *Social Work Today*, vol. 21, no. 47, pp. 16–17.

Jones, C. (1983) *State Social Work and the Working Class*, London, Macmillan.

Jones, C. (1996) 'Anti-intellectualism and the Peculiarities of British Social Work Education', in N. Parton (ed.), *Social Theory, Social Change and Social Work*, London, Routledge.

Jordan, B. (1972) *The Social Worker in Family Situations*, London, Routledge & Kegan Paul.

Jordan, B. (1987) 'Fallen Idol', *Community Care*, 12 February, pp. 24–5.

Kaufman, P. (1966) 'Helping People who Cannot Manage their Lives', *Children*, vol. 13, no. 3.

Kell, B. L. and Mueller, W. J. (1966) *Impact and Change: A Study of Counselling Relationships*, New York, Meredith Publishing.

Kelly, G. A. (1955) *The Psychology of Personal Constructs*, New York, Norton.

Langrish, S. V. (1981) 'Assertiveness Training', in C. Cooper (ed.), *Improving Skills in Interpersonal Relations*, Aldershot, Gower.

Lau, A. (1984) 'Transcultural Issues in Family Therapy', *Journal of Family Therapy*, vol. 6, no. 2, pp. 91–112.

Lindemann, E. (1965) 'Symptomatology and Management of Acute Grief', in H. J. Parad (ed.), *Crisis Interventions: Selected Readings*, New York, Family Service Association of America.

Lindon, V. and Morris, J. (1995) *Service User Involvement: Synthesis of Findings and Experience in the Field of Community Care*, York, Joseph Rowntree Foundation.

Lishman, J. (1995) *Communication in Social Work*, Basingstoke, BASW/ Macmillan.

Liverpool, V. (1986) 'When Backgrounds Clash', *Community Care*, 2 October, pp. 19–21.

Loney, M. (1983) *Community Against Government*, London, Heinemann.

Luft, J. (1963) *Group Processes*, Palo Alto, California, National Press.

Lupton, C. and Gillespie, T. (eds) (1994) *Working With Violence*, Basingstoke, BASW/Macmillan.

Lyons, J. (1977) *Chomsky*, London, Fontana/Collins.

Magee, B. (1982) *Men of Ideas*, Oxford, Oxford University Press.

Mahrer, A. R. (1989) *The Integration of Psychotherapies*, New York, Human Sciences Press.

Mainprice, J. (1974) *Marital Interaction and some Illness in Children*, Institute of Marital Studies, London, Tavistock Institute of Human Relations.

Marris, P. (1986) *Loss and Change*, London, Routledge.

Marsh, P., and Fisher, M. (1992) *Good Intentions: Partnership in Social Services*, York, Joseph Rowntree Foundation.

Marshall, M. (ed.) (1990) *Working with Dementia: Guidelines for Professionals*, Birmingham, Venture Press.

Marziali, E. (1988) 'The First Session: An Interpersonal Encounter', *Social Casework*, vol. 69, no. 1, pp. 23–7.

Mattinson, J. (1975) *The Reflection Process in Casework Supervision*, Institute of Marital Studies, London, Tavistock Institute of Human Relations.

Mattinson, J. and Sinclair, I. (1979) *Mate and Stalemate: Working with Marital Problems in a Social Services Department*, Oxford, Basil Blackwell.

Maximé, J. E. (1986) 'Some Psychological Models of Black Self-Concept', in S. Ahmed, J. Cheetham and J. Small (eds), *Social Work with Black Children and their Families*, London, B. T. Batsford/British Agencies for Adoption and Fostering.

Mayer, J. E. and Timms, N. (1970) *The Client Speaks: Working Class Impressions of Casework*, London, Routledge & Kegan Paul.

McNay, M. (1992) 'Social Work and Power Relations', in M. Langan and L. Day (eds), *Women, Oppression and Social Work*, London, Routledge.

Means, R., and Smith, R. (1994) *Community Care: Policy and Practice*, Basingstoke, Macmillan.

Meichenbaum, D. (1978) *Cognitive Behaviour Modification: An Integrative Approach*, New York, Plenum Press.

Membership Notes (1990) British Association of Counselling, Rugby.

Merry, T. (1990) 'Client-centred Therapy: Some Trends and Some Troubles', *Counselling*, vol. 1, no. 1, pp. 17–18.

Minuchin, S. (1974) *Families and Family Therapy*, London, Tavistock.

Mitchell, J. (1984) *Women: The Longest Revolution: Essays in Feminism Literature and Psychoanalysis*, London, Virago.

Monach, J. and Spriggs, L. (1994) 'The Consumer Role', in N. Malin (ed.), *Implementing Community Care*, Buckingham, Open University Press.

Morgan, S. (1986) 'Practice in a Community Nursery for Black Children', in S. Ahmed, J. Cheetham and J. Small (eds), *Social Work with Black Children and their Families*, London, B. T. Batsford/British Agencies for Adoption and Fostering.

Moyes, B. (1988) 'The Psychodynamic Method in Social Work: Some Indications and Contraindications', *Practice*, vol. 2, no. 3, pp. 236–42.

Mullender, A. (1996) *Rethinking Domestic Violence: The Social Work and Probation Response*, London, Routledge.

Mullender, A. and Morley, R. (eds) (1994) *Children Living with Domestic Violence: Putting Men's Abuse of Women on the Child Care Agenda*, London, Whiting & Birch.

Mullender, A. and Ward, D. (1991) *Self Directed Groupwork: Users take Action for Empowerment*, London, Whiting & Birch.

NAPO (1995) *Good Practice Guide*, London, National Association of Probation Officers.

Neill, J. (1989) *Assessing Elderly People for Residential Care: A Practical Guide*, London Institute for Social Work.

Nelson-Jones, R. (1983) *Practical Counselling Skills*, New York, Holt, Rinehart & Winston.

Neville, D. and Beak, D. (1990) 'Solving the Care History Mystery', *Social Work Today*, vol. 21, no. 42, pp. 16–17.

Noonan, E. (1983) *Counselling Young People*, London, Methuen.

Northen, H. (1969) *Social Work with Groups*, New York, Columbia University Press.

Northen, H. (1982) *Clinical Social Work*, New York, Columbia University Press.

O'Brian, C. (1990) 'Family Therapy with Black Families', *Journal of Family Therapy*, vol.12, no. 1, pp. 3–16.

O'Connor, G. G. (1988) 'Case Management: System and Practice', *Social Casework*, vol. 69, no. 2, pp. 97–106.

O'Hagan, K. (1986) *Crisis Intervention in Social Services.*, London, Macmillan.

Orme, J. (1995) *Workloads: Measurement and Management*, Aldershot, Avebury (in association with CEDR).

Orme, J. (1996) 'Participation or Patronage: Changes in Social Work Practice Brought About by Community Care Policies in Britain', *Participating in Change – Social Work Profession in Social Development,*

Proceedings of the Joint World Congress of IFSW/IASSW, Hong Kong, pp. 250–2.

Orme, J. and Glastonbury, B. (1993) *Care Management*, Basingstoke, BASW/Macmillan.

Orten, J. D. and Rich, L. L. (1988) 'A Model for Assessment of Incestuous Families', *Social Casework*, vol. 69, no. 10, pp. 611–19.

Papell, C. P. and Rothman, B. (1966) 'Social Groupwork Models: Possession and Heritage', *Journal of Education for Social Work*, vol. 2, no. 2, pp. 66–77.

Parad, H. J. and Caplan, G. (1965) 'A Framework for Studying Families in Crisis', in H. J. Parad (ed.), *Crisis Intervention: Selected Readings*, New York, Family Service Association of America.

Parkes, C. M. (1986) *Bereavement: Studies of Grief in Adult Life*, London, Tavistock.

Parry, G. (1990) *Coping with Crises*, Leicester, British Psychological Society/Routledge.

Payne, M. (1986) *Social Care in the Community*, Basingstoke, Macmillan.

Payne, M. (1991) *Modern Social Work Theory: A Critical Introduction*, Basingstoke, Macmillan.

Payne, M. (1995) *Social Work and Community Care*, Basingstoke, Macmillan.

Pearson, G, Treseder, J. and Yelloly, M. (eds) (1988) *Social Work and the Legacy of Freud: Psychoanalysis and its Uses*, Basingstoke, Macmillan.

Penn, P. (1982) 'Circular Questioning', *Family Process*, vol. 21, no. 3, pp. 267–79.

Perelberg, R. G. and Miller, A. C. (eds) (1990) *Gender and Power in Families*, London, Tavistock/Routledge.

Perlman, H. H. (1957) *Social Casework: A Problem-Solving Process*, Chicago, University of Chicago Press.

Perls, F. (1973) *The Gestalt Approach and Eye Witness to Therapy*, Ben Lomond, Cal., Science and Behaviour Books.

Perrott, S. (1994) 'Working with Men who Abuse Women and Children', in C. Lupton and T. Gillespie (eds), *Working With Violence*, Basingstoke, BASW/Macmillan.

Pilalis, J. (1986) 'The Integration of Theory and Practice: A Re-examination of a Paradoxical Expectation', *British Journal of Social Work*, vol. 16, no. 1, pp. 79–96.

Pilalis, J. and Anderton, J. (1986) 'Feminism and Family Therapy: A Possible Meeting Point', *Journal of Family Therapy*, vol. 8, no. 2, pp. 99–114.

Pincus, A. and Minahan, A. (1973) *Social Work Practice: Model and Method*, Itasca, Ill., Peacock.

Pincus, L. (1976) *Death and the Family*, London, Faber & Faber.

Preston-Shoot, M. (1987) *Effective Groupwork*, London, Macmillan.

ProCare (1996) *Interpersonal Skills*.

Prochaska, J. O. and Diclemente, C. (1984) *The Transtheoretical Approach: Crossing the Traditional Boundaries of Therapy*, Dow, Jones/Irwin.

Rack, P. (1982) *Race, Culture and Mental Disorder*, London, Tavistock.

Randall, P. (1990) 'Too Old to Learn New Tricks?', *Community Care*, 1 March, pp. 20–1.

Raphael, B. (1984) *The Anatomy of Bereavement: A Handbook for the Caring Professions*, London, Unwin Hyman.

Raphael, B. (1986) *When Disaster Strikes: A Handbook for the Caring Professions*, London, Hutchinson.

Rapoport, L. (1970) 'Crisis Intervention as a Brief Mode of Treatment', in R. W. Roberts and R. H. Nee (eds), *Theories of Social Casework*, Chicago, University of Chicago Press.

Redgrave, K. (1987) *Child's Play: 'Direct', Work with the Deprived Child*, Cheadle, Boys' and Girls' Welfare Society.

Redl, F. (1951) 'Art of Group Composition', in S. Schultze (ed.), *Creative Living in a Children's Institution*, New York, Association Press.

Reed, B. G. and Garvin, C. D. (eds) (1983) *Groupwork with Women, Groupwork with Men: An Overview of Gender Issues in Social Groupwork Practice*, New York, Haworth Press.

Rees, S. (1991) *Achieving Power: Practice and Policy in Social Welfare*, Sydney, Allen & Unwin.

Reid, W. J. (1978) *The Task-Centred System*, New York, Columbia University Press.

Reid, W. J. and Epstein, L. (1972) *Tast-Centred Casework*, New York, Columbia University Press.

Reid, W. J. and Epstein, L. (eds) (1977) *Task-Centred Practice*, New York, Columbia University Press.

Reid, W. J. and Hanrahan, P. (1981) 'The Effectiveness of Social Work: Recent Evidence', in E. M. Goldberg and N. Connolly (eds), *Evaluative Research in Social Care*, London, Heinemann.

Reid, W. J. and Shyne, A. W. (1969) *Brief and Extended Casework*, New York, Columbia University Press.

Remington, B. and Barron, C. (1991) 'Working with Problem Drinkers: A Cognitive Behavioural Approach', *Probation Journal*, vol. 38, no. 1, pp. 15–19.

Renshaw, J. (1988) 'Care in the Community; Individual Care Planning and Case Management', *British Journal of Social Work*, no. 18, pp. 79–105.

Rich, J. (1968) *Interviewing Children and Adolescents*, London, Macmillan.

Richmond, M. (1922) *What is Social Case Work?*, New York, Russell Sage.

Rogers, C. (1980) *A Way of Being*, Boston, Mass., Houghton Mifflin.

Rojek, C. (1986) ' "The Subject", Social Work', *British Journal of Social Work*, vol. 16, no. 1, pp.65–77.

Rojek, C., Peacock, G. and Collins, S. (1988) *Social Work and Received Ideas*, London, Routledge.

Rothman, J. (1968) 'Three Models of Community Organization Practice their Mixing and Phasing', in F. M. Cox *et al.* (eds), *Strategies for Community Organization*, 3rd edn, Itasca, Ill., Peacock.

Rueveni, U. (1979) *Networking Families in Crisis*, New York, Human Sciences Press.

Runciman, P. (1989) 'Health Assessment of the Elderly: A Multidisciplinary Perspective', in R. Taylor and J. Ford (eds), *Social Work and Health Care*, London, Jessica Kingsley.

Sainsbury, E. (1986) 'The Contribution of Client Studies to Social Work Practice', in P. Wedge (ed.), *Social Work – Research into Practice*, Birmingham, British Association of Social Workers.

Schless, A. P., Teichman, A., Mendels, J. and Di Giacomo, J. N. (1977) 'The Role of Stress as a Precipitating Factor of Psychiatric Illness', *British Journal of Psychiatry*, vol. 130, pp. 19–22.

Schon, D. A. (1987) *Education the Reflective Practitioner Toward a New Design for Teaching and Learning in the Professions*, California, Jossey-Bass.

Schutz, W. C. (1966) *FIRO: The Interpersonal Underworld*, New York, Science and Behaviour Books.

Scott, M. (1983) *Group Parent-Training Programme*, Liverpool Personal Service Society, Stanley Street, Liverpool, L1 6AN.

Scott, M. (1989) *A Cognitive Behavioural Approach to Clients' Problems*, London, Routledge.

Scott, M. J. and Stradling, S. G. (1990) 'Group Cognitive Therapy for Depression Produces Clinically Significant Reliable Change in Community-Based Settings', *Behavioural Psychotherapy*, vol. 18, pp. 1–19.

Scrutton, S. (1989) *Counselling Older People: A Creative Response to Ageing*, London, Edward Arnold.

Seebohm Report (1968) *Report of the Committee on Local Authority and Allied Personal Social Services*, Cmnd 3703, London, HMSO.

Sharkey, P. (1989) 'Social Networks and Social Service Workers', *British Journal of Social Work*, vol. 19, no. 5, pp. 387–405.

Sheik, S. (1986) 'An Asian Mothers', Self-Help Group', in S. Ahmed, J. Cheetham and J. Small (eds), *Social Work with Black Children and their Families*, London, B. T. Batsford/British Agencies for Adoption and Fostering.

Sheldon, B. (1983) 'The Use of Single-Case Experimental Designs in the Evaluation of Social Work', *British Journal of Social Work*, vol. 13, no. 5, pp. 477–500.

Sheldon, B. (1984) 'Behavioural Approaches with Psychiatric Patients', in M. R. Olsen (ed.), *Social Work and Mental Health*, London, Tavistock.

Shulman, L. (1979) *The Skills of Helping: Individuals and Groups*, Ithaca, Ill., Peacock.

Simmonds, J. (1988) 'Thinking about Feelings in Group Care', in G. Pearson, J. Treseder and M. Yelloly (eds), *Social Work and the Legacy of Freud: Psychoanalysis and its Uses*, London, Macmillan.

Siporin, M. (1975) *Introduction to Social Work Practice*, New York, Macmillan.

Skinner, B. F. (1938) *The Behaviour of Organisms*, New York, Appleton.

Smale, G., Tuson, G., Biehal, N. and Marsh, P. (1993) *Empowerment, Assessment, Care Management and the Skilled Worker*, National Institute for Social Work Practice and Development Exchange, London, HMSO.

Smale, G., Tuson, G., Cooper, M., Wardle, M. and Crosbie, D. (1988) *Community Social Work: A Paradigm for Change*, London, NISW.

Social Information Systems (1990) *Social Services and Quality Assurance*, Manchester, SIS Ltd.

Solomon, B. B. (1976) *Black Empowerment: Social Work with Oppressed Communities*, New York, Columbia University Press.

Specht, H. and Vickery, A. (eds) (1977) Integrating Social Work Methods, London, Allen & Unwin.

Speck, R. V. (1967) 'Psychotherapy of the Social Network of a Schizophrenic Family, *Family Process*, vol. 7, pp. 208–14.

Spurling, L. (1988) 'Casework as Dialogue: A Story of Incest', in G. Pearson, J. Treseder and M. Yelloly (eds), *Social Work and the Legacy of Freud: Psychoanalysis and its Uses*, Basingstoke, Macmillan.

SSI/SWG. (1991) *Care Management and Assessment: Practitioners Guide*, London, HMSO.

Stanley, L. (1990) *Feminist Praxis: Research, Theory and Epistemology in Feminist Sociology*, London, Routledge.

Stevenson, O. (1963) 'The Understanding Caseworker', *New Society*, 1 August, pp. 84–96.

Stevenson, O. and Parsloe, P. (1993) *Community Care and Empowerment*, York: Joseph Rowntree Foundation.

Stewart, I. (1989) *Transactional Analysis Counselling in Action*, London, Sage.

Thoburn, J. (1988) *Child Placement: Principles and Practice*, Aldershot, Wildwood House.

Thomas, D. H. (1983) *The Making of Community Work*, London, Allen & Unwin.

Timms, N. and Timms, R. (1977) *Perspectives in Social Work*, London, Routledge.

Traux, C. B. and Carkhuff, R. R. (1967) *Towards Effective Counselling and Psychotherapy*, Chicago, Aldine.

Treacher, A. and Carpenter, J. (eds) (1984) *Using Family Therapy*, Oxford, Basil Blackwell.

Tsoi, M. and Yule, J. (1982) 'Building up New Behaviours: Shaping, Prompting and Fading', in W. Yule and J. Carr (eds), *Behaviour Modification for the Mentally Handicapped*, London, Croom Helm.

Tuckman, B. W. and Jensen, M. A. C. (1977) 'Stages of Small Group Development Revisited', *Group and Organisation Studies*, vol. 2, no. 4, pp. 419–27.

Tully, J. B. (1976) 'Personal Construct Theory and Psychological Changes Related to Social Work Training', *British Journal of Social Work*, vol. 6, no. 4, pp. 481–99.

Tuson, G. (1996) 'Writing Postmodern Social Work', in P. Ford and P. Hayes (eds), *Education for Social Work: Arguments for Optimism*, Aldershot, Avebury (in association with CEDR).

Twelvetrees, A. (1991), *Community Work*, 2nd edn, London, Macmillan.

Van der Velden, H. E. M., Halevy-Martinin, J., Ruhf, L. and Schoenfield, P.

(1984) 'Conceptual Issues in Network Therapy', *International Journal of Family Therapy,* vol. 6, no. 2, pp. 68–81.

Vernon, S., Harris, R. and Ball, C. (1990) *Towards Social Work Law: Legally Competent Professional Practice,* Paper 4.2, London, CCETSW.

Vickery, A. (1976), 'A Unitary Approach to Social Work with the Mentally Disordered', in M. R. Olsen (ed.), *Differential Approaches in Social Work with the Mentally Disordered,* Birmingham, British Association of Social Workers.

Walker, L. (1978) 'Work with a Parents', Group, in N. McCaughan (ed.), *Group Work: Learning and Practice,* London, Allen & Unwin.

Walrond-Skinner, S. (ed.) (1979) *Family and Marital Psychotherapy: A Critical Approach,* London, Routledge & Kegan Paul.

Ward, H. (ed.) (1995) *Looking After Children: Research into Practice,* 2nd Report to the Department of Health on Assessing Outcomes in Child Care, London, HMSO.

Webb, S. A. and McBeath, G. B. (1990) 'Political Critique of Kantian Ethics: A Reply to Professor R. S. Downie', *British Journal of Social Work,* vol. 20, no. 1, pp. 65–71.

Whan, M. (1983) 'Tricks of the Trade: Questionable Theory and Practice in Family Therapy', *British Journal of Social Work,* vol. 13, no. 3, pp. 321–38.

Whitaker, D. S. (1975) 'Some Conditions of Effective Work with Groups', *British Journal of Social Work,* vol. 5, no. 4, pp. 423–40.

Whitaker, D. S. (1985), *Using Groups to Help People,* London, Routledge & Kegan Paul.

Winnicott, D. W. (1957) 'The Capacity to Be Alone', paper read at a meeting of the British Psychoanalytical Society, 24 July.

Wise, S. (1990) 'Becoming a Feminist Social Worker', in L. Stanley (ed.), *Feminist Praxis: Research, Theory and Epistemology in Feminist Sociology,* London, Routledge.

Wittenberg, I. S. (1970) *Psychoanalytic Insight and Relationships: A Kleinian Approach,* London, Routledge & Kegan Paul.

Wootten, B. F. (1959) *Social Science and Social Pathology,* London, Allen & Unwin.

Yalom, I. D. (1970) *The Theory and Practice of Group Psychotherapy,* New York, Basic Books.

Yelloly, M. A. (1980) *Social Work Theory and Psychoanalysis,* Wokingham, Van Nostrand Reinhold.

York, A. (1984) 'Towards a Conceptual Model of Community Social Work', *British Journal of Social Work,* vol. 14, pp. 241–55.

Zastrow, C. (1985) *Social Work with Groups,* Chicago, Nelson-Hall.

Index